SPIRIT COUNTRY

SPIRIT COUNTRY

CONTEMPORARY AUSTRALIAN ABORIGINAL ART

Jennifer Isaacs

Fine Arts Museums of San Francisco

Hardie Grant Books

Spirit Country: Contemporary Australian Aboriginal Art
is published on the occasion of the exhibition
Spirit Country: Australian Aboriginal Art from the Gantner Myer Collection

Fine Arts Museums of San Francisco
California Palace of the Legion of Honor
18 September 1999 - 9 January 2000

Explorers Hall
National Geographic Society
Washington, D.C.
28 June - 14 August 2000

Spirit Country: Australian Aboriginal Art from the Gantner Myer Collection has been organized by the
Fine Arts Museums of San Francisco. Support for the exhibition and catalogue has been
provided by Netcom and Friends of Ethnic Art.

First published in the United States of America in softcover in 1999 by the Fine Arts Museums
of San Francisco, Golden Gate Park, San Francisco California 94118
Reprinted in 2000

First published in Australia in 1999 by Hardie Grant Books, Level 3, 44 Caroline Street, South
Yarra, Victoria 3141

National Library of Australia Cataloguing-in-Publication Data:
Isaacs, Jennifer.
Spirit country.
ISBN 1 86498 049 4

1. Aborigines, Australian — Painting — Exhibitions.
2. Painting, Modern — 20th century — Australia — Exhibitions.
3. Paintings, Australian — Exhibitions.
I. Title.

759.99407479461

Museum edition produced by Hardie Grant Books in Association with the Fine Arts Museums
of San Francisco: Michael Callaghan (Redback Graphix), cover and text design; Gregory
McLachlan, type styling; Mark Ashkanasy, photography for the Gantner Myer Collection;
Richard Woldendorp, landscape photography; Joseph McDonald, photography for the Fine Arts
Museums of San Francisco

Frontispiece: PLATE 96 (detail)
Gertie Huddlestone, b. c. 1930
Ngukurr Sunset, 1996
123 x 100 cm (48.5 x 39.5 in.)
Acrylic on canvas

Printed in China

Contents

Director's Foreword

The last two decades have seen a great awakening in the appreciation of contemporary Australian Aboriginal art. Contemporary Aboriginal paintings are avidly sought by collectors, but at the same time they have deep religious meanings to Aboriginal peoples who have occupied Australia for more than 40,000 years. This exhibition, which focuses primarily on recent works, includes dazzling acrylic and ocher paintings from the Australian Central Desert and Western Australia, together with remarkable bark paintings and sculptures from the artists of Arnhem Land and the Tiwi Islands in the Northern Territory.

The creation of ancestral designs, worked on a multitude of materials, has long been a part of Aboriginal sacred tradition. Although Western canvases and paints are often now used, the resulting compositions and designs have been handed down over generations. Each painting compresses sacred symbols relating to ancestral land, epic journeys, totemic relationships, metaphysics, mythology, and law.

This exhibition, developed for the spiritual insight and pleasure of American audiences, has been co-curated by an American and an Australian. Fine Arts Museums curator Kathleen Berrin has had wide experiences as both an educator, museologist, and interpreter of the arts of Africa, Oceania, and the Americas. Noted Australian authority and author on Aboriginal art Jennifer Isaacs is the curator for the Gantner Myer Collection of Australian Aboriginal Art and has spent years working with Aboriginal artists.

The Gantner Myer Collection of Australian Aboriginal Art, brought together by Baillieu Myer and Carrillo Gantner, reflects their enthusiastic responses to the vibrancy of contemporary painting that they experienced first-hand on a visit to seventeen Aboriginal community centers. Most of the works were purchased directly from Aboriginal communities. They bear testament to a bold and resilient culture that creates images replete with spiritual power.

The presentation of this exhibition in San Francisco marks long-standing ties between the cities of San Francisco and Melbourne and the Gantner and Myer families. The exhibition also forms part of the Sydney 2000 Olympics Arts Festival, Reaching the World. We particularly welcome the indigenous Australians who came to San Francisco to share and interpret their culture for us: guest speakers Djon Mundine and Hetti Perkins in addition to the Walpiri artists from Yuendumu who created a breathtaking ground painting during opening week.

There are many whom we wish to thank for the success of this project. From Australia, we wish to acknowledge the outstanding staff of Hardie Grant Books, in particular editors Tracy O'Shaughnessy and Jenny Lee, and designer Michael Callaghan. From the Fine Arts Museums of San Francisco, heartfelt thanks go to Ann Karlstrom, Director of Publications; Karen Kevorkian, Managing Editor; Kathe Hodson, Director of Exhibitions Planning; Bill White, Exhibitions Designer; Vas Prabhu, Director of Education; Pamela Forbes, Director of Media Relations; Andrew Fox, Media Relations Assistant; and Alyce Waxman, Special Project Intern. Financial support from Netcom and Friends of Ethnic Art made this exhibition and catalogue possible.

Harry S. Parker III
Director of Museums
Fine Arts Museums of San Francisco

Our Painting Is a Political Act

At the close of the twentieth century, Australia has witnessed the renaissance of the world's oldest living art tradition. Indigenous artists have brought their culture to the international stage from the breadth of the Australian continent and its surrounding islands. From the Torres Strait Islands, birthplace of the historic *Mabo* decision of 1992 that recognized the native title of indigenous peoples, to the goldfields of Kalgoorlie in Western Australia and the cities of the southeast, artists are drawing on their heritage to express their contemporary reality.

Through their work, Aboriginal artists invite a more appreciative understanding of their world and its diversity. Among the collectors who have responded are the Gantner and Myer families, whose outstanding representative collection of contemporary Aboriginal art from the communities in the Central Desert, the Kimberley, and Arnhem Land is being shown for the first time at the California Palace of the Legion of Honor in San Francisco.

One of the most exciting developments in contemporary indigenous arts practice over the past few decades is the consolidation of regional diversity. Several art centers have emerged in the Western Desert since the beginnings of the art movement out of Papunya in the early 1970s. Among them is Warlukurlangu Artists, serving the Warlpiri artists of Yuendumu, which is well known for its elaborate and vibrantly colored paintings, often executed communally by custodians of the particular Jukurrpa (Dreaming story) being depicted. The unique landforms of the Kimberley and surrounding regions frequently occur in the work of northwestern Australian artists such as the late Rover Thomas. Thomas and fellow artists such as Queenie McKenzie and Freddie Timms have developed idiosyncratic yet distinctively Aboriginal interpretations of the country to which they belong and the histories it contains. In Arnhem Land, the center at Maningrida is the collection point for artists from many small communities, including James Iyuna, whose paintings capture the often mischievous or formidable personalities of the spirit beings that dwell in the region's lagoons and caves.

In the mid–1980s, when I began working in the indigenous visual arts arena, most exhibitions at Aboriginal art galleries, including the one where I worked in Sydney, were focused on communities and emphasized the cultural, communal context of Aboriginal art practice. Now, the presence of the individual is increasingly being asserted through the visual arts, as artists express their identity in relation to ceremony and community, and great artists are acknowledged for their special gifts and power of visual communication.

Art and politics are often inextricably intertwined. As Galarrwuy Yunupingu, leader of the Gumatj people and head of the Northern Land Council, has written:

> We are painting, as we have always done, to demonstrate our continuing link with our country and the rights and responsibilities we have to it. We paint to show the rest of the world that we own this country and the land owns us. Our painting is a political act.

Aboriginal artists have been at the forefront of political and social change for indigenous communities. In the metropolitan centers of Australia, part of this struggle has been an ideological campaign to achieve recognition of the changing face of indigenous identity. The emergence of a distinctive and strong indigenous voice through the visual arts over the preceding few decades has been a catalyst for a re-evaluation of Australia's history and its potential to emerge into the twenty-first century as a nation reconciled with its past.

Hetti Perkins
Curator of Aboriginal and Torres Strait Islander Art
Art Gallery of New South Wales

The Myer and Gantner Families: Bonds across the Pacific

The exhibition of the Gantner Myer Aboriginal Art Collection at the California Palace of the Legion of Honor in San Francisco is being held to celebrate the trans-Pacific links between the Myer and Gantner families and to mark the centenary of Sidney (Baevski) Myer's arrival in Australia from his native Russia.

Born in Krichev, Belarus, in 1878, Sidney Myer joined his elder brother Elcon in Australia at the age of twenty-one. Although penniless on arrival, by 1904 the brothers had opened a small shop in the prosperous gold-mining town of Bendigo. The business expanded rapidly, and in 1911 Sidney purchased a store in central Melbourne. This became the Myer Emporium, the largest store in the Southern Hemisphere and the nucleus of an Australia-wide retailing empire.

Sidney Myer visited the United States in 1918 and formed a friendship with Reverend Brewster Adams, a prominent Baptist minister in Reno. In January 1920, Adams officiated at Sidney Myer's marriage to Merlyn Baillieu at the Palace Hotel in San Francisco. Sidney and Merlyn Myer spent a great deal of time in San Francisco during the 1920s, and their four children — Kenneth (deceased), Neilma, Baillieu, and Marigold — were all born there.

In America, Sidney Myer studied retailing and investment practices, becoming a member of San Francisco's Commercial Club and New York's Department Store Research Bureau. He introduced many innovations into his business, which he directed from California, constantly traveling by ship to and from Australia. The family had homes on both sides of the ocean until 1929, when Sidney and Merlyn Myer decided to return permanently to Australia. Nevertheless, they continued to visit San Francisco frequently until Sidney's sudden death in 1934.

In San Francisco, Sidney had often met his friends and business associates at the Bohemian Club and the Californian Golf Club. Among his closest friends was John Oscar Gantner, a wellknown knitwear manufacturer.

John Oscar Gantner's father, John Gantner (1823 – 1889), had left his native Switzerland at the age of eighteen. In 1849 he arrived in California, where he spent many years working as a blacksmith on various mines before purchasing the Schweitzerhof (Swiss Hotel) on Commercial Street, San Francisco, with his wife, the former Nannette Kalenback. They had two sons, John Oscar (b. 1868) and Frederick (b. 1870).

For a time John O. Gantner worked as a book-keeper/secretary to the hotel. Then, in the early 1890s, he took up an offer from a family friend, J. J. Pfister, to help run his knitting mill. Ten years later, keen to modernize, John decided to go into business with the superintendent, Mr. Mattern. They purchased a small knitting mill and began trading as Gantner and Mattern in September 1900. The business flourished. Though the San Francisco earthquake of 18 April 1906 destroyed their first retail store soon after it opened, by 1909 they had established a new store downtown. The firm's catalogues went to department stores throughout the United States, and in the 1930s its "waterlovers" billboards became a feature of the Californian landscape.

In 1908 John O. Gantner married Adela Isadora Frisby, whose great-uncle, General Mariano G. Vallejo, had been the last Spanish military commander of Northern California. Eight years later, the couple and their three children — John O. Gantner jnr., Vallejo, and Adela — moved to Pacific Heights. By the 1920s the Gantner and Myer families were close friends, and in 1941 John Gantner's second son, Vallejo, married Sidney Myer's eldest daughter, Neilma, cementing the links between the two families.

In the seven years of their marriage, Neilma and Vallejo Gantner lived in San Francisco and had two sons, Vallejo and Carrillo. They were later divorced, and in 1954, after studying creative writing at Stanford University, Neilma returned to Australia with her sons. Young Vallejo died in an accident in 1962, having just completed his first year at university. Carrillo graduated from the University of Melbourne, then returned to the Bay Area in 1966 to obtain a graduate degree in drama at Stanford. He went back to Melbourne in 1969 to follow a career as an actor and producer. Carrillo founded the Playbox Theatre Company and later built the Malthouse arts complex. In recent years he has been increasingly involved in Myer family business and philanthropic activities. He followed his uncle Baillieu Myer as chairman of the private family investment company and is also a vice-president of the Myer Foundation.

The idea of forming a collection of contemporary Aboriginal art to be shown in San Francisco was the inspiration of Sidney Myer's son, Baillieu Myer, who is known for his patronage and love of the arts. For more than thirty years Baillieu has acted as a trustee of the Sidney Myer Fund, a philanthropic trust established by his father, and in 1959 he and his brother Kenneth cofounded the Myer Foundation, of which his sister Marigold is now the president. The brothers also served

the public company, the Myer Emporium Ltd., now Coles Myer Ltd., with great distinction for more than sixty years. Baillieu's eye for contemporary painting was apparent in the Baillieu Myer Collection of the 80s, which was donated to the Museum of Modern Art at Heide in Melbourne. Baillieu is also a member of the National Council of the Fine Arts Museums of San Francisco. He and his wife Sarah follow the family's long-standing tradition of broad philanthropy towards science, social welfare, the arts, and cultural programs.

Baillieu, Neilma, and Carrillo have joined together in building this collection of contemporary Australian Aboriginal art to mark the strong bonds between the Myer and Gantner families, San Francisco and Melbourne, and to pay tribute to their forebears who forged these lasting links of family and friendship. To this end, it seems most fitting to celebrate the distinctive creativity of Australia's indigenous people and share it with the citizens of San Francisco and beyond.

The Gantner Myer Aboriginal Art Collection

Spirit Country presents Aboriginal art that continues to express people's essential relationship with their Spirit Ancestors, the land and their spiritual beliefs concerning the Tjukurrpa or Dreaming, the creation era. The collection has been formed over a four-year period, and is purposely designed to reveal the best of recent contemporary Aboriginal art practiced in the main art centers on indigenous lands from the Desert, the Kimberleys and the tropical Top End. Selected works from previous eras have been included as reference points to show the sources of contemporary Aboriginal art and the way in which it has changed over the decades.

The paintings and sculptures in the Gantner Myer Aboriginal Art Collection are the work of major indigenous Australian Aboriginal artists, many of whom have significant careers as solo exhibiting artists. The collection also encompasses community work that expresses people's continuous sense of history

and spirituality relating to the land through art. The artists deal with individual themes in relation to their knowledge and the law relating to their own spiritual connection to a particular tract of land. In some paintings, notably the major abstract works from the desert regions, an interplay can be discerned between individual painterly inventiveness and ancient spirituality that already has its own symbolic code.

The rich, often surprising, always bold and dynamic collection largely reflects the taste and vision of its patrons, Carrillo Gantner and Sidney Baillieu Myer, and guidance from the curator Jennifer Isaacs. Using paint from the earth itself, the ground substances left by the Creative Ancestors, or the bright colors of modern acrylic paints, indigenous artists have moved to the forefront of mainstream Australian contemporary art.

Compiled from information by
Baillieu Myer and Carrillo Gantner

Impressions of an American Curator in the Outback

As a curator, I have had a long-standing interest in the arts of the Pacific. Although I had traveled to the big cities of Australia several times in my career, these trips had always been for other purposes and never to concentrate solely on Australian Aboriginal art. That's what made my November 1997 trip with noted author and Aboriginal arts authority Jennifer Isaacs so special. We were collaborating on an exhibition of Australian Aboriginal art for American audiences. I was thrilled at the prospect of traveling through Australia's famed "outback," that remote, inner wilderness I had long heard about but never experienced. What better way to get a sense of this ancient country and its people?

As a kind of orientation for our desert journey, we went gallery-hopping in Sydney and Melbourne so that I could begin to get an idea of how things work. By the time Aboriginal paintings and sculptures get to the big auction houses in the cities, they can be many times the price originally paid for them in distant Aboriginal communities. The artists often have delightfully graphic names — Long Tom Tjapanangka, Rover Thomas, Ginger Riley, or Helicopter Tjungurrayi — and the titles of the paintings are poetic — *Flying Ant Dreaming, Death of the Tjampitjin Fighting Man at Tjunta,* or *Yingarna, the Rainbow Serpent.*

The scene in the galleries was a familiar one. There were many canvases hanging on the walls, with marked prices or keyed price lists. Books and catalogues were everywhere, as were slick brochures pitching a particular artist or Contemporary Aboriginal Art in general. As I was to find out, the atmosphere in the Aboriginal arts co-operatives, where canvases originate, is completely different. There, the artists calmly obtain their supplies of canvas and acrylic paint, brush the flies away, sit on the ground or floor, and get to work. Both men and women paint, and some paintings are group efforts. The co-operatives provide the space, guidance, and

materials for making artworks. They store the works, sell them for the artists, and give them a percentage of the price. They are run by art managers, most of whom are non-Aboriginal, and the best of them are available at all hours to assist the Aboriginal community with any personal crisis. It is demanding work, and the managers who are most emotionally involved generally leave after about five years, depleted by responsibilities and concern.

Some Western buyers may have little interest in the meaning of what they are collecting, but to Aboriginal painters, these paintings are not just pretty pictures. They are expressions of an entire view of the cosmos, replete with meaning about the origins of life, ceremony, and law. What we see as bold color and form denotes the presence of Ancestral beings who are permanently linked to the living — beings who came out of the earth, moved around in important patterns, and formed the landscape, creating all the physical and social aspects of the known world. Aboriginal images are not attempts to capture appealing views of nature or to create magnificent saleable designs. In Aboriginal terms, every bit of landscape is somebody's home. Everything, from a rugged desert mountain to a seemingly insignificant mark on the land, is of profound importance. Coming from a culture in which size is equated with significance, I quickly learned to cultivate an appreciation for a wide range of dimensions.

I was not prepared for the tremendous diversity and individuality of the painters. There appear to be no stylistic constraints, only limitations in the subject matter that are specific to particular artists. There is as much stylistic freedom in Aboriginal painting as there is in contemporary Western art, but because Aboriginal art looks like abstract expressionism, conceptualism, primitivism or other isms in Western art, some people look on the works as affordable Jackson Pollocks or Mark Rothkos.

Here is how I, an American curator, experienced the Australian outback. It was a series of transitions — from one culture (American), to another culture (Australian), to yet another culture (Aboriginal), and into its art.

The Aboriginal people have occupied the ageless terrain of Australia for at least 40,000 years, knowing in their specific homelands the habitats of all food plants and animals, the possible sources of sub-terranean water, and ancestral maps of totems that link the people to their country and keep them alive. They have depended on this knowledge for their lives. Call these ancestral maps songlines or lifelines; as much as we want to see or penetrate them, they are all invisible to Westerners. We are too devoted to directed thinking and the logic of what we see. If you think of the landscape as a massive accordion, folded back and forth on itself, you can begin to understand how this great, ancient land turns many things inward. I was amazed when an overnight electrical storm with a deluge of rain left only a hint of wet sand in the morning. Where had those vast quantities of water gone? Of course. They went inward.

The Ancestors gave the Aboriginal people the knowledge of where to find these inward things, which are marked by the subtlest of "signposts," providing the sustenance for their basic life. The land and everything in or on it is animate. To say Aboriginal people live by their wits doesn't begin to explain it. Meanwhile, we Western visitors do not seek out underground water sources ("water-soaks"). Instead, we cart our water around in giant containers, hauling it in an air-conditioned Toyota Landcruiser 4WD, with a 4.2-liter diesel engine, a radio if we need to call for help, extra tires, and food supplies for two weeks.

Out in the bush, where everything seems red, spiky, distant, close-up, or baked, there are no edges. We could be anywhere, we could be nowhere. Roads are meaningless, and there is no program of Western signage. Perhaps we are in the land of the burrowing skink (a new word I jot down with delight, a kind of short-legged lizard, a totemic creature with great meaning to Aboriginal communities).

As if I am in kindergarten, Jenny takes me out for a walk in the bush. First we see the bloodwood tree, housing juicy moth larvae. Then I am shown the edible portulaca plant, with minute black seeds that Aboriginal women make into bread, and leaves that can be eaten in times of drought. We walk past the occasional rabbit burrow or goanna hole, see the telltale marks where a kangaroo sat or scuffled in the reddish dust before dawn, and make a left to the grevillea tree, its frondy yellow flowers dripping with nectar. Next comes the witchetty bush, whose roots seasonally provide the succulent and highly nutritious witchetty grub, a kind of comfort food. On the rest of the walk we find bush banana plants, mulga apples, desert raisins and bush tomatoes. All of this is here on this vast, red desert but my eyes aren't trained to see it. Isn't that little animal cute? No. Aboriginal people don't emotionalize food or animals. But here's something I can see, and it brings me to a screeching halt: a hot-pink parakeelya plant with stunning flowers, a perfect succulent. Suddenly, a mother and baby camel run, startled, from the road. (Wild camels in Australia? Camels and their Afghan owners used to deliver mail and supplies in the outback, where they were considered more reliable than cars.) I learn that mulga trees provide the best shade on hot or muggy days, that clumps of spinifex are ubiquitous — these are related to those endless dots that appear on some acrylic paintings. Spinifex was and is still used by Aboriginal people for adhesives, resins, and, more recently, baskets.

Many desert Aboriginal people prefer to sit (or lie) directly on the earth. Direct contact with the land is important; touching the earth is a sign of reverence. But for us there are folding chairs to keep the red dust off our clothing. After we have had lunch and traveled on, our tables and chairs will leave odd patterns in the dust for smaller creatures to ponder over. Then, when night falls, we will haul out our termite-proof swags with puffy pillows and sleep under the stars in complete bliss.

Peter, our guide, has driven around for hours to find the perfect place for our night camp. Jenny and I are nearly cross-eyed with exasperation, but to him the optimal campsite is important — among other things, you certainly don't want to choose a place near a cattle crossing. He also wants me to have the best orientation to the sunrise when I wake. The camp position he finally chooses is worth it. Just a few hundred yards away, standing like a specter, is a stunning ghost gum *(Eucalyptus papuana)*, the like of which I've never seen. There are hundreds of varieties of gums in Australia, but surely the willowy ghost gum is the Ancestors' most magnificent creation.

In the outback, you must learn about ocher. Ocher is a clay colored by iron oxide. It is found in veins, in various tones and hues — usually a version of yellow or reddish brown. The Aboriginal people use it as a pigment, and not just for painting canvases. For painting bodies. For painting up the country. It occurs in Rover Thomas's canvases as soft hunks on the swirling surface. Some ochers are so important that groups of Aboriginal men will travel for hundreds of miles just to obtain them. There are heavy fines for unauthorized ocher removal. Blocks or pebbles of ocher are ground on small palettes or stones, crushed into a fine powder, then mixed with water or fixatives. Jenny tells me that ocher and its properties are sacred. That red ocher is the most important color, and that every area of Aboriginal land has its own characteristic ocher colors. It would be possible to chart the country by its ocher hues.

The next day, as we drive on, I notice that there are an extraordinary number of car wrecks all over the seemingly timeless landscape — rusting old bodies that have been dragged into the bush, and turned over on their sides or backs like beetles. I want to

laugh. Is this a joke, an art piece, an ancient custom? Jenny explains that when Aboriginal people buy cars, they're often sold patched-up lemons — cars calculated to go only just so far and then to break down. There is little protection of consumer rights in the outback, and material maintenance is alien to the Aboriginal way of life. Being possessed by possessions, as we are in the West, is not part of this communal culture. A thing has its life, and it is used for the benefit of the community. Then it is left to return to the land and the life cycle. Except that these cars are not part of a food chain or a cosmic plan. They rust and rot but cannot decompose. Their overturned carcasses are initially sniffed for petrol fumes (a dangerous pursuit among young Aboriginals wanting to get high). Ultimately, however, the car parts are useless. Do not treat this as a subject for art, I tell myself. Do not aestheticize human tragedy. Put your camera away.

To try to grasp the size and geography of Australia, one must grossly oversimplify. You can superimpose the Australian continent over the whole of Asia. Basically, the European Australians (who came about 210 years ago) now occupy most of the southeastern and southern edges of the continent, where they lead a sophisticated, citified existence. The inner country, the hinterland — the northern, central, and western parts of the continent — is considered less choice. Aboriginal people are found everywhere on the continent, but have best maintained their way of life in the outback, especially in the central and western parts of the country. Almost in the center of the continent is a town called Alice Springs, or simply "Alice" to the locals. Here is our last opportunity to get Western delicacies and gear before heading to the desert. From Alice, if you plan to drive for miles to remote Aboriginal communities, you must have a special government permit. There may or may not be roads, and you'd better have a two-way radio. These areas are very much like our Indian reservations in the States, but they seem much more immense.

Always remember, the land and everything in or on it is animate. The more you learn, the more you realize that the Aboriginal Ancestors really outdid themselves in their creations of organisms and landforms. What they didn't count on was the devastating effects of European culture — the thirst for land, the desire for ownership, the diseases, the debilitating liquor, the rot of civilization when things don't work or aren't fixed. No ceremony takes care of these. Who could have predicted they'd drop a cattle station on top of your grandmother's sacred site? Who foresaw that cattle would destroy the habitats of your ancestral kangaroos, goannas, or yams? Or that dialysis machines would be sorely needed in Aboriginal communities, as a result of alcohol-related disease? Things have gone radically wrong for rural Aboriginal people. The Ancestors could not have foreseen this heart-breaking predicament in their wildest dreams.

Coming from a country that has neglected and decimated its indigenous peoples in the name of progress, I see many parallels in Australia. In the central outback in the late nineteenth century, horsemanship and skill in cattle work ultimately became a source of pride for dispossessed Aboriginal people, just as it did for some displaced Native American peoples. This cattle work has provided a way for Aboriginal people to stay close to nature, be left to themselves, perpetuate their ceremonies, be near their homelands, and remember their past. In Alice, you can buy spiffy cowboy clothes, and look like you're part of a rodeo. The Aboriginal men like that. Some of them still dress this way, and they really look good.

Aboriginal women in the far outback communities like Haasts Bluff or Yuendumu are likewise distinctive and splendid-looking. Often they are barefoot, wearing Western-style clothes in splashy prints. The combinations of tops and bottoms are eye-catching, and to our eyes outrageously matched. Some wear bandannas on their heads. It is touching that they will not look at you directly. That would be rude, I suppose, to look directly, but they are always watching. Anxiety time — do I shake hands or hug? On Jenny's advice I do as the mood takes me. Whatever I do is all right. I feel awkward, bumbling, and stupid. They are poised and relaxed. Together, we brush away flies.

In these Aboriginal outback communities, there's barely a general store. "Men's and Women's Keeping Places," someone's idea of indigenous museums, have long been ransacked, and are boarded up. There is usually some kind of church with a tin roof. Luckily, the old-time missionaries considered Aboriginal art as "useful toil." Habitations range from battered-looking Western-style houses to hovels; maybe there's running water, maybe not. I try to forget how they stack the French fries at the Ritz Carlton; there's no parallel here.

We visit the Ikuntji Women's Centre in Haasts Bluff and the Warlukurlangu Artists Co-operative in Yuendumu. Both these art co-operatives work more or less in the same manner. The artists are middle-aged to elderly, working independently or in groups. They sit directly on the ground and paint. It is rude to take pictures of them without their permission, especially while they are painting. They use whatever canvas size has been provided and whatever paint colors are available. Maybe they paint just a tiny patch of iridescent red, so as not to use it all up. No one worries about frames. When the works are done, they are rolled up and stored on cinder-block shelves. After the works are sold by the co-operative, the artists get a percentage, perhaps 40 per cent of the fee. The rest of the money goes back into the co-operative to pay for exhibitions or more supplies. (I don't see a single young painter; if the elders are the only ones who paint and the young people generally aren't interested; what will be the future of Aboriginal painting in these communities?)

Now, why, given all the ways that Aboriginal and Western (European-Australian) cultures are wildly out of whack, would painting be such a joyful crossroads of these two vinegar-and-oil cultures, something that each, for its own reasons, can heartily embrace? I have always been interested in the rare, brief but ecstatic intersection of complementary aesthetic values between otherwise disjunctive cultures. The reality, however, is disconcerting. Westerners look at Aboriginal acrylic canvases and joyfully see artworks in the modern tradition. Aboriginal artists are more than happy to paint these works because there is "nothing whitefella" in the activity of painting or in the images they create. Their works proclaim land rights, panoramas of life, the life force, animated landscapes, and sacred identities. They mean many untranslatable things at once. They aren't giving away tribal secrets (or if they are, we can't decode them); they are showing Westerners what they believe we are able to see, in an effort to educate our sorry souls. This is serious work. This is one area that does not require compromise. They want big money for their paintings, and why shouldn't they get it?

What would an Aboriginal artist see, I idly wonder, if he or she were shown a Rothko or a Pollock? Has any aspiring Ph.D. candidate ever tried to ask Aboriginal artists their opinions of Western contemporary art? Do they have thoughts or discussions about aesthetics? Who do they consider their best painters? Are there indigenous categories of aesthetic evaluation?

Later, back in the States, I spoke to Fred Myers, an anthropologist interested in these questions. We met in 1998 at a conference celebrating the Kluge Collection of Aboriginal Art in Charlottesville, Virginia. Myers and other speakers at the conference confirmed that, for a Westerner, Aboriginal painting collapses a number of different ideas, concepts, experiences, and symbols on a two-dimensional surface plane. A single element or group of elements can articulate a ritual object, a particular place, a clan or body design, an ancestral being, a historical event, and/or a totemic plant. Yet the analysis only goes so far; the paintings can't be intricately defined. They don't stand for or mean something else. As the saying goes, the paintings mean themselves.

Yet what the Western brain wants to do with Aboriginal painting is to chop it into understandable categories:

1. Broad conceptual frameworks
2. Cultural symbols
3. Communication systems
4. Abstract art
5. Land rights and politics

We want to spread meaning out, but we can't. The more you chop it up in our Western analytical manner, the further away you get from the reality of experiencing the actual work.

According to Fred Myers, no conscious vocabulary has been found in Aboriginal speech for analyzing beauty or art. But just because the vocabulary may not exist does not necessarily mean that there are no evaluations or judgments made about paintings. Myers suggests that, for some painters, the "expressive" or aesthetic function of their painting predominates, while for others the "poetic" function (the message, the rhythm, or the rhyme) may be the key. A tremendous amount of experimentation, invention, and freedom seem to be at work in Aboriginal paintings. Personal style is absolutely allowed. The diversity of the paintings suggests that aesthetic judgments are at work, even if people do not articulate them. Many artists will consciously experiment with the composition of a painting; others will not.

Creativity, innovation, and resourceful adaptation have always been characteristics of Aboriginal life At Sotheby's in Sydney I was amazed to see a collection of exquisitely and ingeniously made spear points, in various hues, fabricated from discarded glass telegraph wire insulators that had been found by resourceful Aboriginals, and delicately chipped into great works of art.

For much of my trip I struggled with the false problem of "traditional art" versus "contemporary art." I thought of what American audience expectations would be for an exhibition of Aboriginal art. Most people in the United States are not deeply aware of the contemporary Aboriginal painting movement and don't often have the chance to see a work of Aboriginal art. When we think of Aboriginal art, many of us are more likely to think of historic objects from the outback — boomerangs, rock engravings, secret charms, feather headdresses, or body decorations we've seen on TV or in the movies. Seasoned collectors or connoisseurs might wish to see "fine old Aboriginal objects" — pure and intact, made of indigenous materials, with good age and patination — exotic objects, highly crafted, revealing tribal secrets, imbued with sacred beliefs. Their "sensitometers of the authentic" might reject an acrylic painting instantly, but they would be wrong.

Yet here we are, surrounded by works of reasonably clean surfaces, synthetic materials, and Westernized-looking paintings. And they sure aren't copying our modern art. I wonder how such different journeys have brought both cultures to roughly the same visual place. Is it possible to appreciate Aboriginal art as mainstream and contemporary, and also as religious and traditional? I think that this is a question that people have to answer for themselves. Most Aboriginal contemporary painting that I have seen seems to speak from a true and authentic voice. At the same time, to Western eyes these canvases appear not only sophisticated but beautiful. Why are we surprised?

We have ended our outback journey and have now returned to the town of Alice. Exhausted and spent, we yearn for showers and are gradually winding down. In town, we come upon Walimpirrnga Tjapaltjarri and his brother Walala, members of the last small band of nomadic desert people, who became a media sensation when they "came in" in 1984. They are dressed in Western clothes and have a Western smoke. We shake hands and talk on the edge of a city park. I cannot understand a word they are saying, but I know that this meeting is important and that we have hit upon good fortune. I wonder if these men were, in a sense, the Australian equivalents of Ishi, the famous Yahi Indian declared to be the last living descendant of his kind in California. But as Jenny says, "To whom were any of these so-called 'Lost Tribe' people ever considered to be lost? Certainly never to themselves."

Kathleen Berrin
Curator in Charge
Africa, Oceania, and the Americas
Fine Arts Museum of San Francisco

Kathleen Berrin wishes to thank
Baillieu Myer of Melbourne and
Peter Yates of Alice Springs for their friendship
and support in the preparation of this essay.
Special thanks to Karen Kevorkian and,
of course, Jennifer Isaacs.

SPIRIT COUNTRY

Spirit Country

The art of Australian Aboriginal people is a modern, vibrant expression of many indigenous nations. Yet it is also ancient, as old as humankind's first mark-making. Contemporary paintings exploring Aboriginal people's spiritual connection to their special tracts of land are part of a continuum from ancient rock engravings and cave paintings, through a continuing tradition of ground designs and body art, to the expressive canvas and bark paintings of today.

The works in this volume have been selected specifically to explore that extraordinary spiritual continuum among communities in the central desert, the Kimberley to the northwest, and Arnhem Land and the offshore islands in the far north. All the artists represented here are working from a deep religious base, but in recent years they have pushed and extended the form of their work in ways that excite critics and collectors of contemporary art. Among the desert communities, the formal process of laying down ground designs, which were subsequently translated into dotted canvases, has now become a painterly, abstract art movement. In the Kimberley, artists have developed a unique style of ocher paintings on canvas, blending stories of the land and the ancestral characters with recent social history. The Arnhem Land bark painters have also moved their art into contemporary forms, elaborating their characteristic cross-hatching into fine, mesmerizing webs that are being read simultaneously as religious works, titles to land, and abstract art.

The People and the Land

The Australian continent extends from tropical wetlands in the far north through a vast expanse of desert terrain in the center, to coastal riverine environments that once sustained very large Aboriginal populations. The offshore islands, including Tasmania, were also home to indigenous peoples. As the climate and natural environment

(previous page)
Ghost gum country, Northern Territory
PHOTOGRAPH: Richard Woldendorp

PLATE 42 (detail)
Rover Thomas, c. 1926–1998
Gulgoodji, 1988
60.5 x 105.5 cm (24 x 41.5 in.)
Natural earth pigments and bush gum on canvas

varied, so did the resources for humankind and the cultural practices that arose from interaction with such widely different types of country.

Archaeological records indicate that Aboriginal peoples probably came to Australia by sea from the islands to the north. When this occurred is unknown; estimates range anywhere from 40,000 to 100,000 B.P. Aboriginal peoples' religious account of their origin is much more cataclysmic. Spirit Ancestors emerged from beneath the central desert and moved overland, creating as they went. In the far north, however, the story of the origin of human beings retains the theme of travel over the sea by canoe.[1]

Linguists differ, but it is generally thought that more than two hundred distinct languages were once spoken throughout the continent. There are now fewer than fifty in daily use, although local literacy programs and bilingual education schemes are reintroducing and affirming the importance of continuing culture through language.

Most Aboriginal people moved across their lands, traveling to particular tracts of their country according to the season. In rich coastal areas the homelands could be quite small, perhaps the area bounded by two creeks, but in arid lands where food was scarce, people were much more mobile within their prescribed territories, traveling over hundreds of square miles. Food was gathered seasonally, and people sometimes moved daily in search of sustenance for the family, using a basic repertoire of weapons and utensils.

When Europeans first came to settle in Australia about two hundred years ago, Australian Aboriginal people were regarded as "the last of the stone age peoples." This was partly a product of ignorance prevalent in the eighteenth century (and in many quarters still today) that some races were "superior" to others as measured by such things as agricultural practices, inventions, technology, and social practices or "civilization." Aboriginal peoples' widespread use of stone technology — spear heads, axes, and cutting

tools — to provide for their daily needs was seen as an indication of cultural inferiority.

Trade in stone objects was an important part of the extensive trade cycles that existed throughout Aboriginal Australia before colonization. Here too there are elements of continuity with the present day. Contact between peoples and trade in property of importance remains a significant way in which Aboriginal peoples interact with the wider world. In many ways, a new cultural exchange system that involves making portable art has replaced earlier forms of trade, but the key parameters of the process have been retained.

Spirit World, Dreamings, and Tjukurrpa

Throughout Aboriginal Australia, the religious philosophy of the land and the Ancestors provides answers to the fundamental question of creation and existence, and hence of the meaning of life. This system of belief is given many different names, depending on the language of the speaker. The Anmatyerre and related peoples refer to it as the Altyerre, while the peoples of the Kimberley call it the Ngarrangkarni. Among the Pitjantjatjara and related desert peoples it is the Tjukurrpa, the term that is widely used in this book.

The common English translation, Dreaming, is evocative but inadequate to encompass the scope and multiple levels of the concept. Broadly, Tjukurrpa is spoken of in terms of both the past and the present. It was the original Creation era, the time during which the land, all its features, and the life upon it were created by spiritual beings, the great Creation Ancestors. These spirit beings took many forms — human, animal, and plant — and in some places they were objects, substances, or forces. For example, in some places people speak of hail Tjukurrpa or honey Tjukurrpa, of lightning or wind Tjukurrpa.

During the Tjukurrpa period, these ancestral beings or forces traveled widely across the land and performed remarkable feats of creation and destruction. The journey pathways or routes along which they traveled are remembered and celebrated wherever they went, at particular sites along their routes. The present Aboriginal groups across the country trace their descent directly from these great Spirit Ancestors.

The Tjukurrpa is therefore a creative force from the distant past, but it is also a constant and pervasive force in present-day life. The record of the Tjukurrpa events is apparent in the natural features of the land, be they large mountains, river systems, waterholes, a particular mark on a tree, or a pattern on the surface of a stone. Each is a form of immutable evidence and a manifestation of the Ancestor that speaks to present-day people. Tjukurrpa is omnipresent, and the term is used in a variety of contexts that Westerners sometimes find confusing. Discussing a painting, an artist might say, "That's my Tjukurrpa." When someone is absent for ceremonies involving men's law, his relatives might say, "He's gone for Tjukurrpa." On waking from an intense dream, a person could indicate that a visionary character in the dream had sung to him, giving him new Tjukurrpa.

Tjukurrpa is also a synonym for Aboriginal religious law, which must be observed properly to ensure the balance of the elements and the continuation of life in all its forms. During their epic journeys, the Spirit Ancestors sang and performed ceremonies. In the far north these song cycles are handed on from generation to generation along with body designs, which were also painted on the chests of the first Creation Ancestors at the time of the first songs. In the desert, the Ancestors left their spirit essence, their power, in the form of sacred stone objects, which (until they were plundered by traders and opportunists in recent times) remained at the sacred sites, being brought out only for sacred ceremonies exclusive to highly initiated men. These stone or wood tablets are shown to novices only after certain rites of passage, and never to women; they bear the geometric markings that underpin so much

of today's contemporary desert art by men. In the far north, the central desert, and the Kimberley, it can be said that ancient mark-making from caves, rocks, and ceremonial life continues as the reference point and structure behind much contemporary art, which expresses the spirit of the land.

Concepts of Identity, the Land, and Designs

To understand Aboriginal concepts of life, it is necessary to comprehend as a first premise that the land or earth itself is not static. It also is a living thing. It can and does interact with human beings, animals, plants, the elements, and the constellations above.[2]

Aboriginal explanations of the way an individual relates to the world contain remarkably unified concepts, such as that embodied in the word "djalkiri," used by the Yolngu of northeast Arnhem Land. Djalkiri, which literally means "foot" or "footprint," is translated by the more poetic and philosophical Yolngu in their bilingual literature center as "foundation," referring to culture, society, and individual identity.[3]

The range of concepts involved can be glimpsed in a remarkable diagram produced by Yolngu school students at Yirrkala to explain their cosmos. At the center of this diagram was an image of a footprint with the word "Djalkiri." All around it were radiating lines with words in their own language that translated into the following: paintings, stories, women's business, singing, circumcision, kinship relations, languages, special land sites connected to the creator beings, sacred law, time, events, creatures of the land at the time it was created, ritual dances, symbols of clan identity, groups of people, and rules of everyday behavior. The land, therefore, contains all these for each person.

As Dhayirra Yunupingu, a Yolngu writer, has put it:

> This land of ours, it provided our ceremonial objects ... and it wasn't only the sacred things which were given but the land also provided the sacred names, the

kinship, the sub-sections, the homelands, and whatever language you might speak. So wherever we Yolngu people see this land, we must care for it, even as if it were our mother.[4]

A fundamental aspect of Aboriginal being is the integral connection between expressing thought, communicating details of religious ancestry, and stating land ownership. In this, Australian Aboriginal people have much in common with other indigenous peoples of the world. The land is the basis of who and what they are, and is essential to their survival as separate peoples. They repeatedly insist in every forum — in publications, at conferences, in the media — that people cannot be separated from other living things. All living things are connected to the land in which they grow, and knowledge of the land and its resources is an integral part of the culture. They plead for intellectual integrity, not just understanding and acceptance, but recognition, respect, and most importantly deference within the context of their own lands. This is a crucial part of their art. Making paintings is an integral part of expressing oneself, and therefore one's land or "being."

The ownership of "designs" is at the center of Aboriginal intellectual property. Common Western notions of property in dwellings or objects were not a part of traditional Aboriginal society, but intellectual knowledge, religious in its base, held significant value. Indeed, its value was such that those who devalued it through social or cultural transgressions, or by acting against the rules of Tjukurrpa — for example, by stealing sacred information or exposing sacred men's business to women — were punished by death.

In this context, designs were used as a means of achieving influence and power over others. The successive revelation of designs formed part of young men's gradual age-grading rituals. In the desert, the large ground designs that form the basis of today's acrylic painting movement were progressively revealed to initiates at sacred ceremonies away from the eyes of women. In Arnhem Land, under different laws and visual traditions, the magnificent designs painted in ocher on initiates' chests and bodies were visible to most of the community, but the successive and deeper layers of meaning, each a metaphor for the one beneath, were the province of older law-keepers.

The sacred information about such designs was contained in songs or song cycles recording the journeys, speech, and actions of the Creation Ancestors and the making of the first designs. Like the designs themselves, these songs had to be learned by initiates at increasing levels of complexity, according to age and training.

Women's ceremonies and designs were different from men's, yet the two were complementary. This reflected the wider separation of roles in Aboriginal cultures, particularly in desert areas. On a daily basis, women talked, sat, worked, hunted, and cared for children in the company of other women. This separation of roles extended to ownership of aspects of the Tjukurrpa. Men and women owned different aspects of the same "story."

This division continues today, and is reflected in the subject matter of contemporary paintings. Men's paintings detail aspects of "men's business" — the journeys of male Ancestors gathering in novices for initiation. Women's paintings may depict the same ceremony, but be about the water site the Ancestors made and the women ancestors who gathered food, dug for small game, or sang love-magic songs using their potent spindles to make handspun fur string for their hair-belt lures.

Sometimes, men and women help each other with paintings, but women will not paint some key

PLATE 95 (detail)
Willy Gudabi, c. 1916–1996
Grandfather's Paintings, 1995
160 x 122 cm (63 x 48 in.)
Acrylic on board

elements belonging to the men, or will soften the colors. Ceremonial life retains aspects of secrecy, and women are not allowed access to "inside" men's religious knowledge or practice. Similarly, men do not approach or participate in "women's business." Among the Anmatyerre people, for example, men own the emu Dreaming and the associated emu ceremonies and designs; but emus have to eat, and they love to feed on yam flowers and seeds, for which the Tjukurrpa is owned by women.

In Aboriginal Australia, both designs and songs were exchanged with nearby peoples. When people traveled around, negotiating over hunting, marriages, and care of country, and trading in other items such as ocher, gum, weapons, stones, and utensils, the gifting or sharing of sections of religious knowledge formed part of the system of traditional trade.[5] Just as the Creation Ancestors moved across the country, the long song cycles recording their journeys moved from area to area across regions of Australia. The story of two Creation women's travels, for example, might take a particular form in Arnhem Land, but similar themes occur again throughout the desert, where they reappear on the landscape as two women or Minyma Tjukurrpa (women of the Creation era). The exchange of knowledge that linked songs, ceremonies, and mythology over vast tracts of country remains a living tradition. When Aboriginal people gather in contemporary settings, perhaps to discuss land rights, health, or education, one of the first points of exchange is a discussion of their kinship and connections. This is often done by tracing stories or songlines that have been handed down to them and for which they are responsible.

What happens when sacred art or designs are placed in the art market and "traded" for money? It is important to understand that Aboriginal artists' connection with the paintings they make continues after the works are sold. This has been explained by comparing Aboriginal thought processes with Polynesian practices of gift-giving, known among Maori as "hau," "the spirit of things."[6] In these exchange systems,

> *The obligation attached to a gift itself is not inert. Even when abandoned by the giver, it still forms a part of him. Through it he has a hold over the recipient, just as he had, while its owner, a hold over anyone who stole it … We can see the nature of the bond created by the transfer of a possession … it is clear that in the Maori custom this bond created by things is in fact a bond between persons, since the thing itself is a person or pertains to a person. Hence it follows that to give something is to give a part of oneself … In this system of ideas one gives away what is in reality a part of one's nature and substance, while to receive something is to receive a part of someone's spiritual essence.[7]*

Aboriginal people naturally want recognition of their art, which represents their great knowledge of the content of the land and the right way to live and act within it. In selling, exchanging, and exhibiting their works, they are also obviously hoping to improve their economic position within Australian society. The money earned by selling art is significant, but in the context of their own culture this exchange has another explanation. It is clear that Aboriginal artists are saying to Australians and to the world at large that they are the landholders and law keepers on their own lands, because the land is integral to their beings, because they have the kinship with it and the knowledge of it. They are saying that, if we understand this, we should defer to that prior and superior connection, and to the integral relationship they have with their country.

"Authenticity" and Innovation

At the closing ceremony of the Atlanta Olympic Games in 1996, members of the Gumatj clan of Yirrkala performed music and dance while their uncles and brothers were completing huge bark paintings — visual texts about the religion of their land, many thousands of miles away. Is this irreconcilable? Is one a more authentic expression of culture than another? Not in the Aboriginal world; both are just expressing culture in a very modern way. Both settings, the world stage and the local community, provide a forum for spiritual and ancestral cultural voices to be heard and seen.

In the past, arguments about the "authenticity" of Aboriginal art were linked to notions of antiquity, which was a synonym for purity. Aboriginal art was valued insofar as it was seen as uncontaminated, the product of a static, "primitive" culture in which designs were handed down intact, unchanged over generations. When the ethnographer Baldwin Spencer first exhibited the bark paintings he had collected near Oenpelli in 1912, the exhibition was called *The Primitive Art of Australian Aborigines*. While Spencer thus applied the term "art" to objects that had previously been seen as mere artifacts or items for trade, the exhibition also placed them in an anthropological, museological domain, where they stayed for many decades.

The category "primitive art" excluded art forms that were breakaways, contemporary visual expressions using new materials or new ideas. Any works deemed to have been influenced by and adjusted to Western tastes were viewed as unauthentic. Aboriginal paintings and ceremonial arts therefore stayed in museums of ethnography, along with the arts of Africa, Oceania, and other pre-colonial cultures, as though they were in some way primordial, rather than the changing and highly responsive art forms of modern non-Western peoples.

What does the use of the word "authentic" signify? In the Western art world, it means a genuine painting by the artist. In the world of "tribal art" or in the ethnographic sense, it means something else as well — closer to "a true statement from within the culture it comes from." The artist might be anonymous, or there might be multiple artists, but for an object to be "authentic" in this sense it must be made to be used, or preferably have been used, within the society it

came from, and not be "influenced" by the society from which it is being viewed (or bought). Aesthetic criteria for excellence of the "authentic" include age, patina, decorative qualities, precision of technique, and rarity. In the latter twentieth century, as relationships between world peoples change, these museological attitudes have belatedly had to readjust. It has become clear that such notions were mostly based on race, and on the erroneous assumption that in most indigenous cultures art does not represent individual creativity.

Part of the wonder experienced in Australia and around the world at the explosion of art activities in Aboriginal communities all around Australia during the past three decades was a result of the widely accepted misconception that there was no prior Aboriginal art, a misconception promulgated at length by earlier writers. In 1962 Douglas Fraser's book *Primitive Art* was published by Thames and Hudson. It became a standard reference work for English-speaking art students throughout the world. The art of the entire Australian continent was represented by just one plate — a rock-art painting of three running mimih figures from western Arnhem Land.

According to Fraser, Australian Aboriginal people lived in "unbearable" conditions, without homes, clothing, metal, pottery, or crops. So they wandered in small groups over a vast territory "searching for . . . wild game and other food."[8] He attributed the absence of portable art to the lack of private property. Sacred designs on objects were simply "memory aids for elders." He claimed that "the idea of organizing large scale patterns seems to have been lacking in ancient Australian art," which he described as "a more or less fossilized survival of art of the Old Stone Age."[9]

Such writers unfortunately created an international conceptual framework into which Aboriginal paintings had to fit. The international art philosophers, the ground-breakers from London,

Paris, and New York, spread the word about the ability of indigenous Australians in the art department (or their lack of it). How wrong they were!

Even when Fraser wrote, spectacular collections of Aboriginal bark paintings and ceremonial arts had been acquired by major Australian galleries. By the 1960s, museums in several cities held thousands of objects that today would be considered fine examples of work by Aboriginal artists throughout Australia. Then, in 1971, nine years after Fraser's book appeared, some of the most remarkable artwork of the twentieth century began pouring from the hands of the Pintupi, Warlpiri, Anmatyerre, and Luritja people camped at the small desert community of Papunya. What the commentators had missed was the fact that art did not have to be portable in order to be art. A single glimpse of the body art of Arnhem Land, with its fine cross-hatched filigree designs from head to toe, would have dispelled the notion that Aborigines did not fill a ground with design.

If the body is a ground, so also is the earth. In the central desert, huge sand paintings and constructions were made, chanted over and danced through until they were annihilated during frenzied and spectacular night-time performances employing every theatrical device — sound, movement, color, and light, with the added drama of fire. These formed the basis for the new paintings on boards. The contemporary Aboriginal art movement did not therefore appear suddenly and inexplicably from nowhere. The Papunya artists had simply shown a new way in which to elaborate on their "cosmological preoccupations,"[10] which they also share with other peoples of the region.

The rise of the desert painting movement coincided with a sea change in Australian government policies towards indigenous people. Since the nineteenth century, the main thrust of Aboriginal policy had been to "absorb" or "assimilate" indigenous people into mainstream Australian culture. This was never an objective that indigenous people held themselves, and in the late 1960s their voices were at last listened to. By 1969 an Australian Council for the Arts had been established, with an Aboriginal arts committee that was given a brief to try to reverse the process of cultural absorption and encourage Aboriginal artists in their work.

The Aboriginal Arts Board was quick to recognize the significance of the new painting movement at Papunya, and provided art advisers and funds to supply services to remote artists. The Board also began to support artists through an active exhibition program. Their acquisitions, now held in the National Museum in Canberra, resulted in many exhibitions in major American and European museums and galleries during the 1970s. They were not yet, however, conceived as exhibitions of contemporary art.

Aboriginal people began to explore their individual creativity within the bounds of custom, tradition, and law. From Papunya, the art movement rapidly spread to other desert communities. The mid-1970s also saw the beginning of the outstation movement, in which groups of Aboriginal people were provided with grants and subsidies to enable them to move back closer to their traditional country. Wells were made and artesian bores sunk to provide water, and the logistics of providing supplies and services to remote communities were investigated. Many established Papunya artists were among those who took the opportunity to return to their own land, continuing to paint and receive art supplies from Papunya Tula.

During the 1970s Aboriginal art began to recover ground in public opinion. The notion of unchanging traditional designs and subject matter became impossible to sustain. Exhibitions such as *Oenpelli Paintings on Bark*, first shown in 1978, made it clear that artists working with traditional materials and

PLATE 59 (detail)
Mick Kubarkku, b. c. 1925
Dibdib Spirit, 1997
138 x 46 cm (54.5 x 18 in.)
Earth ochers on bark

designs could nevertheless display individual creativity and poetic imagination. Even when depicting a single Dreaming figure such as the kangaroo or rainbow serpent, the artists had varied the internal patterning, posture, and general impact from painting to painting in remarkable ways.

By 1979 there was a discernible change in the mainstream Australian art community's attitudes towards Aboriginal art. At the 3rd Biennale of Sydney, a survey exhibition of contemporary art at the Art Gallery of New South Wales, several Aboriginal bark paintings from Ramingining artists were exhibited alongside other contemporary artists. There was also a new willingness to recognize that indigenous art forms had parallels in the most advanced forms of Western art. In 1981, the first ground design executed for the public was made by Dinny Nolan and Paddy Carroll at the National Trust gallery on Observatory Hill in Sydney. In the following year, as part of the 4th Biennale of Sydney at the Art Gallery of NSW, another ground design was executed by Morris Luther and others from Lajamanu; this was an example of a ceremonial installation, as well as modern performance art.

In 1988 a major survey exhibition, *Dreamings*, was mounted by the South Australian Museum at the Asia Society Galleries in New York City and drew wide acclaim. The efforts of the prominent Melbourne gallery-owner Gabrielle Pizzi also brought Aboriginal art to the attention of international art museums. Works were acquired by key museums, including the Brooklyn Museum (Yala Yala Gibbs Tjungarrayi, 1988), the Art Institute of Chicago (Joseph Jurra Tjapaltjarri, 1989), and the Metropolitan Museum of Art (Anatjari Tjakamarra, 1989). In 1989 Papunya paintings were shown at the prestigious New York-based Weber Gallery, known for its minimalist and conceptual exhibitions. To date, there have been perhaps a hundred exhibitions of Aboriginal contemporary art that present the work as mainstream contemporary art, including the

remarkably successful *Aratjara, Art of the First Australians,* at the Hayward Gallery, London, and also at Kunstsammlung Nordrhein-Westfalen in Düsseldorf, in 1993.

Aboriginal art is now a significant component of collectable Australian art, with numerous attendant specialist galleries. The artists of the desert, the north, and the Kimberley work through art centers in their communities, or by direct arrangements with their agents or galleries. The art centers handle materials, business arrangements, and copyright, collect data, and maintain records. They also liaise with galleries and collectors and arrange and manage exhibitions. Often they act as "banks," advancing artists money if necessary. They also play a role in titling the works; when a painting is completed, the artist usually gives a brief explanation of its meaning, which community advisers then abbreviate into a title for the painting.

Balancing the cultural needs of the local artists against outside pressures is a constant difficulty. The managers or advisers in the art centers must drive long distances to maintain contact with artists in their outstations and homelands. It is an arduous, time-consuming but highly rewarding vocation. Increasing numbers of young art and anthropology graduates have welcomed the opportunity to gain a first-hand, intensive education in Aboriginal culture, and to support and promote Aboriginal aspirations to the wider community.

Aboriginal contemporary art is clearly in a category of its own, and resists easy definition. Although it is tempting to use modern art criteria to assess these works — and many critics succumb — Aboriginal art does not fit neatly into the mold of art in a Western sense. Australian critics attempt analysis, but their response is generally one of wary excitement:

> As with so much of Aboriginal art, the deeper you delve, the more you find yourself rubbing your eyes in amazement, befuddled by the usual brew of faint misgivings and deep, abiding wonderment.[11]

Many have found it difficult to come to terms with such an extraordinary art movement when the channels through which it has emerged are so little understood. In its formality and strength, as well as its abstract painterly qualities, the work bore striking similarities to certain international art movements or schools, particularly minimalism and op art. (In reference to the more recent paintings, one could add gestural abstraction and expressionism to the list.)

At the age of eighty, Emily Kame Kngwarreye (see page 102) became perhaps the most famous of the contemporary Aboriginal artists. Charting commentaries on her work over ten years, one can see that critical response was enthusiastic at first, when the recognizable Aboriginal animal tracks and linear structures were clearly visible, but as she moved towards full abstraction, people were dumbfounded. Was this really Aboriginal art, or was she fooling people? Perhaps the dealers were making suggestions to adjust her succeeding styles?

Certainly, like many artists, she changed colors and style, often in response to interest or commissions, but she always retained the essential interior content of what was being expressed — what she called "merne" or "everything", or "kame", the yam seed, the Altyerre (or Tjukurrpa) for which she was the custodian on her land. Speaking virtually no English, and without access to extraneous Western art history, Emily Kngwarreye remained a fully traditional and religious woman all her life. Yet she made marks that have been described as at the cutting edge of abstraction itself.[12]

This power of mark-making and visual resonance has been a hallmark of Aboriginal spiritual arts for millennia. The linear patterns and sculptured bodies of dancers glowing in the moonlight as they move and flash are the antecedents of today's luminous abstract paintings. Geometric stripes may pertain to the marks left by receding water around a waterhole, or they may be stripes on the bark of a tree. The fully abstracted fine rarrk or cross-hatching in a bark painting may resonate with a subliminal, chattering power that reflects the phosphorescence of the scales of the great Rainbow Serpent. The power that emanates from the design is what Aboriginal artists regard as the essential quality of the work, deriving from the spiritual beings themselves. So, when Aboriginal people from a traditional background enter exhibition halls where such paintings are hung, their response is directly related to the power or immanence of the design.

The continuation and vibrancy of desert paintings, and the new work from artists such as the senior women at Kintore or Billy Thomas in the Kimberley, have proved the fecundity of the painting movement.[13] Once only painted or made for ceremonial display, Aboriginal art is now transposed onto new supports and enlivened through individual visual imagination and access to the spectacular color range of modern pigments. These paintings are new ways of expressing life, land, and Tjukurrpa in a visual form.

Aboriginal Art Making

Watching Aboriginal artists at work can be revealing. To sit silently, watching and appreciating the rhythm of the work, is to become part of the process and enter into the mental world the painted surface conjures.

Pintupi and Warlpiri painters sit on the ground, the canvas spread out before them. Working from each side, they first mark out the main pathway in strong lines, circles linked by parallel lines, often dark red on a black ground or black on a red ground. The special symbols that mark waterholes or ancestral places go down first, fixing the journey to be undertaken on the painted "map." Then the "country" takes form and becomes alive through color fields of dots, meanders, textured painted zones, and all the other painterly devices that give each work its singular hand.

This is the laying down of the Tjukurrpa, conjuring images from thoughts. Although the formal configurations of Pintupi art are recognizable as being a particular design — that is, for a particular "story" or Tjukurrpa at a particular place or in an area owned by the artist — the design may be depicted in ways that make it a different work from the viewer's perspective. It might be reconfigured by showing more of what happened in between sections of the journey, by adding the country a little further on from an earlier painting, or by including parts of another Tjukurrpa or journey that intersects the pathway. The women's role might be included, or seasonal changes suggested — for example, by adding a patch of color to show the ceremony took place when yams were flowering.

Desert paintings are seldom closed or complete views. The canvas to be painted is laid on the ground so it becomes a section of the earth itself, the skin of the land. The designs on top are just what the artist allows to show. The paintings are open-sided, suggesting that they lead off to connecting journeys and country. The hieroglyphs or symbols used as a sort of shorthand to tell of people, animals, and events are also drawn from what the earth's surface reveals — animal and bird tracks, U-shapes for the marks left by seated figures, and indentations of coolamons and shields beside each figure to show that it is a man or woman.

There is also another quality that artists bring to the process — the aspect of putting the maker into direct physical contact with the ancestral power by touching the surface, calling to mind the Ancestors, marking the sacred places. Artists often sing quietly as they work, in what could be termed a gentle trance.

Large, important works, especially those covering sites connected to men's business or initiation journeys, are usually painted by the site custodians but watched over by "kurdungurlu," sometimes translated as "policemen" or "guardians" for the place being painted. The kurdungurlu are there to ensure that the designs are done correctly; if they are not, and the Tjukurrpa beings are angered, it will rebound on the living. Outsiders too are drawn in through song and instruction as to the meaning of the painting, a process that makes the act of painting a central technique for imparting information about Aboriginal law, country, and knowledge.

In the far north too, bark painters work seated on the ground, but they lean closer to the work to paint the fine lines of cross-hatching, guiding the long hair brushes laden with wet ocher paint as they are laid down on the bark surface, then drawn through, away from the body. This is time-consuming work, requiring peace, concentration, and close co-ordination of hand and eye. The building up of patterns produces a similar sense of timeless trance. At Port Keats this state is called "dadirri." In the words of Miriam-Rose Ungunmerr:

> *"Dadirri" recognizes the deep spring that is inside us … It is inner, deep listening and quiet, still awareness … The stories and songs sink quietly into our minds and we hold them deep inside. In the ceremonies we celebrate the awareness of our lives as sacred … I love to see the painted bodies and to watch the dancers. I like the sound of the didgeridoo and clap sticks. I never feel alone at the ceremonies …*
>
> *Quiet listening and stillness, dadirri, renews us and makes us whole. There is no need to reflect too much and to do a lot of thinking. It is just being aware. My people are not threatened by silence. They are completely at home in it. They have lived for thousands of years with nature's quietness … We wait for the right time for our ceremonies and our meetings … Sometimes many hours will be spent on painting the body before an important ceremony. We don't like to hurry. There is nothing more important than what we are attending to.*[14]

The material substance of modern paintings has changed. They are now painted on canvas or board with acrylics, or transferred from the body onto bark strips, yet they continue to reaffirm the identity of Aboriginal people in the spiritual and temporal world. Although the modern paintings are dynamic and individual, they stay contained within the indigenous worldview, as a Gandhian form of passive resistance to the full onslaught of Western attitudes.

Generally artists do not keep their paintings. It is not a common way of life to stretch and hang canvases on walls, or to keep bark paintings. The physical object need not remain with its maker, because the substance within it, the images and intellectual content, is always his or hers. The painting itself can go on its journey, bringing back good things to the maker: money to distribute, perhaps with increasing reputation a Toyota, or a trip to Sydney or Paris. It becomes an object for trade, but those receiving it, as has been explained, will be affected and will have reciprocal responsibilities.

The Aboriginal contemporary painting movement is therefore a way of spreading information and knowledge, and strengthening Aboriginal power. It could almost be viewed as the proselytizing arm of Aboriginal religious thought.

As the senior Yolngu artist Wandjuk Marika has said:

> I am not painting just for my pleasure; there is the meaning, knowledge and power. This is the earthly painting for the creation and for the land story. The land is not empty, the land is full of knowledge, full of story, full of goodness, full of energy, full of power. Earth is our mother, the land is not empty.
>
> There is the story I am telling you — special, sacred, important.[15]

THE DESERT

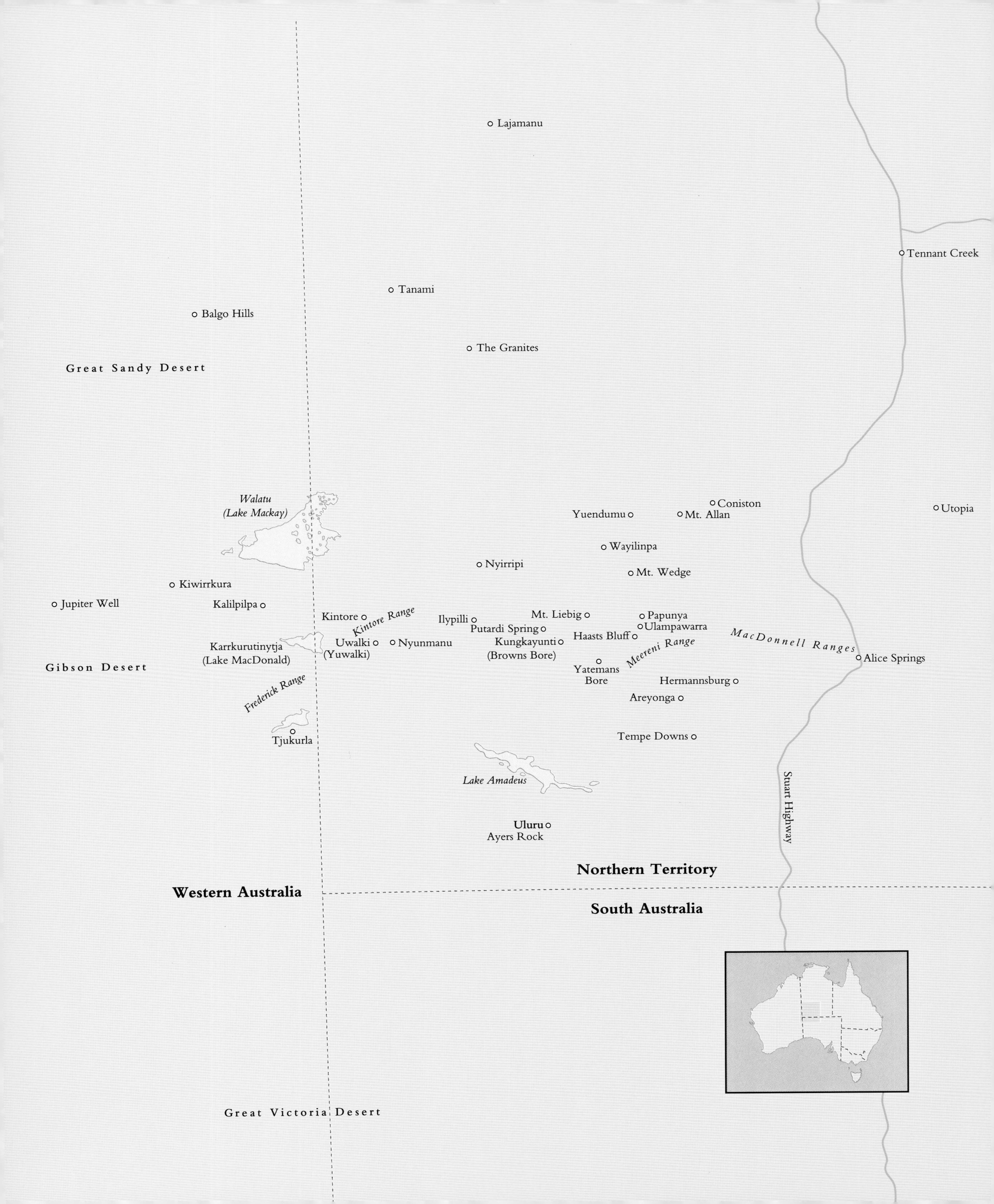

○ Lajamanu

○ Tennant Creek

○ Tanami

○ Balgo Hills

○ The Granites

Great Sandy Desert

Walatu
(Lake Mackay)

○ Coniston
Yuendumu ○   ○ Mt. Allan   ○ Utopia

○ Wayilinpa

○ Nyirripi   ○ Mt. Wedge

○ Kiwirrkura

○ Jupiter Well   Kalilpilpa ○

Kintore ○   Mt. Liebig ○   ○ Papunya
          Kintore Range   Ilypilli ○   ○ Ulampawarra
                              Putardi Spring ○   *MacDonnell Ranges*
Karrkurutinytja   Uwalki ○   ○ Nyunmanu   Kungkayunti ○   Haasts Bluff ○   *Meereni Range*   ○ Alice Springs
(Lake MacDonald)   (Yuwalki)   (Browns Bore)
                                                  Yatemans ○
Gibson Desert   Bore   Hermannsburg ○
                    Frederick Range   Areyonga ○

Tjukurla ○

                              Tempe Downs ○

                    Lake Amadeus

                                             Northern Territory

Uluru ○
Ayers Rock

Western Australia   **Northern Territory**

                              South Australia

Stuart Highway

Great Victoria Desert

Dune formations of the Australian desert
PHOTOGRAPH: Richard Woldendorp

The Desert

The town of Alice Springs is at the geographical center of Australia. It is situated on the land of the Arrernte people, but is now home to large numbers of Aboriginal people whose lands extend for many hundreds of miles in all directions through the surrounding desert. The art "boom" of recent decades has provided some artists with significant income. Most prefer to live in the major community towns or in their own country, in kinship-based communities known as outstations, occasionally visiting Alice Springs.

Until the late nineteenth century, Aboriginal people moved about the desert region without incursions from outsiders. From 1870 on, however, their country was gradually invaded. First, an overland telegraph line bisected the country from Adelaide to Port Darwin. Then prospectors and pastoralists arrived, hoping to make their fortunes. Most failed, but not before they had changed the lives of the Anmatyerre, Warlpiri, Pintupi, Luritja, and Arrernte peoples. The lands along the telegraph line and around Alice Springs, at that time known as Stuart, were leased for sheep and cattle stations. The newcomers established themselves on the most productive grasslands close to water, usurping the nomads' land, often by force. Sheep, cattle, and camels polluted and destroyed natural watering holes, and the impact of their hooves damaged the walls of the traditional wells.

Alice Springs grew from the first telegraph station settlement, which had been set up at a permanent Arrernte waterhole. In a pattern that was repeated across the continent, Arrernte people were drawn to the new settled community at their own waterhole, initially by the food there but, most importantly, by the permanent water supply.

Further inroads occurred with the establishment of a Lutheran mission at Hermannsburg, and other missions and government depots to the east and north. In times of drought, when there was a limited supply of wild foods, the mobile desert peoples gathered at ration depots, wells, and welfare stations. These are still the sites of many Aboriginal communities today. Some began as mixed-language communities, and a few sought to develop sheep and cattle businesses with local Aboriginal labor.

Aboriginal people soon began to trade with the newcomers, selling or bartering boomerangs, spears, spear-throwers, and shields. These were marked with geometric designs: circles, barred lines, tracks of animals, birds, or snakes. Some were incised, some painted with red ocher, white clay, and black charcoal. This trade intensified during World War II, when many troops were stationed in Alice Springs and a road was built across the desert to enable goods and troops to travel north to Darwin.

Ethnographic interest in desert people was sparked by early exploration, notably the journeys of John McDouall Stuart, who traversed the center from 1860 and noted the presence of many Aborigines. During a scientific expedition to Central Australia in 1894, the biologist and ethnographer Baldwin Spencer met F. J. Gillen, a former Alice Springs telegraph station master and "sub-protector of the Aborigines," and the two men subsequently collaborated to produce a series of works on the desert peoples. Principal among these writings was a volume on ceremonial life published in 1899, illustrated with numerous photographs of ceremonial activities and drawings of sacred designs.[1]

Publications such as this, and many more that followed, showed no understanding of or respect for the secrecy of sacred knowledge. As a consequence, in the early twentieth century many sacred stones passed into public collections in Australia and elsewhere. Today these are no longer displayed in public. Belatedly, the wider community has come to understand that these objects are extremely important to Aboriginal people, for whom they are the sacred essence of the Creation Ancestors of the Tjukurrpa or Dreaming. Traditionally, such objects were brought out only during appropriate rituals, and always hidden from non-initiated men, outsiders, women, and children.

The designs etched on the surface of these emblems, drawn and photographed by ethnographers such as Spencer, were widely regarded as the desert peoples' only form of artistic expression. It was often stated that the desert people had no tradition of painting. Yet the caves of the MacDonnell Ranges and other outcrops contain numerous paintings, and many sacred places have rock engravings, particularly the circular roundel denoting water.

The art of the desert was of necessity made to be ephemeral. It was and is a spiritual expression of country or Tjukurrpa marked on the body, on the ground as giant sand "paintings," and on portable objects such as weapons and utensils. The provision of canvas boards and paints in the 1970s gave it a new realm and freed many highly creative individuals to express their designs, country, and stories in new ways.

Traditional Life

Before settlements were established, most desert people traveled considerable distances in small family groups, hunting and gathering vegetable foods. Larger groups, sometimes numbering two or three hundred, would assemble for ceremonies. During droughts the permanent waterholes became major gathering points. Ilypilli was one such center for the Pintupi.

Men hunted with spears and spear-throwers, clubs and fighting boomerangs. Their quarry included large goannas and other reptiles, swift but flightless emus, and marsupials such as kangaroos, wallabies, and euros. Women concentrated on gathering food in large, curved wooden dishes, which are commonly called coolamons. They foraged for wild desert fruits, root vegetables, and witchetty grubs, the nourishing larvae of a moth. Grasses and acacia seeds were dry-ground and baked in the ashes to make a type of bread, or wet-ground into porridge.

People followed the available water supply, and the location of water dominated their lives. On the vast desert horizon, rain was visible perhaps eighty miles away, so people knew where water would be found. The water sources ranged from permanent catchments in deep gorges containing thousands of gallons to small soaks hidden under the sand at the foot of rocky outcrops, or tiny rock basins and tree cavities that yielded a few mouthfuls at a time.

The people understood where rock-holes and water soaks were situated even if they had not passed that way before. They had learned the source of water through oral history and song cycles that were chanted at ceremonies into the night. In major ceremonies such as the initiation of young men, these song cycles would continue for weeks.

Chains of waterholes or "soaks" follow the great Tjukurrpa or Dreaming routes. The sequences of locations are memorized, and each location is visited by custodians, who care for it as a sacred site. The sites are also recorded in paintings, some of which even map subterranean watercourses and channels. Concentric circles and tracks marking water sources of the desert appear in rock engravings and paintings produced between 10,000 and 20,000 years ago.

The desert people's knowledge of the botanical environment was, and is, immensely detailed. The paintings record some of this Tjukurrpa knowledge,

as well as the journeys and deeds of the Creative Ancestors who made the plants and animals, great rocks and other formations of the desert country.

Sand Paintings — The Origins of the Modern Paintings

For thousands of years the people expressed the Tjukurrpa in symbolic art on the body, on weapons, and in their great sand paintings. Many of the sand painting designs are sacred and secret. The paintings are not seen by women and are known only to those who attend the ceremonies at which they are made.

Tjukurrpa sand-painting ceremonies continue to be held. Although most are regarded as "men's business," women participate in the early stages. Over days or even weeks, large groups of people gather at a campsite connected with the Tjukurrpa Ancestor involved in the ceremony. When all are assembled, the singing begins. At dusk each day, women begin the verses of the song cycle that tell of the Ancestor coming to that place. The song "brings" the power closer, with each verse naming the country or plants and telling of incidents along the way. Women paint their upper bodies with ocher during this phase and sing and "dance" the Ancestor along. These Ancestors may appear as super-powerful humans, or in the form of animals such as honey ants or snakes.

Meanwhile, men begin their preparation in secret. A large ground mosaic or painting is constructed of ocher, blood, animal fat, and pulverized plant substances. When the women's role is over, they retire or hide, and the men sing and dance, miming the Ancestral characters. Their bodies and faces are covered with plant down and ocher. At the conclusion of the ceremony, men dance through the sand painting, obliterating it but freeing its powerful essence.

In the 1970s modern paints provided the people with a new, portable way of expressing the great stories of the creation of the land and Tjukurrpa law. Many of the first Papunya paintings almost replicate

Albert Namatjira, Mt Sonder, *n.d.*
26 x 36.5 cm. (10 x 14.5 in.), watercolour on paper
PHOTOGRAPH: Mark Ashkanasy

the sacred Tjukurrpa works viewed from above. The modern paintings are often called "dot" paintings because many are constructed of linear symbols against overall patterns of dots, much as the ground paintings were made of daubs of plant down and ocher. The patterns and symbols derive mostly from the sand paintings, although the symbols are universal among the desert cultures. Tracks and an aerial perspective are essential features. Most paintings tell of the Ancestral journeys from one sacred place to another, or depict bush food and vegetation in the artist's country. The Ancestors' journey and camps are traced in symbols. Kangaroo, emu, dingo (native dog),

or goanna tracks are easily recognized. Wavy lines might be rivers; concentric circles are campfires, sacred sites or waterholes. U-shapes are seated figures, the symbol marking the indentation their haunches leave in the desert sand.

Hermannsburg Watercolors

The first Aboriginal "modern artist" was Albert Namatjira, an Arrernte-speaking man from Hermannsburg Mission, west of Alice Springs. His gentle and exceptional watercolor landscapes, which were first exhibited in 1939, may seem out of step with the spectacular acrylic paintings of the past three decades, yet to Australians he not only represents the beginnings of a modern Aboriginal art tradition, but is also a painter who expressed the close and loving bond between Aboriginal people and their "country" in a visual idiom that was accessible to outsiders.

Albert Namatjira's story has tragic elements, like the histories of many other Aboriginal artists who have been caught between "two laws."[2] Although he achieved fame and popular commercial success, his paintings were not widely shown in public art institutions. Most were bought privately. Further-more, despite his public stature, Namatjira was refused permission to take up a pastoral lease or build a house in Alice Springs.

At that time Aboriginal people were not citizens of Australia, the nation that had occupied their lands. Because of his artistic success, in 1957 Namatjira was legally pronounced an Australian citizen, a gesture that was a source of pride to him, but also created severe problems. Aboriginals were forbidden access to alcohol at the time, but Albert Namatjira, being a citizen, became the exception. Under Aboriginal law, property must be shared. In 1958 he was charged with supplying alcohol to relatives. He was shamed in court and served a period in detention at Papunya. In 1959, shortly after his release, he died of heart failure in the hospital in Alice Springs. Today the "school" Namatjira founded thrives among Arrernte at Hermannsburg, who regard his achievements with great pride. His name is still very widely known among Aboriginal people throughout the country some forty years after his death.

Papunya

Papunya was set up as an official government settlement in 1959 in order to gather disparate nomadic peoples from the remote Western Desert into one community. Under the assimilationist government policy of the day, it was expected that these groups would somehow absorb European ways within a short period of time. With education,

housing, training, and the introduction of technology, it was imagined that they would miraculously throw off their "primitive" existence and blend into the wider society.

The Aboriginal communities resident at Papunya in the 1960s had come in from all directions. From the west came the Pintupi; closer by were the Warlpiri; from the east came the Anmatyerre; and from the south and southwest the Arrernte and Luritja. The Welfare Branch of the Northern Territory administration sent out patrols during drought time to persuade these groups to move to Papunya. Those who "came in" were moved far from their sacred sites and Tjukurrpa country. At the new settlement, alienation from their lands and former life, boredom, grief, ill health, and appalling food produced a miserable and disenchanted community.

By 1970 there were approximately 1,500 people resident at Papunya. Geoff Bardon, who came to work there around that time, has written a poignant description of the place:

> red dust billowed along the streets. All to be seen were the scalds and sandhills, and little whirlwinds about the settlement; there was a sense of barrenness in all you beheld. In that place the sand was close to all that was said or done; the Aboriginal people made the sand speak as they drew it in their hieroglyphs. There was a strange sense of people's abject gentleness, and soft, quiet dismay in realizing where they were … The glory, as I came to understand, surged forth in the immense, almost desperate, creativity of people seeking only to be themselves.[3]

A small school provided limited education in difficult circumstances, the local police were kept very busy, and the place was run by the manager, known significantly as the "superintendent."

Against this backdrop, Bardon, a dedicated young teacher, arrived at Papunya to teach the children. He observed the rhythmic patterns marked in the sands around the community, and occasionally the

Grafitti on Papunya store wall, 1983
PHOTOGRAPH: Jennifer Isaacs

older men told him a little of their sacred knowledge of their country when they were out hunting kangaroos. Bardon felt that if he could encourage some sort of creative expression, he might find art that was more interesting than the Europeanized trees and animals that the children were drawing in the school. He initiated a school mural project with the children, but was pleased when some old men who were employed in the grounds of the school came to watch, then took over the mural. They subsequently refined it until it represented a minimal concentric circle honey ant design. This is the Tjukurrpa of Papunya itself, which is situated on an important site along the route of the honey ant Tjukurrpa Ancestors.

Within a short space of time these older men and many others had begun drawing and painting for Bardon at his home. They painted on any materials they could find — small boards, housing materials, plywood, composition board, occasionally even parts of wrecked cars. Bardon tried to encourage the wider art world to appreciate these remarkable drawings, reveries of desert people far from their country.

As well as telling children's stories and water stories, many of the paintings referred to the Tingari ceremonial cycle, a journey undertaken by a group of Creation Ancestors, who traveled over vast areas of desert country performing rituals, singing the animals, plants, and natural features into being and forming particular sites, which are now regarded as sacred to their descendants, today's custodians of these places. The Tingari took different forms, some human, some animal. They also laid down social custom and law as it should be practiced today to ensure harmony. Their journeys form the basis of sacred and secret men's law.

Some of the early paintings inadvertently included special and secret motifs, which soon caused trouble. Bardon was accused of encouraging the men to exhibit sacred and potentially dangerous information. Revealing sacred men's law is a punishable offense in the desert, and the threat of retribution hung over the future of the painting movement in the early 1970s.

Bardon came under pressure from several directions. It was argued that he had no right to encourage adults in a private enterprise while employed to teach the children in the community. Competing commercial interests also began to see the value of the paintings, and wanted to take over the management and sale of the work. Bardon left the community reluctantly, and with some disillusionment, but he has remained a pivotal figure in the history of the desert art movement. By the time he left, more than 1,200 paintings had been produced, and these today offer an extraordinarily full visual record of Aboriginal iconography and religious thought. Bardon had consistently worked with the artists during his time at Papunya, encouraging them to free their imaginative thought and express "stories" with different visual elements on the board, devising their own mnemonics.

The desert art movement at Papunya did not abate. In 1972 the artists had formed a company, Papunya Tula Artists Pty Ltd, with a permanent art adviser. For most of the 1970s, however, the paintings were largely supported by local buyers and government agencies. The Aboriginal Arts Board and the national Aboriginal arts marketing company consistently made large purchases and arranged exhibitions in major Australian cities. Critical success did not follow until Papunya artists began to paint large canvases. The first large work, *Warlugulong*, was successfully produced in 1976 by Tim Leura and his brother Clifford Possum. The move to larger canvases gained impetus with the involvement of the Aboriginal Artists Agency, which arranged exhibitions in private galleries in Sydney and Melbourne.

Government policies had also changed as assimilation fell into disrepute. From the mid-1970s, many of the desert people responded to the government's new willingness to assist them to leave mixed-language settlements and move back to their own country. The Pintupi, the last of the desert people to move into Papunya, were the first to leave, heading west to Kintore on the border of Western Australia, then on to Kiwirrkura. Many other outstations were also established. It was now the onerous task of Papunya Tula field officers to travel vast distances overland, handing out canvases and paint and collecting the finished paintings one week later.

During the early years of the art movement only ocher-colored paints were supplied. The outcry that had greeted the work of 1971 and 1972 arose partly out of resistance to the "corruption" of Aboriginal traditional values and the destruction of "traditional" arts. The colors representing nature — earth, plants, blood, clay — seemed somehow to retain the link with the land and its spirituality. Once a full color range was available, however, individual artists went their own way.

In the 1980s, Pintupi paintings from Papunya Tula were seen as being the archetypal Australian Aboriginal contemporary art. The National Gallery of Australia in Canberra embarked on a vigorous acquisition policy, and this stimulated other galleries throughout the country to follow suit. The attention and mood of critics also altered, and Aboriginal contemporary art from the desert was increasingly accepted as mainstream Australian contemporary art.

Kintore

In the 1970s, when the Aboriginal land rights movement gained momentum, many Pintupi families opted to move back to their homelands close to their sacred sites, where they could care for the country, collect bush food if vehicles were available, and join with other remote peoples in the celebration of the Tingari ceremonies. Small groups of families first moved to the more permanent waterholes. Bores were sunk, enabling people to maintain a settled lifestyle at the outstations, although the use of vehicles to travel long distances was now the norm.

Community stores made periodic trips to the outstations to trade goods for the money people had obtained through pensions and other sources, including the sale of canvas paintings. Settlements were established at Yai Yai Bore, Ilypilli (a permanent Pintupi waterhole that often features in the art), Muyinga, and Yamunturrngu. A number of important artists took up residence in the majestic Kintore Ranges on the border of Western Australia, carrying the painting movement west. At first Kintore received supplies from the art adviser at Papunya, but as numbers increased and the social conditions at Papunya worsened, Papunya Tula Artists moved its headquarters into Alice Springs and dealt with Kintore directly from there. In 1981 Kintore had become a fully fledged township of more than 300 people, and by 1985 an even larger number had formed a settlement at Kiwirrkura.

A notable event occurred in 1984. Word had spread that there were Pintupi still living a nomadic life who had not been contacted during the 1960s government patrols, nor in subsequent attempts to round up the remaining stragglers in the 1970s. Walimpirrnga Tjapaltjarri and his brother Walala (see page 48) were part of a group of eight people who had chosen to remain in the Gibson Desert on their own country. They had survived droughts and enormous difficulties, but their lives changed radically when they finally allowed Europeans to make contact.

The group was taken back to camp at Kiwirrkura. At first they were sheltered from media attention, but the story was soon leaked to the press, who reported it under headlines such as "Last of the Stone Age Men" and "The Lost Tribe". Tragically, several members of the group died within a short time. The psychological shock took its toll, as did the enormous, almost unimaginable learning process that was expected of them.

In the past ten years Kintore and Kiwirrkura have become the centers for outstanding paintings by male Pintupi artists. Those whose work is represented here are Anatjari Tjampitjinpa, Yala Yala Gibbs Tjungarrayi, Ronnie Tjampitjinpa, Mick Namerari Tjapaltjarri, Walala Tjapaltjarri, and Pinta Pinta Tjapanangka.

Until 1994, it was mostly senior men who painted at Kintore. Women occasionally helped to fill in backgrounds or areas of color, but the designs and country depicted belonged to the male artists, and the paintings were marketed as men's paintings. Then, after a series of stimulating visits and cultural exchanges with their female relatives from Haasts Bluff between 1993 and 1995, a number of senior Kintore women began painting. The women from Haasts Bluff, Narputta Nangala and Eunice Napanangka (see pages 62 and 72), encouraged the Kintore group to paint large canvases, some painted by as many as eight people working together.

Kintore women artists have now exhibited together in Adelaide, Melbourne and Sydney with considerable success. Included in this volume are Tatali Nangala, Wintjiya Napaltjarri, Tjunkiya Napaltjarri, Makinti Napanangka and Nyurupayia Nampitjinpa.

Eschewing the dots that have become the hallmark of men's work, the women artists have produced expressive and painterly works with a liberal use of pastel colors, achieved by mixing white with the acrylic pigment and continuously working over the surface of the painting while wet. As in the men's paintings, the themes relate to waterholes, the nomadic life, and the sacred areas the artists have inherited through kinship and for which they are custodians in the temporal world.

Haasts Bluff

Haasts Bluff is situated on the land of the Luritja and Kukatja people, and is approximately 150 miles west of Alice Springs. It is in a picturesque setting on the plains between two mountain ranges, which turn purple in the evening light, creating archetypal

Narputta Nangala with her painting Two Women *outside Ikuntji Arts Centre, 1997*
PHOTOGRAPH: Kathleen Berrin

Central Australian scenic views in the hues of Namatjira. To the north are Ulampawarru and Anyali, and to the south the Mereeni Range. The hills are dotted with clumps of spinifex grass and white ghost gums, while the plains support river gums and patches of mulga. To the west are stands of desert oak against red sandhills.

The Coniston Massacre of 1928, in which a large number of Aboriginal people were slaughtered by police on a cattle station to the north, sent many Warlpiri and Anmatyerre people fleeing south to Haasts Bluff and Hermannsburg. The numbers increased as a result of drought and resource competition with cattle. By the time a permanent Lutheran settlement was established in 1935, the

Haasts Bluff community included Pintupi, Ngalia, Warlpiri, Pitjantjatjara, and Arrernte people. The Lutherans ran a cattle industry there, and in 1941 the area was declared an Aboriginal Reserve. In the 1970s a number of key artists at Haasts Bluff painted for Papunya Tula, including Gideon Jack Tjupurrula (see page 76), Riley Major, Timmy Tjungarrayi Jugadai, Barney Raggatt Tjupurrula, and Limpi Tjapangarti. When Papunya Tula ceased supplying materials to the settlement, only a few people at Haasts Bluff continued to paint, buying their art materials at the local store.

The role of providing local artists with materials was later taken on by the Ikuntji Women's Centre, which began operating in August 1992, providing

27

School door, Yuendumu, 1994
PHOTOGRAPH: Jennifer Isaacs

health education and child care, supplying art materials and conducting painting workshops. The center was officially opened with a large women's ceremony in April 1993. At this time a number of women traveled from Kintore, Papunya, and Mount Liebig to join with their relatives at Haasts Bluff and perform the appropriate dances and songs for the country. A series of subsequent painting workshops with female Pintupi relatives from Kintore became known as the Minyma Tjukurrpa Project (Women's Dreaming Project), which culminated in late 1995 with a large group exhibition at Tandanya in Adelaide.

Today the women of Haasts Bluff continue to make lively and vital art, characterized by a free use of paint with little dotting and a textured quality. The stories and Tjukurrpa remain a powerful undercurrent of their work.

The Ikuntji center is a happy and vital place. The walls are covered with diagrams of the usual fruits and vegetables, along with their wild bush food equivalents, to educate people in nutrition. Among groups of women painting on the floor, children troop to and from the shower, cleaning the desert dust from their bodies.

This is the first community where artists, stimulated by art advisers who are also painters themselves, are freely exploring the tactile qualities of paint with exuberance and colorful invention. It was this vitality among the women of Haasts Bluff that influenced their older relatives at Kintore to produce a similar wave of exciting modern work for Papunya Tula.

The women artists of Haasts Bluff included in this collection are Katarra Nampitjinpa, Narputta Nangala, Marlee Naparrula, Mitjili Naparrula, Anmanari and Mantua Napanangka, and Eunice Napanangka. The center provides services to male artists as well, principal among them being Gideon Tjupurrula (page 76) and Long Tom Tjapanangka (page 80).

Yuendumu

Yuendumu is approximately 200 miles northwest of Alice Springs. In its early years, the settlement functioned as a cattle station and government settlement for Warlpiri people, but today the community also includes Anmatyerre and Pintupi members.

Warlpiri artists whose traditional lands are northeast of Papunya witnessed and participated in the beginnings of the painting movement in the 1970s while visiting relatives at Papunya or camping at outstations. Occasionally individuals at the Yuendumu community also utilized available surfaces to make paintings of their own, but there were no formal arrangements for supplying materials or paint to Yuendumu until the 1980s.

Contemporary painting at Yuendumu began in 1984, when several old men, including Paddy Jupurrurla Nelson, Paddy Japaljarri Sims, Paddy Japaljarri Stewart, and Larry Jungarrayi Spencer, were encouraged by the schoolteacher to paint the Yuendumu school doors in order to encourage the young people of the community to pay more attention and respect to the law and authority of their elders and their spiritual life. An artists' association, Warlukurlangu Artists Aboriginal Association, was incorporated in 1986. Approximately two hundred artists, both men and women, are now actively painting for Warlukurlangu Artists.

Interestingly, although the men took the initiative with the doors project, women began painting at Yuendumu immediately afterwards; the artists' company, unlike Papunya Tula, was not perceived as being just for men. A number of Warlukurlangu artists also live at the outstations of Ngarna, Yinjirrmardi, Nyirrpi, and Wayililinpa.

Warlukurlangu Artists is an organization with a very strong sense of collective purpose and cultural pride. Since about 1993 the center has specialized in major commissions for large institutions. These are group paintings executed by a number of kin, and are generally undertaken as a way of revisiting their country, teaching and explaining designs and stories to the young, and showing how large tracts of the country are connected through Tjukurrpa (among Warlpiri spelt Jukurrpa). These commissioned works have entered public collections at the Glasgow Art Museum, Art Gallery of New South Wales, Art Gallery of Western Australia, and major private collections such as the Kluge-Ruhe Aboriginal Art Collection in Charlottesville, Virginia, the Kelton Foundation in Los Angeles, and the Gantner Myer collection (see page 84).

Initially, paintings by Warlpiri artists from Yuendumu were distinguished by their unfettered use of color and detailed patterning in shimmering zones. In the 1980s it was revolutionary to fill background vegetative areas with bright pink, grass green, purple, and sky blue. Early Yuendumu works by men also marked out the important routes of Tjukurrpa Ancestors in strong black linear designs, called kuruwarri, which held the overall composition and gave it dynamism and movement. Undulating water Dreamings, bush fruit Dreamings, and sinuous vine Dreamings employed kuruwarri quite unlike those of the more formal Pintupi works with which the market had become familiar.

Utopia

Utopia is an area of Aboriginal freehold land on the Sandover River, about 150 miles northeast of Alice Springs. A former cattle station, it was named Utopia by Sonny and Trott Kunoth, who were early lease-holders of this choice stretch of desert land. Centered on the traditional lands of the Anmatyerre people, the station was handed back to its Aboriginal owners in the late 1970s.

For a period, the Anmatyerre community and their close relatives the Alyawarre kept up the cattle enterprise at several outstations. For the most part, however, people preferred to separate into extended family groupings, and today a variable number of up

Painted school building at Lajamanu
PHOTOGRAPH: Jennifer Isaacs

to eighteen outstations are spread across the region according to kinship ties to particular tracts of land. Supported and reinforced by a centralized school and store, Anmatyerre people maintain contact with their relatives by road, each family owning a vehicle. Ceremonies continue across Anmatyerre country and with their neighbors the Warlpiri. A life of working on cattle stations has produced artists with strong personalities and an independent style.

It was at Utopia that the most famous Central Australian artist, Emily Kame Kngwarreye, first learned batik painting in the late 1970s. Late in life, after a career as a batik artist, she went on to have a spectacular flowering as an abstract painter (see page 102).

For Anmatyerre people, the Tjukurrpa, or in their own language the Altyerre, remains strong, and

ceremony is a major component of life. A significant number of contemporary painters are women who are inventively exploring the sacred body marks used when making Awelye, women's dances and ceremonies. At these ceremonies, women's breasts, arms, and torsos are painted with ocher stripes and curves. Each formation is specific to the wearer and the ceremony being conducted, and the design is for and about the particular plant, animal, or subject for which the dancers are owners or custodians. Sometimes, a senior female custodian conceives the designs and paints them with the help of her kin (see Mary Kemarre and family, page 96).

Whereas the paintings by women such as Emily Kngwarreye and Gloria Petyarre often utilize free abstraction, the paintings of Anmatyerre men such as Lindsay Bird Mpetyane and Freddy Kngwarreye Jones have remained true to the ancient system of iconographic mark-making for ceremony. These paintings are bold, strong, and geometric.

The nearby cattle station of Delmore Downs also provides artists with materials for painting. At Delmore Downs a privately run gallery is operated by the Holt family, descendants of some of the first Europeans to settle on Anmatyerre and Alyawarre country. Because of their long association through several generations, painters sometimes prefer to work on commission from outside agents such as the Holts for specific exhibitions or when undertaking assignments.

Lajamanu

Lajamanu is predominantly a Warlpiri community and lies in the Tanami Desert, north of Yuendumu and east of Balgo. The ties of kinship, ritual, and Ancestral journey routes connect the community to Balgo. Many Warlpiri were moved here from their own country near Yuendumu more than thirty years ago. Abie Jangala, a community leader, has described the forced transportation of Warlpiri to Lajamanu as an abduction:

> *"About 200 people were collected by truck. Nobody was asked if they wanted to go, they were just told."*

Individuals at Lajamanu have been painting since the mid-1980s, but the community council did not succeed in its early attempts to organize an art center, and the artists' organization, the Warnayaka Art Centre, was only formed in 1991. Since then, despite several phases when painting ceased because of organizational problems, Lajamanu artists, particularly senior women such as Lorna Fencer, have persevered to make distinctive paintings, often working independently through the contacts they have built up over several decades. Lorna Fencer's new work represents a breakthrough. Expressionistic and joyful, it marks a stylistic change that may influence other artists in the years to come.

Uta Uta Tjangala

Untitled

This work is among the first contemporary paintings by Australian desert people specifically made for trade and for communication with the world about land owner-ship. Completed at Papunya when the art movement began in 1971, it was part of the fifth consignment sent to the small shop in Alice Springs that sold the work of the senior men who had just begun painting under the guidance of the teacher Geoff Bardon.

The design, painted with materials supplied by Bardon, is an archetype. It is a direct rendition of sacred symbols usually incised on wooden or stone emblems, or painted in ocher on weapons and shields. The iconography refers to part of the Tingari ceremonial cycle (see page 24). The artist has marked out a section of the Tingari journey and associated events in his own desert country.

PLATE 1
Uta Uta Tjangala, 1920–1990
Untitled, 1971
60.5 x 35 cm (24 x 14 in.)
Polymer powder paint on composition board

Biographical Notes

Uta Uta Tjangala was born about 1920 and lived much of his life until adulthood on his own desert country in the Lake MacDonald area, close to the Western Australian border. Along with many others, he moved into the government settlement at Papunya soon after it was established. He was one of the first Pintupi painters to visit Geoff Bardon in his quarters at Papunya and ask for painting materials. In his book *Aboriginal Art of the Western Desert,* first published in 1979, Geoff Bardon described his early association with Uta Uta:

> *I first met Uta when he was a gardener in the Papunya Park, where he worked with his friend Yarta. These two men would see me coming and going between my quarters and the school. Occasionally they would visit me at my quarters where there was a quite secluded veranda.*
>
> *Several times I prepared a billy of tea for them the way they liked it. It just so happened one time that they started scribbling concentric circles and loops in various combinations on square paper that just happened to be available with old pencils that I lent them. What seemed to be scribbles had quite a neat order and interesting variations, drawn sensitively, of which the men were immensely proud. Soon that is all they wanted to do.*[4]

These first attempts to express country and stories in painting gave rise to a widespread contemporary Aboriginal art movement, which is now common to all Aboriginal communities of the desert.

Uta Uta's paintings are known for the strength of their circular forms. In the 1980s he became one of the leading artists who moved to large-scale canvases. His work *Yumari* (1981) is a spectacular painting depicting many sites with a large central goanna-like form. It was executed under Uta Uta's direction by a group of eleven other painters, and was the forerunner of many subsequent group works.

Uta Uta Tjangala won the National Aboriginal Art Award in 1985. He died in 1990. He is considered a pre-eminent painter from the original Papunya men's group, and his work is held in major Australian collections, including the National Museum of Australia; National Gallery of Victoria; Art Gallery of South Australia; Art Gallery of New South Wales; Queensland Art Gallery; and the Museum and Art Gallery of the Northern Territory.

Women's Ceremony

The original documentation of the meaning of the iconography in this painting has been lost, and the following is a compilation of possible interpretations.

The painting may represent the "Two Women Dreaming" — an epic saga concerning the travels of two women across vast stretches of the Western Desert. They stopped at various sites or waterholes and are depicted in different places, gathering bush food and singing songs associated with particular areas. The women traveled north and east from an area close to Lake Mackay. The broad U-shapes depict seated women, while the concentric circles represent campfires and significant sites. The parallel striped lines presumably represent the body paint employed during women's ceremonies or love-magic rituals. During such ceremonies women first oiled their bodies — with goanna oil, for example — then applied linear patterns in yellow, red, and white ocher as shown in this work.

A key theme in the paintings of Uta Uta's descendants concerns two women at Kampurranpa (Henty Hills) who were continually followed by an old man. The illicit coming together of these great Creation figures is the subject of many songs and love-magic themes in Western Desert Aboriginal art. The lines connecting the U-shapes and concentric circles are also reminiscent of the stick structure of the woman's spindle — a significant love-magic emblem — which was used to hold string spun from human hair.

The painting can also be viewed as representing two women within the central motif of a reconfigured hair-string belt (an item of clothing made and worn by women). It is the opinion of many older Pintupi women today that in Tjukurrpa or Creation times, a woman in such a magic belt would have been irresistibly attractive to men.

PLATE 2
Uta Uta Tjangala, 1920–1990
Women's Ceremony, 1972
51 x 50 cm (20 x 19.5 in.)
Polymer powder paint on composition board

Johnny Warangkula Tjupurrula

Children's Story

This is one of the first paintings the art teacher Geoff Bardon elicited from senior Pintupi and Luritja men at Papunya. Bardon asked the artists to produce paintings for or about children, works that would not carry dangerous or secret information. The subjects include cautionary tales, accounts of ceremonies, and children's versions of Tjukurrpa or Dreaming activities in the artist's country, far beyond the confines of the Papunya settlement. It is a particularly important painting, because it shows the artist's response to an outsider when he was asked to depict important religious knowledge and law as it would be told to children.

The story of this painting, a water Dreaming, was not fully elaborated by the artist at the time of its execution, but in recent years Geoff Bardon has given an interpretation of the painting. It shows a ritual elder dancing in the center of a cleared camping ground, surrounded by objects associated with the ceremony: shields, coolamons (large wooden dishes), and the sacred stone emblem denoting water (the large oval inscribed with three concentric circles situated beneath the main participant's feet).

The white meandering tracks show the watercourses, both above and below ground. Several concentric circles mark waterholes or soaks. Smaller meandering lines indicate running water. Watching, or at the side of the ceremonial dancer, are two young children, one enclosed within a watercourse, perhaps an initiate preparing to learn the sacred songs and law. The parallel straight white lines are a row of spears. Artists such as Turkey Tolson Tjupurrula and Mick Namerari Tjapaltjarri later used rows of spears to denote important men's business.

This is one of the earliest paintings in which the artist uses a dotting technique to cover the surface of the board. Components of the overall design were later to be developed and embellished by Pintupi artists as they extended their visual repertoire. Although the top right-hand corner has been damaged, earlier photographs of this work show that the white meandering waterline finished in a rounded end similar to a snake's head.

PLATE 3
Johnny Warangkula Tjupurrula, b. 1925
Children's Story (Water Dreaming for Two Children), 1972
41 x 45 cm (16 x 17.5 in.)
Acrylic on composition board

Biographical Notes

An eminent artist who first painted for Papunya Tula in 1971, Johnny Warangkula was born at Minjilpirri in the Western Desert about 1925. He speaks several languages, including Luritja and Warlpiri.

He is the owner of Ilypilli, a large, permanent waterhole that was the center of the known world for nomadic Pintupi people before the appearance of outsiders. When smaller soaks in sandy watercourses dried up, people moved to semi-permanent rock-holes, but in lengthy periods of drought all would converge at Ilypilli. The site continues to be a major ceremonial area, and for a period in the late 1970s it was an active outstation, with services supplied from Papunya.

In his accounts of his early life, Warangkula has recalled his fear at his first sight of a plane, which he took to be an evil spirit or mamu. His family came from the Western Desert into Hermannsburg Mission, where as a young man he worked building the airstrip. Along with many others, he moved on to Haasts Bluff and worked as a laborer, receiving only rations in return for his work. In 1954, while he was living at Haasts Bluff, he met the young Queen Elizabeth II on her visit to Australia.

In 1960, Johnny Warangkula moved to Papunya, where he became an active leader of the community because of his extensive contact with outsiders and his understanding of their ways. He was a member of the Papunya Council, and became interested in obtaining art materials when he observed a mural being painted on the school wall (see page 24). Throughout the 1970s and 1980s, he was one of the foremost Western Desert artists. His paintings frequently depict watercourses and subterranean channels and his Dreaming places include the important waterholes at Kampurarrnga and Kalilpilpa.

He later took up residence in Alice Springs. For some years he only painted intermittently because of his failing eyesight and ill health, but acclaim for his early works, particularly those executed in 1971 and 1972, has recently rekindled his inclination to paint, and he has held several solo exhibitions.

Johnny Warangkula's paintings are held in State galleries throughout Australia, including the Queensland Art Gallery; National Gallery of Victoria; Art Gallery of Western Australia; Art Gallery of South Australia; National Museum of Australia; National Gallery of Australia; and the Museum and Art Gallery of the Northern Territory.

PLATE 3 (detail)
Johnny Warangkula Tjupurrula, b. 1925
Children's Story (Water Dreaming for Two Children), 1972
41 x 45 cm (16 x 17.5 in.)
Acrylic on composition board

Anatjari Tjampitjinpa

Tingari Cycle at Tjuwal

This composition of mesmerizing roundels is an archetypal Pintupi mapping of the Tingari journeys (see page 24). It conveys the power embodied in the sacred sites left by the Creation Ancestors, whose journeys are now part of sacred men's law, associated with the initiation of youths. Water sources in this area of Australia are immensely important. In recounting the journeys of the Tingari, these song cycles also plot out the whereabouts of soaks, rock-holes, and ancient wells. Religious knowledge is thus an integral part of survival in the desert.

This painting was produced in the late 1980s, at a time when the principal painters of the Papunya Tula artists' company were achieving significant success, moving to larger canvases and exhibiting in contemporary art spaces. Its resonance marks it as one of Anatjari Tjampitjinpa's major works. The vibrating circles have become almost hallucinatory in their evocation of the shimmering, mirage-like manifestations of waterholes in the desert.

Biographical Notes

Anatjari Tjampitjinpa was born around 1927. He came into Papunya from his Pintupi homelands in the far Western Desert in the early 1960s, and he was one of the original group of artists who painted for Geoffrey Bardon at Papunya in 1971. With the strengthening of the outstation movement (see page 11) and the return of groups of Pintupi to form settlements closer to their far country, he subsequently left the small Papunya outstation at Yai Yai Bore and moved first to Kintore and then further west to the remote community of Kiwirrkura.

Anatjari Tjampitjinpa's elaborate yet strong roundels have a "magic eye" effect on the viewer, giving visual sensations of depth and movement. This form of sensory stimulation is regarded by many elders of the desert as evidence of Tjukurrpa power interacting with temporal life. His work has been featured in numerous group exhibitions, and is included in the collections of the Queensland Museum; South Australian Museum; Museum and Art Gallery of the Northern Territory; and numerous private collections.

PLATE 4
Anatjari Tjampitjinpa, b. c. 1927
Tingari Cycle at Tjuwal, 1989
152 x 122 cm (60 x 48 in.)
Synthetic polymer paint on canvas

Yala Yala Gibbs Tjungurrayi

Kaarkurutinytja, Lake MacDonald

This work is a major painting in the classic Pintupi style showing the ceremonial activities of the Tingari (see page 24). The circles and connecting linear tracks represent the activities of the Tingari men at the site of Kaarkurutinytja. Around several of the main campsites and ceremonial areas are connecting U-shapes, representing seated people. Men's ceremonies today repeat and celebrate the Tingari journeys in dances, songs, and ground designs during the training and initiation of young men.

The specific Tjukurrpa Ancestor connected to this painting is a small, poisonous snake that lives in a rock-hole at the lake. The artist does not explain the events surrounding this snake and the other sacred designs, which are depicted as small sequences of circles. Their ovoid formation and symbolism, however, are linked to the ancient design language used by Pintupi artists in ground designs and on sacred emblems of stone and wood.

Biographical Notes

Born about 1925 in the country west of Lake MacDonald, Yala Yala Gibbs spent his early life moving with his family around the vicinity of this vast salt lake. He walked into Papunya with his family, but returned to his country in the 1980s, living at Kintore. He was involved in the contemporary painting movement at Papunya from the beginning, and for a period lived in his outstation at Muntardi, west of Kintore, in the Western Australian desert.

Yala Yala, who died in early 1999, was one of the most authoritative senior Pintupi men. His paintings are held in the National Gallery of Victoria; National Gallery of Australia; Museum and Art Gallery of the Northern Territory; Queensland Art Gallery; and Art Gallery of New South Wales.

PLATE 5
Yala Yala Gibbs Tjungurrayi, 1925–1999
Kaarkurutinytja, Lake MacDonald, 1997
153 x 122 cm (60 x 48 in.)
Acrylic on canvas

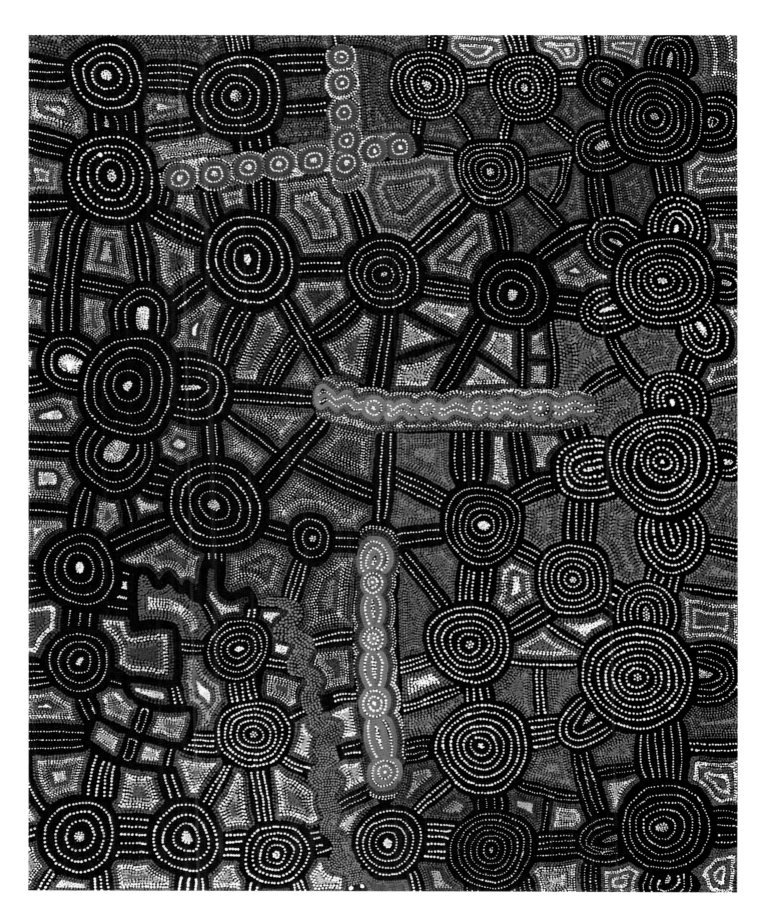

Ronnie Tjampitjinpa

Emu Dreaming at Tumpilpungkul

This design is an abstracted contemporary rendition of men's ceremonial body designs associated with the rock-hole at Tumpilpungkul, west of Lake MacDonald. The Tingari Emu Ancestors came to visit this site in the Tjukurrpa or Creation time. Today, emu song cycles and ground designs form part of the initiatory procedures for young men. Details of the ceremony and its meaning are regarded as sacred men's business and are not divulged to outsiders. The Tingari cycle (see page 24) provides the basis for Pintupi law.

Biographical Notes

Ronnie Tjampitjinpa was born around 1943 in the country west of the Kintore Range in Western Australia. His family traveled extensively across Pintupi country, then walked into the Haasts Bluff settlement about 1956. Ronnie Tjampitjinpa later went to Yuendumu, then traveled on to Papunya, where he joined the Pintupi who were camped there in the 1970s. At Papunya, he worked as a laborer. He recalls his early life there as somewhat sedentary; food was readily available, but it was difficult to fulfill others' expectations. He observed the Papunya painting movement during its early years and began to paint in about 1974.

Contemporary art critics have been impressed with Ronnie Tjampitjinpa's large, linear, abstracted works, which essentially blow up small segments of his earlier detailed paintings into compellingly strong geometric forms, some using brilliant color. In 1988 he won the Alice Springs Art Prize. His paintings are in the collections of the National Gallery of Australia; National Gallery of Victoria; Art Gallery of South Australia; Art Gallery of Western Australia; Museum and Art Gallery of the Northern Territory; Art Gallery of New South Wales; Supreme Court, Darwin; and the Musée National Des Arts Africains et Oceanians, Paris.

PLATE 6
Ronnie Tjampitjinpa, b. c. 1943
Emu Dreaming at Tumpilpungkul, 1997
122 x 183 cm (48 x 72 in.)
Acrylic on canvas

Mick Namerari Tjapaltjarri

Golden Bandicoot Dreaming

This painting, executed the year before the artist died, is a simplified and minimal rendering of a major theme in his art — the Golden Bandicoot (Mingatjurru) Dreaming journey, which culminates at the site of Nyunmanu, east of the Kintore community.

The bandicoot is a small marsupial that usually forms a nest by gathering grasses together in a scraped-out area of sand under a spinifex hummock or among tussock grass. The rectangular section in the top right-hand corner of the painting represents the Mingatjurru's home.

Biographical Notes

As a small boy in the late 1920s, Mick Namerari traveled on foot with his family from camp to camp in Pintupi country, across sandhills and acacia-studded plains. He was born at the soak at Marnpi in 1916 and camped at various times at Putarti Spring, then arrived at Haasts Bluff in the 1930s, when it was a ration depot supplying nomadic Aboriginal families with food, including flour, sugar, and tobacco. When Haasts Bluff became a cattle station, he was employed in the industry, and later worked at Tempe Downs and Areyonga. Throughout the 1970s he was one of the principal painters at Papunya. He later moved out to Kintore on the border of Western Australia, then set up his own outstation southeast of Kintore.

Mick Namerari began painting typical Pintupi designs of Tingari cycles and journey paintings, but he was one of the first to explore abstract motifs — dots or straight lines — to represent the Tjukurrpa subject matter. He won the National Aboriginal Art Award in 1991 with a version of his Bandicoot painting, and has had numerous solo exhibitions in South Australia, Melbourne, and Sydney. He is represented in most Australian art gallery collections and at the National Gallery of Australia.

A frequent visitor to Alice Springs over the final decade of his life, Mick Namerari often welcomed visitors to the Papunya Tula Gallery, where he became something of a landmark in his tweed sports coat, enjoying the public accolades for the work that had flowed from the pioneers of the 1970s.

Mick Namerari died in 1998.

PLATE 7
Mick Namerari Tjapaltjarri, 1916–1998
Golden Bandicoot Dreaming, 1997
153 x 91 cm (60 x 36 in.)
Acrylic on canvas

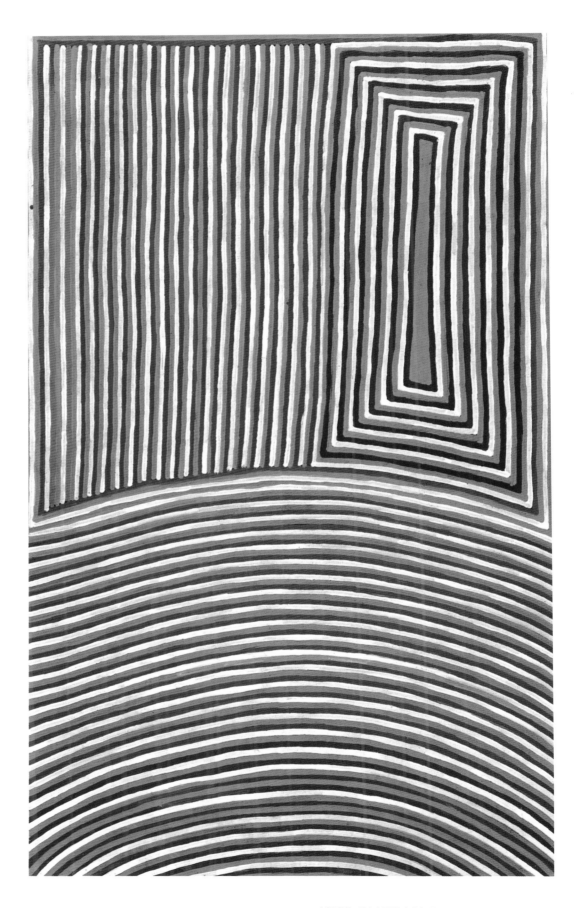

Walala Tjapaltjarri

Tingari at Wanapatangu

In a minimal linear style, the artist has depicted a particular site known as Wanapatangu, which is recorded as being northeast of Wilkinkarra (Lake Mackay) in Western Australia. This was one of the points where the Tingari Ancestors stopped for ceremonial and social activity in their long journey across the desert. According to the artist, the rectangles mark the watery areas that surround Wanapatangu, which is represented by the double bars in the center of the painting.

Biographical Notes

Walala Tjapaltjarri was born in the 1960s and spent his childhood as one of only nine remaining Pintupi people who lived a fully nomadic existence without any contact with the outside world. In 1984 the group allowed contact to be made, and his family moved to the community at Kiwirrkura, the remote Pintupi community in the Great Sandy Desert.

It was in 1997 that Walala first began painting. Initially his work was minimalist, with archetypal circular symbols depicting the sacred men's Tingari site formations. Then, later in 1997, he began working on canvas for a gallery in Alice Springs, producing bold, simple, individual work with strong graphic forms derived from body painting, sand paintings, sacred stone and wood objects, and engravings on weapons. He thus continues to encode geographic information through the ancient mark-making practice. Walala has retained the absolute simplicity of Pintupi design, exactly the same as has been used on weapons, shields, and spear-throwers for centuries.

PLATE 8
Walala Tjapaltjarri, b. c. 1960
Tingari at Wanapatangu, 1997
200 x 49 cm (78.5 x 19.5 in.)
Acrylic on linen

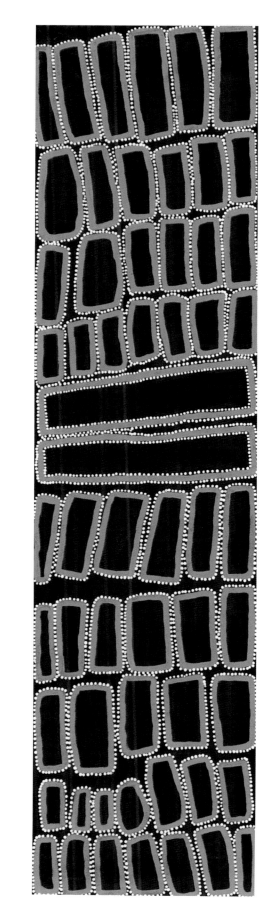

Pinta Pinta Tjapanangka

Ralyalnga

This painting shows a group of soakages at the site of Ralyalnga, north of Mt. Webb in Western Australia. The Tingari men and women (see page 24) made these in Creation times on their journey towards Lake Mackay from further west.

Tingari information is part of the teachings of young men during "men's business" — sacred ceremonies, song, and ritual, which are kept secret within Aboriginal society.

Pinta Pinta Tjapanangka's work, with its singular focus, has returned to the clarity of religious statement of the first Pintupi paintings on board. As such it is a direct continuation of classic ancient religious art expressed in vigorous, strong, black-and-white contemporary media.

Biographical Notes

Pinta Pinta Tjapanangka is one of the oldest Pintupi men living at Kintore. He has painted intermittently since 1973 but has increased his output in the past three years, finding particular pleasure in refining his symbolic range to classic Pintupi Tingari symbols — concentric circles and tracks in either linear or radiating spoke formation. This painting shows the artist's delight in the tactile qualities of the thick texture and surface and the clarity of white on black.

His works are held in several major collections, including the National Gallery of Victoria.

PLATE 9
Pinta Pinta Tjapanangka, b. c. 1928
Ralyalnga, 1997
107 x 28 cm (42 x 11 in.)
Acrylic on canvas

Linda Syddick Napaltjarri

Ancestral Spirits at Lake Mackay

This painting resonates with the spirits of the artist's two fathers — her biological father, Rintje Tjungarrayi, and stepfather, Shorty Lungkata. Although they are deceased and have returned to their tribal lands, they have manifested themselves for their daughter. These figures represent the Creation Ancestors, emu and kangaroo men, who are closely associated with the formation of Lake Mackay. The four circles and the connecting lines that enclose the spirits symbolize important rock-holes and Ancestral tracks at Lake Mackay. The radiating lines on the edge of the painting are the dunes and sandhills of the region. Linda Syddick's paintings of this period resonate with the power of Ancestral beings, but also explore themes that interact with temporal life, Christian spirituality, fantasy, and hyperreality.

Biographical Notes

Linda Syddick's Pintupi name is Tjunkiya Wukula Napaltjarri. She has been married several times and her name reflects her complex interaction with the wider world. She uses the family name of her second husband, Musty Syddick (Cedick), whose father was one of the Afghan cameleers who transported goods over the Australian desert during the early twentieth century. Her first husband was Tony Walpinta, with whom she has seven children. Her stepfather, Shorty Lungkata Tjungarrayi, was one of the principal Papunya painters. His work had an influence on Linda Syddick, who assisted him in his later works and watched the development of his art. Now a great-grandmother, she continues to paint in her home outside Adelaide, South Australia.

Born around 1940 in the Gibson Desert near Lake Mackay, Linda Syddick lived a traditional life until the late 1960s. As a young woman she embraced Christianity, which continues to influence her worldview and her painting. Many of her works imbue contemporary events with biblical associations.

The primary inspiration for her paintings is the interconnectedness of Christian and Aboriginal mythology. Central to her work is the notion that spirit beings dwell in the sky, come to earth and interact with human beings, then return to their celestial home. She achieved a breakthrough in her work after she saw the film *ET* more than twenty times. The film's theme paralleled her own beliefs, and ET became for her a Creation Ancestor from the sky. She painted this theme constantly for a period but recently has returned to more recognizable traditional Ancestral beings.

On four occasions Linda Syddick has been a finalist in the Blake Prize, the national Australian award for religious art. Her paintings are included in the collections of the National Gallery of Australia; Art Gallery of South Australia; Museum and Art Gallery of the Northern Territory; Araluen Art Centre, Alice Springs; Art Gallery of New South Wales; and the Berndt Museum of Anthropology, Western Australia.

PLATE 10
Linda Syddick Napaltjarri, b. c. 1940
Ancestral Spirits at Lake Mackay, 1996
112 x 137 cm (44 x 54 in.)
Acrylic on canvas

Tatali Nangala

Kaarkurutinytja, Lake MacDonald

Two Creation women came to Kaarkurutinytja hunting goannas. They followed the large reptiles from burrow to burrow, digging energetically, but could not reach them. After leaving this place they traveled east to the Kintore Ranges, where they stopped again at Warman rock-hole.

This painting illustrates the natural appearance of the earth today, as well as the activities of these Ancestors. The U-shapes on the top and bottom edges and right-hand side are the women seated digging for the goanna (visible at top). The journey of the women also takes in two other sites, Lampintja and Walukaritjina, close to Lake MacDonald.

Biographical Notes

A senior Pintupi woman, now resident at the Kintore community, Tatali Nangala came to Papunya sometime in the 1960s and married the notable artist Charlie Tararu, who in 1987 became the first Pintupi artist to have a solo exhibition. Charlie Tararu was also the first Pintupi person to travel outside Australia, visiting England in the early 1980s.

Tatali Nangala later returned to her Pintupi homelands with her husband to live at the new outstation of Kintore. For some years she observed the male artists at work, then in the early 1990s she participated in the Minyma Tjukurrpa Project (Women's Dreaming Project), organized by the Ikuntji Women's Centre (see page 28). Since then she has become an enthusiastic and successful painter for Papunya Tula Artists, the company that provides services to Kintore.

Through Papunya Tula Artists, Tatali Nangala has exhibited at the Aboriginal Art Awards in Darwin and the Alice Prize. Her paintings have been included in several joint exhibitions of Kintore women's work, and have been acquired by the Flinders University Art Museum, South Australia; the National Gallery of Victoria; the Art Gallery of New South Wales; and the Kelton Foundation, Los Angeles.

PLATE 11
Tatali Nangala, b. 1928
Kaarkurutinytja, Lake MacDonald, 1997
153 x 122 cm (60 x 48 in.)
Acrylic on canvas

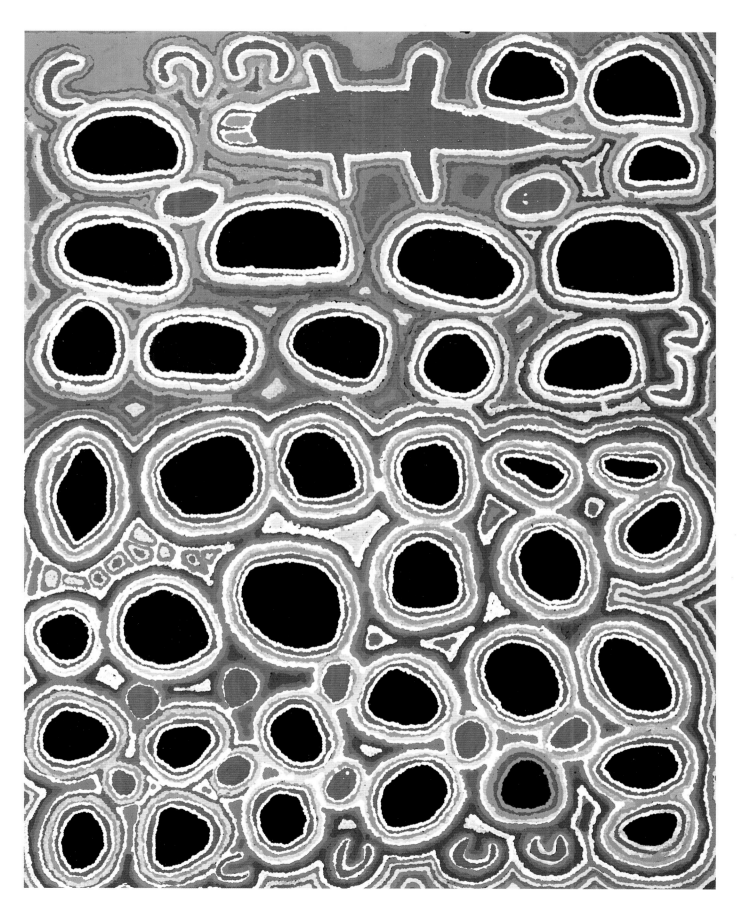

Wintjiya Napaltjarri and Tjunkiya Napaltjarri

Tingari Women at Yuwalki

Yuwalki is a site in the Western Desert south of Kintore associated with the Tingari Ancestors' long Tjukurrpa journey (see page 24). Episodic song cycles of this mythology are repeated at the teaching of youths in religious ritual. Details of the motivations for the Tingari journeys and the events that transpired along the path are of a highly secret nature, and full documentation is rarely given.

The Dreaming track or pathway of the Kungka Tjuta (many women) also connects to the sacred emu Dreaming journeys or Kalaya. The story recounts in detail how one Tingari man chased an emu all the way from Yuwalki to the site of Mitukatjirri, a vast distance to travel on foot. Eventually the emu's superior speed allowed it to elude the man.

Biographical Notes

Wintjiya Napaltjarri and Tjunkiya Napaltjarri are two older Pintupi women artists who now live at Kintore. They were young women when their mother and relatives first came into Haasts Bluff from the more remote desert area to the west.

Tjunkiya's father continued to live out his life as a nomad in his extensive desert country near Ilypilli, the largest permanent waterhole in the region. Some time later, Tjunkiya traveled to Papunya to work as a cook. She remembers making bread and stews, and doing the laundry.

Tjunkiya is the mother of Mitjili Naparrula (see page 70) and Turkey Tolson Tjupurrula, one of the principal painters for Papunya Tula. Her sister, Wintjiya Napaltjarri, is one of three wives of Tupa, the father of Turkey Tolson Tjupurrula. Both Tjunkiya and Wintjiya began painting in 1994 during the Minyma Tjukurrpa Project (see page 28), in which the older women resident at Kintore were visited by their relatives from Haasts Bluff and stimulated to paint. Since that time, Tjunkiya has become one of the principal artists at Kintore. The Creation stories or Tjukurrpa for which she is owner include wangunu or portulaca (small black seeds that are ground to make damper, a type of bread) and arkatjirri, a bush fruit similar to a sultana.

PLATE 12
Wintjiya Napaltjarri, b.1933 and Tjunkiya Napaltjarri, b. 1928
Tingari Women at Yuwalki, 1996
91 x 91 cm (36 x 36 in.)
Acrylic on canvas

WINTJIYA NAPALTJARRI AND TJUNKIYA NAPALTJARRI

Katarra Nampitjinpa

Tjampirrpunkungku

The artist referred to Tjampirrpunkungka, the place described in this painting, as her "borning" place, the place she was conceived, from which her spirit comes. The painting represents a water site surrounded by dunes or ridges. Several Ancestral women are shown as U-shapes. The vibrating visual resonance of this landscape suggests the actual color transformations in this area south of Kintore as it might be seen from above.

Biographical Notes

Katarra was born about 1940 in the Western Desert. In the first twenty years or more of her life she was completely nomadic, traveling on foot to hunt and attend ceremonies. She was a senior ritual leader, participating in many ceremonies and maintaining the traditional law. One of the last women nomads to be brought to a settled life, she first had contact with Europeans in 1965 and subsequently lived at Papunya, Mt. Liebig, Kintore, and outstations, and later at Haasts Bluff. Katarra began painting in 1994. She communicated in Pintupi and sign language, and spoke no English. Her principal Tjukurrpa (Dreamings) were emu, bush tomato or purra, and bush water or yulkapa. Katarra died at Papunya in 1998.

   She is represented in several public art collections, including the Museum and Art Gallery of the Northern Territory, and Darwin Supreme Court. Her work also figures in significant private collections.

PLATE 13
Katarra Nampitjinpa, c. 1940–1998
Tjampirrpunkungku, 1996
182 x 196 cm (71.5 x 77 in.)
Acrylic paint on canvas

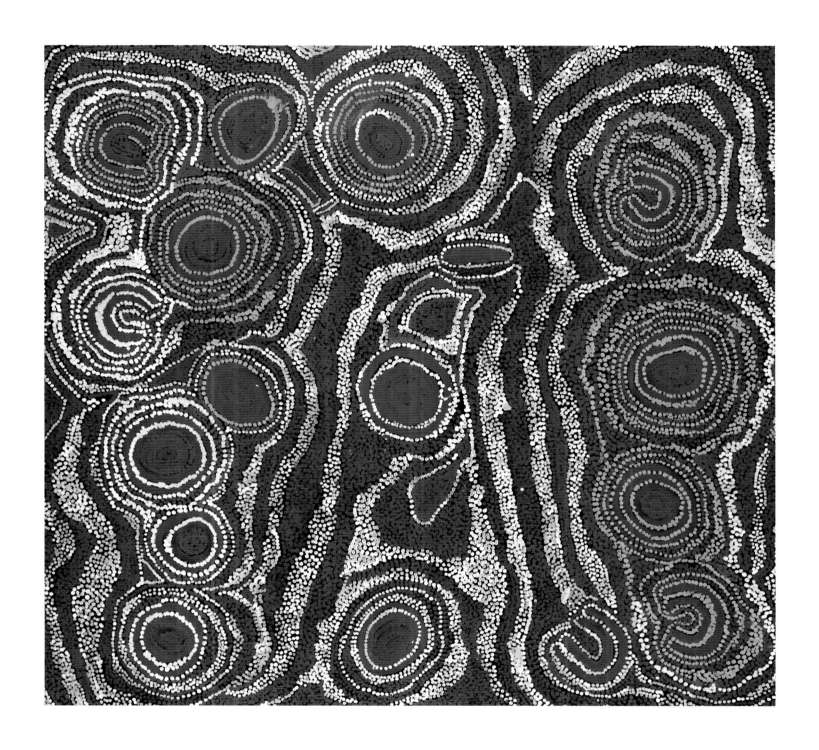

Makinti Napanangka and Nyurupayia Nampitjinpa (Mrs. Bennett)

Kaarkurutinytja Salt Lake

This is a combined work depicting a Tjukurrpa place important to both artists. Kaarkurutinytja (Lake MacDonald) is an elongated salt lake lying south of Kintore, among sand dunes that are usually covered in spinifex grass and other dry vegetation, with occasional desert oaks. Water periodically appears in the salt lakes then disappears again, leaving salt-encrusted earth. These remarkable desert features are often the homes of Ancestral snake beings.

The painting shows a time during the Creation period when the earth was being formed. At Kaarkurutinytja two giant kuniya (carpet pythons) met and carried out their business, the substance of which is not conveyed to outsiders. The snakes are also spoken of as two men of the Tjangala group.

In this dramatically expressive work, the artists have shown a string of circles that represent the tiny holes visible in the salt lake today, said to be the homes where the snakes still dwell. The place is thought of with fear, because the snakes are malevolent; it is said they "eat up to three Toyotas at a time." Beneath the snakes the circles surrounded by half-circles or U-shapes are the traditional depiction of encampments of people gathered at the place.

Biographical Notes

Makinti Napanangka and Nyurupayia Nampitjinpa (also known as Mrs. Bennett) were two of the original women who participated in an important artistic development in 1993/94, when a group of senior women who had not previously painted as solo artists were introduced to a range of art materials at two workshops, the first held at the Ikuntji Women's Centre at Haasts Bluff, then another at Kintore. This initiative has stimulated the vibrant women's paintings that are now produced at Kintore and Haasts Bluff.

Both Makinti Napanangka and Nyurupayia Nampitjinpa now paint at Kintore for Papunya Tula. They are known for pioneering a freer form of expression than their male relatives of the early Papunya movement, who still use careful, formal dotting and linear techniques. The women artists have a distinctively expressionistic style, using strong color and free brushwork.

Plate 14
Makinti Napanangka, b. 1930 and Nyurupayia Nampitjinpa, b. 1935
Kaarkurutinytja Salt Lake, 1995
300 x 150 cm (118 x 59 in.)
Acrylic paint on canvas

Narputta Nangala

Lampintja

South of the Pintupi community of Kintore is Lake MacDonald, a large salt pan known to Pintupi as Kaarkurutinytja. It is an important Tjukurrpa center. Close by is a remarkable geographical area called Lampintja, consisting of a series of huge mounds and deep dips, where it seems generations of nomadic peoples have dug. The crusty, compacted, white terrain, a combination of salt and gypsum, has possibly remained like this for centuries.

The significance of the area in the Creation beliefs is that it was formed by a woman digging for sand goannas. The story and songs recount her digging and digging in search of these large reptiles without success. Today, desert women on hunting expeditions repeat this scenario as they follow goannas' tracks to their burrows and dig — with occasional success.

The circular shapes in the painting are the Tjukurrpa diggings for the goanna. Today Pintupi visit this area and collect water near by. The wavy connecting lines are the goannas' subterranean tunnels; they can also be interpreted as water pathways beneath the surface.

Biographical Notes

Narputta Nangala Jugadai was born about 1933 at Kaarkurutinytja (Lake MacDonald). When very young she was completely nomadic with her Pintupi family. Her father Tjalakuny brought Narputta and her brother in from the desert to Haasts Bluff, then left and returned to the nomadic life. After schooling at Jay Creek, Narputta went through a period of interaction with missionaries, stockmen, and government staff. She worked herding animals, and moved large groups of goats and camels from Jay Creek to Haasts Bluff, where she witnessed successive groups of "bush Pintupi" coming in from the desert ill and weak. Many of these people died.

Subsequently she took on the job of cook for the community. At this time a number of other key figures who still live at Haasts Bluff, including Long Tom Tjapanangka, were working as stockmen. She recalls: "When they used to bring in the cattle for yarding we would cook damper and open tinned meat for them … People came in from the bush and passed away here. But I continued cooking and gave it to those who were ill."

Narputta's husband, Timmy Jugadai, was head stockman during this early period of the Haasts Bluff cattle industry. Perhaps as a result of this history of leadership, Narputta has a strong personality and dominant position among the artists in the community. Her work is confident and bold. She was one of the first women artists to commence solo painting, but previously assisted her husband, who painted for Papunya Tula in the 1970s. Her brothers Riley Major and George Tjangala are also prominent artists.

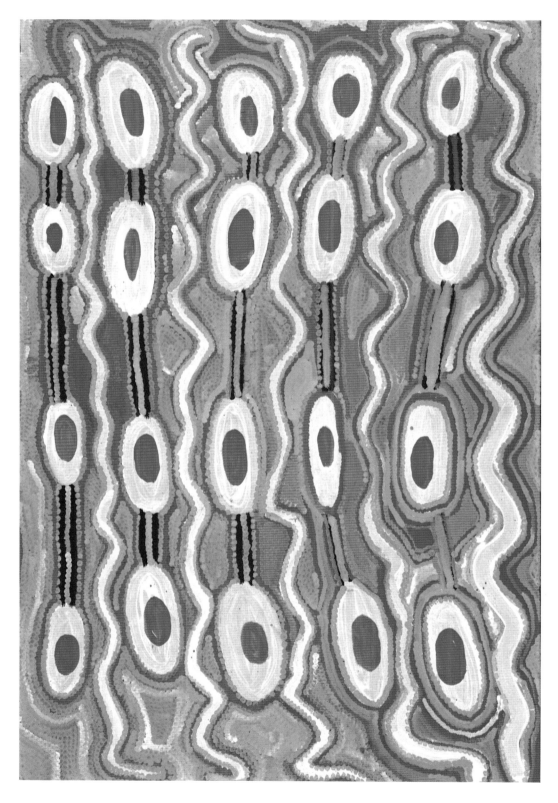

PLATE 15
Narputta Nangala, b. c. 1933
Lampintja, Sand Goanna, 1996
122.5 x 80.5 cm (48 x 31.5 in.)
Acrylic on canvas

Narputta Nangala began painting her father's country around Lake MacDonald in 1992. She won a National Aboriginal Art Award in Darwin in 1997. Her work is held by major Australian art galleries and museums, including the National Gallery of Australia; National Gallery of Victoria; Queensland Art Gallery; and Art Gallery of South Australia.

Two Women

Many of the desert peoples know the Tjukurrpa or Dreaming story of two women Ancestors who traveled vast distances across the Western Desert regions of Australia, gathering food, digging goannas from their holes, collecting berries, witchetty grubs, fruits, and medicines. The exploits of these women as they moved through various landscapes are sung at women's ceremonies across many hundreds of miles, from Pitjantjatjara country on the southwestern edge of Central Australia through to the northern areas beyond Haasts Bluff to Papunya.

Narputta Nangala has shown the women's journey in these expressive works. After crossing sand dunes, rocky ridges, and watercourses, they are approaching her country of Lake MacDonald. In the painting opposite the figures are clearly seen, wearing their hair-string belts. In the image below they are no longer visible, though present in the artist's mind. The humped hills and the expanses of land between them, represented by lines, have been reduced to the rhythmic pattern of a mesmerizing, never-ending journey across the desert.

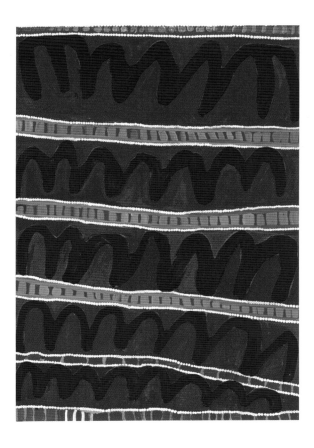

PLATE 16 (left)
Narputta Nangala, b. c. 1933
Two Women, 1997
152.5 x 109.5 cm (60 x 43 in.)
Acrylic on canvas

PLATE 17 (opposite)
Narputta Nangala, b. c. 1933
Two Women, 1997
153 x 121.5 cm (60 x 48 in.)
Acrylic on canvas

Marlee Naparrula

Kungkayunti

Kungkayunti or Brown's Bore is a traditional soakage, a place important to nomadic peoples. In the 1970s it became an outstation consisting of family groups who moved from Papunya and Haasts Bluff to reoccupy their traditional country. At the time of Marlee Naparrula's birth, it was a mixed Pintupi and Arrernte-speaking community.

The tree shapes forming an irregular pattern over the canvas mark out the desert oak country known locally as "the jungle." The depiction of this country is a signifier, a silent representation of a Tjukurrpa event that is connected to this place, although it is not shown or marked. A group of Creation women traveled from Kulpitjarra and passed through Kungkayunti, the name of which means "many women." At Kungkayunti the soakage water is called Pirranga, which means the moon. Details of why this is so are not given. The women were following a group of men engaged in sacred ceremonies, or "men's business," associated with the initiation of youths in religious knowledge and law. The women finally arrived at a place called Ngutjul at a time when it was freezing cold. They did not know how to make fire because they had no fire sticks. They then metamorphosed into a group of rounded rocks, which can still be seen there.

Biographical Notes

Born in about 1930 in Irrimarti, west of Haasts Bluff, Marlee Naparrula is the sister of Gideon Tjupurrula (see page 76), and grew up at Haasts Bluff. She is the first wife of Long Tom Tjapanangka (see page 80), with whom she has two children.

Marlee Naparrula began painting at the end of 1993. Her work has been exhibited widely and is held in numerous collections, including the Art Gallery of New South Wales and the Flinders University Art Museum, South Australia. In 1998 Marlee Naparrula won the Alice Prize, Central Australia's principal Aboriginal art award.

PLATE 18 (below, detail opposite)
Marlee Naparrula, b. c. 1930
Kungkayunti, 1997
71 x 183 cm (28 x 72 in.)
Acrylic on linen

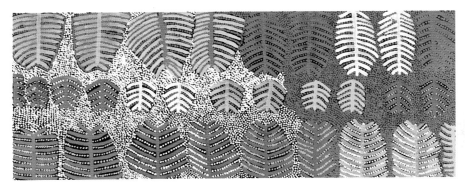

Anmanari and Mantua Napanangka

Mulpu Tjukurrpa at Lupul

This descriptive work, a collaborative painting by two sisters, is a vision of their father's country, depicting a ceremony in place at three campsites (shown as three sets of concentric circles). Around each of the campsites, women are seated in groups of four, with their coolamons and digging sticks. Men's campsites are shown nearby, at either end of the snake form, with two men on each. The greenish circular formation is a water soak. The painting is composed from an aerial perspective, with activities and information radiating around the sites. Two tall white desert gums are shown, each with a dark canopy of leaves. The hair-string belts of the women appear as fringed arcs. Around the painting are the tracks of birds, while irregularly shaped mushrooms or mulpu appear in two corners.

Minyma Tjukurrpa is the generic term for the journey undertaken by Creation Ancestral women who traveled from the place known as Kungkayunti following the Tingari Ancestral men, who were carrying on law and ceremonial business across the country. At each site where these Ancestors stopped, the women held their own separate ceremonies connected to those of the men. The entourage finished at Ngutjul, the name given to the site where the women died from exposure as a result of the extreme cold in the desert.

Biographical Notes

The artists' parents were born in the vicinity of Lupul (Frederick Range), far into the Western Australian desert. They were part of the group of Pintupi who camped at the permanent waterhole of Ilypilli. Anmanari was born some time before World War II at Yateman's Bore, a ration drop where missionaries and others sent expeditions to leave food for desert nomads hit by drought.

This painting concerns Anmanari's father's country, Lupul, where his Dreaming is emu, kunkutakuta (mopoke), and turkey. Anmanari's own Dreaming is mulpu, a type of mushroom or truffle.

From the late 1970s to the late 1980s, Anmanari was married to the Papunya artist Lionel Kantawarra Tjupurrula, and therefore came in touch with the widespread desert art movement. She and her sister participated in Minyma Tjukurrpa, the Women's Dreaming Project at Kintore, in 1994 and 1995. Anmanari now lives at Haasts Bluff.

PLATE 19
Anmanari Napanangka, b. c. 1946, and Mantua Napanangka, 1944–1995
Mulpu Tjukurrpa at Lupul, 1995
182 x 152 cm (71.5 x 60 in.)
Acrylic on linen

Mitjili Naparrula

Uwalki: Watiya Tjuta

The subtitle of the painting, *Watiya Tjuta*, indicates that it relates to men's wooden objects. The Tjukurrpa or Dreaming of this work concerns making spears, an important aspect of men's business. The straightening of spears is a theme frequently painted by Mitjili Naparrula's brother, Turkey Tolson.

Mitjili is known for the strength of patterning in the formal arrangements of her work, as in this representation of the woman's side of this Tjukurrpa, the trees that provide the wood for spear shafts and other objects. The country where the trees are found is Uwalki, Mitjili's father's country. She was taught her father's Tjukurrpa by her mother, who drew images in the sand of Uwalki. She says, "My mother taught me my father's Tjukurrpa; that's what I'm painting on the canvas."[5]

This country, near the Kintore Range west of Haasts Bluff, is rich in bush food, with plenty of native grass seeds for bush damper, as well as animals such as turkeys and kangaroos. Stands of desert oaks form vertical patterns against the shimmering sands.

Biographical Notes

Mitjili Naparrula was born at Haasts Bluff in 1945 and started painting for the Ikuntji Women's Centre in 1993. She is the daughter of Tjunkiya Napaltjarri, a painter at Kintore. Her brother, Turkey Tolson Tjupurrula, is the chairman of Papunya Tula Artists, and she is married to Long Tom Tjapanangka (see page 80). She has exhibited throughout Australia since 1994 and has held several solo exhibitions. Her work is in major Australian collections including the National Gallery of Australia; Art Gallery of New South Wales; and Flinders University Art Museum, South Australia.

PLATE 20 (left, detail opposite)
Mitjili Naparrula, b. 1945
Uwalki: Watiya Tjuta, 1997
137 x 153 cm (54 x 60 in)
Acrylic on linen

Eunice Napanangka

Tjukurla

These three works are abstracted depictions of the artist's birthplace of Tjukurla and her Tjukurrpa or Dreaming of the ninu or bilby. The rock-hole at Tjukurla is a very important water source in the desert country south of the Kintore Range on the border of Central and Western Australia. Surrounded by dunes and sparse vegetation, it was a gravitating point for far-flung nomadic families in drought time.

Tjukurla is one of the centers of the bilby in its journey across the desert during the Creation era. Bilbies, also known as rabbit-eared bandicoots (family *Paramelidae*), are appealing animals with long, soft, silky hair and black-and-white tails. They are ingenious, digging spiral burrows up to six feet long under the desert to escape the daytime heat, then emerging to forage at night. The introduction of rabbits has severely depleted their numbers, and they are now an endangered species. As a caretaker of this native species, Eunice, like many other Aboriginal artists, is concerned to restore and maintain spiritual associations with key sites, lest the destruction of the bilbies' habitat assist in their disappearance. In this way painting becomes an act of both spiritual and environmental maintenance.

Opposite, a distant, aerial view shows the rock-hole from above and the tracks of the thirsty bilby journeying to that site. The dotted lines represent the changes in color of the landscape surrounding the waterhole as the water soaks into the sand and recedes. Curving lines depict the surrounding arid dunes.

In Plate 23, the bilby tracks are again apparent, as are the dune-like formations, represented as strong linear patterns. Within these the four seated Ancestors are visible in the extreme corners as U-forms merging into the hills. The waterhole itself (at bottom right) can be seen to be a "sit down place" for the bilby, also represented by a U-shape. In this painting the country is dry, the waterhole depleted.

In Plate 22, water is abundant, the silted edges of the waterhole sprouting grass after rain. The lines represent the endless sand dunes of the area in an abstracted, painterly depiction of the sacred site.

PLATE 21
Eunice Napanangka, b. 1940
Tjukurla, 1997
151 x 122 cm (59.5 x 48 in.)
Acrylic on canvas

Biographical Notes

Eunice Napanangka was born in January 1940 at Kuruuldu and speaks Pintupi language. Her father, Tutuma Tjapanagarti, was one of the first of the desert artists to paint during the beginnings of the Papunya Tula desert art movement in 1971/72. Tutuma was also the senior member of the Winanpa Pintupi Association. His country, to which Eunice also belongs, includes Tjukurla, Warakuna, Lupul, Punkupirri (also the country of Tutuma's mother, Titurla Nangala), Mantamaru, Wurlilya (west of Tjukurla), Mulpunga, Kuruuldu (Tutuma's father's country and Eunice's birthplace), and many other sites west of Tjukurla.

Eunice began to paint assisting her husband, Gideon Tjupurrula, in the early years when he painted for Papunya Tula. She began to paint her own work in August 1992, when the Ikuntji Women's Centre first opened at Haasts Bluff. From that time until the present she has continued working in acrylic paint on both canvas and paper. Her paintings have been exhibited widely throughout Australia and are held in many significant collections, including the Flinders University Art Museum, South Australia.

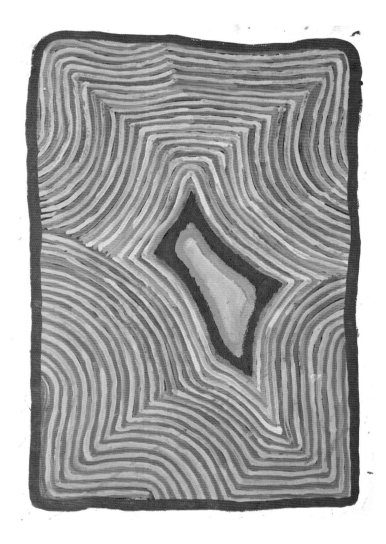

PLATE 22 (left)
Eunice Napanangka, b. 1940
Tjukurla, 1997
106 x 70 cm (41.5 x 27.5 in.)
Acrylic on paper

PLATE 23 (opposite)
Eunice Napanangka, b. 1940
Tjukurla, 1997
75 x 57 cm (29.5 x 22.5 in.)
Acrylic on paper

Gideon Tjupurrula

Lake Mackay

This is a seminal final statement by the artist, a loving depiction of his birthplace and Tjukurrpa, Lake Mackay, a huge lake spanning the Northern Territory–Western Australian border. The artist once said, "You can't drive through there, you'll sink. Biggest lake. My father's place, my grandparents' place. My place. I was born there."[6] In portraying a death scene, the work carries portents of the artist's own imminent death.

The stippled and encrusted white background represents the surface of the salt lake, which is interspersed with many islands, rocks, and sandhills. Lake Mackay and the country around its perimeter have many important Tjukurrpa sites that are of significance to different groups of Pintupi.

The painting is both a map and an event. It shows the road from Docker River to Lake Mackay, which passes near two sacred sites, depicted as concentric circles. It also depicts a killing, both real and mythological. Two men were living on either side of the lake. Each had weapons and fire sticks. As they journeyed towards the lake they separated, one going north, the other south. The man who traveled to the north was killed at a place called Tilkupakan, while the man who traveled south was also struck down and killed.

The two men shown in the work are of the Tjakamarra kinship or skin group. One has been hit with a "killer" boomerang. His severed head appears on the far left of the figures. Above them is a sandy dune area in the lake with trees and vegetation, and a symbolically depicted campsite, with U-shapes denoting people.

PLATE 24
Gideon Tjupurrula, c. 1930–1996
Lake Mackay, 1996
166 x 71 cm (65.5 x 28 in.)
Acrylic paint on canvas

Biographical Notes

Gideon (Jack) Tjupurrula was born about 1930 at Pinarri, Lake Mackay. His family were then living a fully nomadic life, but were later contacted by early mission expeditions led by Pastor Albrecht from Hermannsburg. A group of Pintupi, including Gideon and his family, then moved into Haasts Bluff, where he received his first European food and clothing.

Gideon Tjupurrula was a painter with the Papunya Tula group throughout the 1970s and 1980s. He lived at Haasts Bluff, where the field officers used to supply him with canvas and paint. His traditional dotted paintings in the Papunya mode were exhibited at major Papunya Tula group exhibitions in Australia.

He began painting again at the Ikuntji Women's Centre at Haasts Bluff in 1992. His wife, Eunice Napanangka, is also a prominent artist (see page 72).

In the early 1960s Gideon Tjupurrula accompanied patrol officer Jeremy Long on expeditions to gather together the remaining nomadic Pintupi and encourage them to leave the drought-stricken desert for food and shelter at Papunya. Remembering this emotional time, he said: "After returning with Jerry Long I started painting this Tjukurrpa … The old men danced in honour of their country so far away. They gathered big mobs of tucker, malu [kangaroo] and emu, and made an offering of this to remember their country. All our fathers were there, all the Tjakamarras, all the Tjupurrulas, all the Tjangalas, all the Tjampitjinpas. I'm not there. I'm at Haasts Bluff."[7]

This work is one of several in which the artist departed from the classic dotted technique and formal structure. Shortly after it was completed, Gideon Jack Tjupurrula died of kidney failure in the Alice Springs Hospital.

His work is held in the collections of the Art Gallery of New South Wales; Wollongong Art Gallery; Campbelltown Regional Art Gallery; Flinders University Art Museum, South Australia; and the Supreme Court, Darwin.

PLATE 24 (detail)
Gideon Tjupurrula, c. 1930–1996
Lake Mackay, 1996
166 x 71 cm (65.5 x 28 in.)
Acrylic paint on canvas

Long Tom Tjapanangka

Mikarnta, Irantji and Snake

In Tjukurrpa, the Creation or Dreaming time, Kuniya the carpet snake, who is also called Kartilka, is traveling west of the Irantji Range to Mikarnta Waterhole. The Irantji hills appear on the desert horizon like a row of humps. They are the metamorphosed backs of a band of Tjukurrpa emus that traveled that way in Creation times.

At Mikarnta a large spring offers running water, a scarce and prized desert resource, and one that is guarded by men's law of the Tjukurrpa. Long Tom remarked of this painting: "Biggest spring on top of Mikarnta waterhole. Snake goes right into the water, so the water's running now. Big hole there."

The vast distances of the desert between the rocky desert outcrops have been compressed on the canvas and the vegetation marked as pointers to the place and its resources for traveling people. Although the water spring is not clearly visible in the painting, it is foremost in the artist's mind when he paints this site.

Biographical Notes

Long Tom Tjapanangka was born in 1929 somewhere near his father's country of Lupul (Frederick Range). He speaks the Ngaatjatjarra language, and as a child traveled by foot with his family across vast stretches of desert from Lupul on the border of Western Australia to Areyonga, a small Aboriginal community southeast of Alice Springs. After his father was killed in tragic circumstances the family returned to Lupul.

Long Tom grew up during the early years of the expansion of the cattle industry in central Australia and became a valued stockman on several cattle stations, including his current community, Haasts Bluff. He also worked as a police "tracker," and was renowned for his ability to follow fugitives over hundreds of miles of remote desert. He has been a leading painter at the Haasts Bluff community since 1993.

Long Tom's work is widely held in public collections throughout Australia, including the National Gallery of Australia; National Gallery of Victoria; Art Gallery of New South Wales; South Australian Museum; and the Museum and Art Gallery of the Northern Territory.

PLATE 25
Long Tom Tjapanangka, b. 1929
Mikarnta, Irantji and Snake, 1996
122 x 153 cm (48 x 60 in.)
Acrylic on canvas

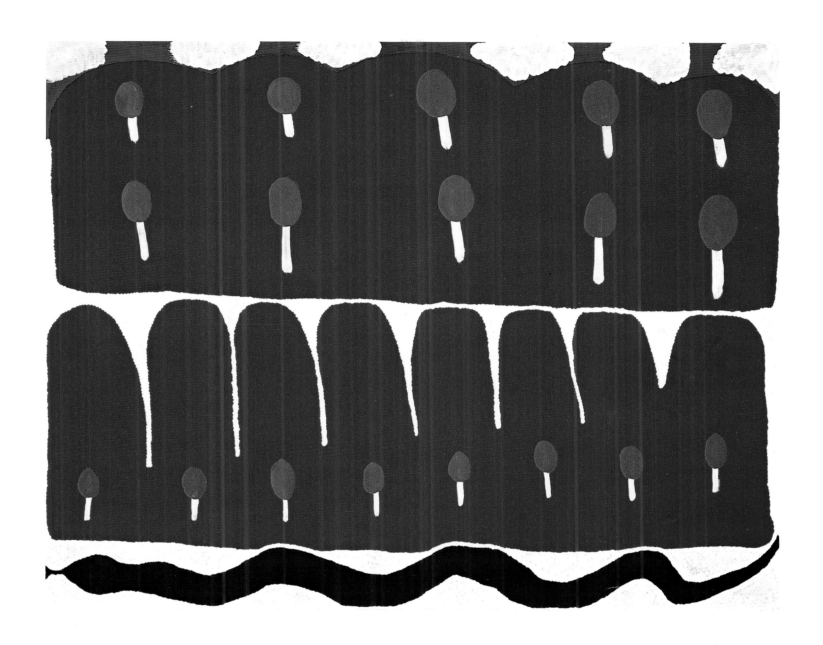

Biddy Napanangka Hutchinson

Majarrdi Jukurrpa (Hair String Belt Dreaming)

During women's ceremonies, all the participants wear hair-string belts — short frontal "skirts" made of string hand-spun from human hair and animal fur. This traditional string is spun on the thigh, then wound on to a stick spindle. These spindles are universal symbols of love magic for desert peoples. The associated image of a string skirt also holds a powerful attraction for men.

The Jukurrpa women depicted in this painting by Biddy Napanangka Hutchinson are the women Creation Ancestors of her own country. In the Tjukurrpa times, two groups of related women, Napangardi and Napanangka, traveled from Mina Mina, west of Yuendumu, eastward to another country, searching for ngarlyipi or snake vine. This vine offers a tough fiber material, which is used to strap parraja or food carriers over the women's shoulders. Tied tightly around the forehead, it also acts as a headache cure.

The circles represent water soaks at which the women stopped or camped during their journey.

Biographical Notes

A prominent Warlpiri artist who mostly lives at Yuendumu, Biddy Napanangka Hutchinson was born at Janyinki, west of Yuendumu, before World War II. She grew up in the area known as the Granites, named for its rounded rock formations. At an early age she learned how to live off the land, traveling through the Tanami Desert, digging up roots and sucking them for moisture. Her family moved to Mt. Doreen and then Mt. Singleton (Wapurtarli), where they worked in a wolfram mine. At that time, Biddy was only thirteen or fourteen years old.

From Wapurtarli, Biddy Hutchinson then walked to Lajamanu, where she married. She later left Lajamanu and moved to Yuendumu, where she became a cook. She also sewed and washed clothes with the other women in the old buildings beside the church.

Biddy Napanangka Hutchinson is the owner of the Jukurrpa or Dreaming for the snake vine, edible fungus, and digging stick. She is one of the founding members of Warlukurlangu Artists and has been painting for the center since the early 1980s, when she helped to produce the first works for the Women's Museum at Yuendumu. Her works have been shown in numerous group exhibitions of Warlpiri artists in Australia, the USA, Tahiti, and Japan.

PLATE 26
Biddy Napanangka Hutchinson, b. c. 1940
Majarrdi Jukurrpa (Hair String Belt Dreaming), 1997
122 x 92 cm (48 x 36 in.)
Acrylic on linen

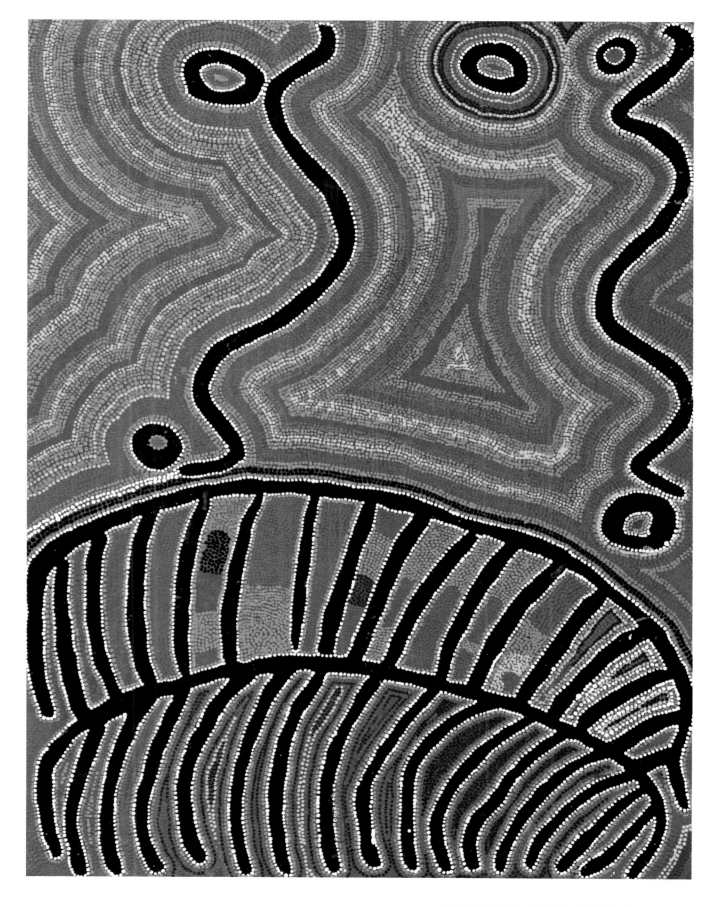

Warlukurlangu Artists

Jack Jakamarra Ross, Paddy Jupurrurla Nelson, Victor Jupurrurla Ross, Sampson Japaljarri Martin, Paddy Japaljarri Stewart, Paddy Japaljarri Sims, Andrea Nungarrayi Martin, Jorna Napurrurla Nelson, Tilo Nangala Jurrah, Dolly Nampijinpa Daniels, Uni Nampijinpa Martin, Judy Nampijinpa Granites, Rosie Nangala Flemming, Lynette Nampijinpa Granites, Jillie Nakamarra Spencer, Bessie Nakamarra Sims, Pansy Nakamarra Stewart, Marlette Napurrurla Ross, Rosie Johnson, Coral Napangardi Gallagher, Judy Napangardi Watson, Ruth Napaljarri Oldfield, Lucy Napaljarri Kennedy, Veronica Napurrurla Williams, Wendy Nungarrayi Brown, Biddy Napanangka Hutchinson, Maggie Nakamarra White, Queenie Nungarrayi Stewart, Ruby Nampijinpa Forest

Liwirringki (Burrowing Skink) Jukurrpa

Liwirringki are small reptiles or skinks that burrow in the ground. They are commonly flushed out of their burrows using small fires, which are lit around mulju (water soakages). When hunting, men wear purdurru (hair-string belts) and tuck the liwirringki under them as they are caught. The men also carry mutu (sticks) to club the skinks as they run out of the spinifex.

This painting traces the path of a large fire across the landscape. A group of liwirringki are fleeing before it. The fire generates large clouds of smoke, which are transformed into a range of sandhills. Several important sites associated with this Jukurrpa have been depicted as concentric circles. The straight lines joining these places together in a grid form are the indentations left by the liwirringkis' tails, with their footprints on either side.

The U-shaped forms interspersed throughout the painting represent Jangala/ Jampijinpa and Jakamarra/Jupurrurla men lighting fires with their ngiji (firesticks).

Ownership of the Jukurrpa is passed from one community to another according to kinship relationships or "skin groups." In this case Jangala/Jampijinpa own one part of the story and Jakamarra/Jupurrurla own another section. As a result, the ownership of the painting is split between the two groups.

The large number of artists who worked on this canvas are the owners and guardians of the areas of country shown, and members of their families. This tract of land is also the natural domain of the liwirringki.

PLATE 27 (detail)
Warlukurlangu Artists
Liwirringki (Burrowing Skink) Jukurrp, 1998
3 x 5 m (118 x 197 in.)
Acrylic on canvas

PLATE 27
Warlukurlangu Artists
Jack Jakamarra Ross, Paddy Jupurrurla Nelson,
Victor Jupurrurla Ross, Sampson Japaljarri Martin,
Paddy Japaljarri Stewart, Paddy Japaljarri Sims,
Andrea Nungarrayi Martin, Jorna Napurrurla Nelson,
Tilo Nangala Jurrah, Dolly Nampijinpa Daniels,
Uni Nampijinpa Martin, Judy Nampijinpa Granites,
Rosie Nangala Flemming, Lynette Nampijinpa Granites,
Jillie Nakamarra Spencer, Bessie Nakamarra Sims,
Pansy Nakamarra Stewart, Marlette Napurrurla Ross,
Rosie Johnson, Coral Napangardi Gallagher,
Judy Napangardi Watson, Ruth Napaljarri Oldfield,
Lucy Napaljarri Kennedy, Veronica Napurrurla Williams,
Wendy Nungarrayi Brown, Biddy Napanangka Hutchinson,
Maggie Nakamarra White, Queenie Nungarrayi Stewart,
Ruby Nampijinpa Forest
Liwirringki (Burrowing Skink) Jukurrpa, 1998
3 x 5 m (118 x 197 in.)
Acrylic on canvas

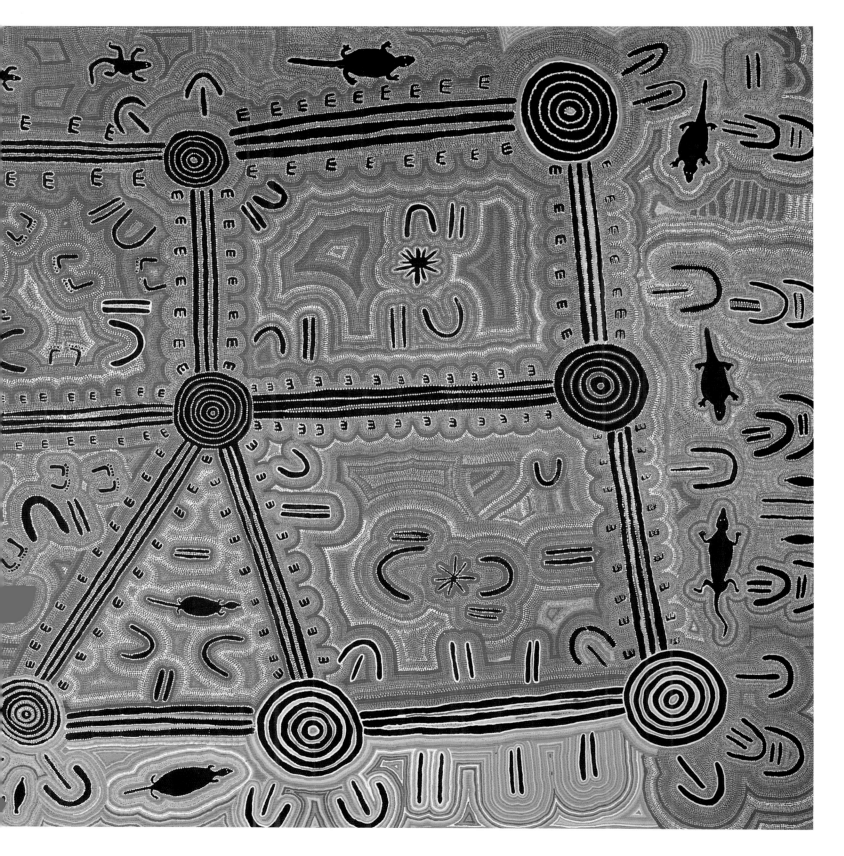

Notes

The following account of the expedition that preceded the making of this painting is drawn from information provided by Warlukurlangu Artists, Yuendumu.

Yuendumu, the home of the Warlpiri, was the first government settlement established north of Alice Springs. It is situated on an Aboriginal reserve (now fully owned Aboriginal land). In the 1950s it was surrounded by cattle stations. On the west was Mt. Doreen, to the north Mt. Denison, the east Mt. Allen, and the south Mt. Wedge. Many of these stations are still in existence. Over the decades since Warlpiri came in to receive rations at Yuendumu, their access to land and sacred places on these cattle stations has varied. While some cattle stations allowed them ready access to sites for important ceremonies, others remained negative or obstructive, claiming that cattle gates would be left open.

It was in this context that in 1998 the Warlukurlangu artists at Yuendumu began discussions with a large number of other artists about making major paintings to record the Jukurrpa of large tracts of land. Each of these would involve several artists, often up to ten or twenty. These large paintings usually require substantial sponsorship, because it is necessary to provide transport and food, not only for the painters and landowners, but also for guardians or kurdungurlu, together with various children and family members. This outing is an opportunity for people to be taught things and shown places that previously they might only have heard about. At a large meeting of the community, it was decided that the liwirringki skink country should be recorded on canvas for the Gantner Myer Collection.

Many people decided to come on the liwirringki journey, and the Warlukurlangu staff were accompanied by filmmakers. Using three vehicles and packing enough food for three days, the party of thirty-three headed for the place known as Kurrkurra-parnta, where a special family place is marked by a large desert oak tree about 500 yards off the Nyirrpi road. The group visited the tree, then moved on to a stony mound, which the people said was the site of a mulju (water soakage). The area was overgrown and unattended, indicating that no one had been there for some time.

This was the first important liwirringki place the expedition visited. People spread out around the area, exclaiming and pointing out tiny formations of stones, which are metamorphosed liwirringki. Some of the rocks exhibited delicate patterns of red and cream oxide markings; these were interpreted as the liwirringki's kuruwarri or Dreaming tracks.

Meanwhile, the women had spread out to hunt and collect bush tobacco. Traveling through country that has not been visited before always serves more than one purpose. Children look for small animals and fruit, and women seek larger reptiles or perhaps a supply of witchetty grubs. Food, travel, religion, and song become a complete way of life.

The expedition then traveled west to the site of Palpin-parnta, following the Jukurrpa journey of the Liwirringki Ancestors. Here and there the remains of old campfires were evident. People had made camps here when hunting during more mobile times. A deep water soakage at Palpin-parnta was once a source of life for the Warlpiri, but on this visit, sadly, it was filled with dirt. It would have taken a full day to dig the soak out, so the group decided to move on, continuing the pilgrimage along the liwirringki route.

The next stopping point was a range of hills called Ngarldindingi. Here the women remained near the road; some rested and others hunted, while the older men, together with Dolly Nampijinpa Daniels and Uni Nampijinpa Martin, drove towards the hills. The men climbed to the top of the range, where there is a special rock-hole and liwirringki rock formations.

The expedition then traveled on to Yinjirrmardi, an old outstation that still had a water tank and some old tin houses. After setting up camp, the men and women rested, immersed in their thoughts of the liwirringki journey they were re-enacting. Some quietly began singing. The liwirringki song cycle had not been performed for some time because the people had not had access to the area. Indeed, the tracks of these small, delicate animals had not been seen for some time in the desert earth. The men feared they were extinct and blamed themselves in part, although there was clear evidence of the ravages caused by cattle on the country.

The next day began at Wilyangkani, an important initiation place for young men. Here the group lit fires, just as the Jukurrpa details, to flush skinks out of the grass, making them easy to catch. The sand dunes that run from east to west in this area are said to be the transformed smoke from the fires. The Jukurrpa of the blue-tongue lizard is closely connected to that of the Liwirringki, so fires were also lit to drive out blue-tongue lizards. Reptiles commonly hide beneath the prickly spinifex grass that grows throughout this rocky country, and it is common practice to hunt them by quickly firing a clump of spinifex and catching them as they flee. Some skinks are also nocturnal, their tracks across the sand visible only in the early hours of the morning, after the dew has settled the sand.

Most of the places the group stopped at also have water soaks, and Wilyangkani was no exception. One more water soakage was visited at Yajarlu, close to an outstation of the same name. The party then returned to Yuendumu three days after they left. The following morning there was a discussion, planning and mapping out the journey and pathway of liwirringki, then the painting was begun. The kuruwarri journey of the liwirringki as they ran from the fire to the various water soaks was first drawn out by Jack Jakamarra Ross and Paddy Jupurrurla Nelson, attended by the guardians. This is the central formation of parallel linear trails connected to concentric circles, forming a strong pathway around which visual detail and information were then assembled. The different hands of various artists are discernible around the canvas.

Twenty-nine people in all assisted with the painting, watched from time to time by their families. The work took about six days.

Lindsay Bird Mpetyane

Ilkatjera and Atapila at Arimala Soak

The painting concerns two plants: ilkatjera, a yellow-flowering, prickly vine, and atapila, a small plum. The Tjukurrpa or Spirit Ancestors of these plants moved across Anmatyerre country from site to site. The artist records their journey as straight lines from roundel to roundel. The largest roundels represent the rock-hole or soak of Arimala, a deep watering point set well beneath the surface of the ground on a large, flat plain. Subordinate roundels represent ritual locations for the ceremonies conducted by ilkatjera and atapila Spirit Ancestors in Creation times.

Biographical Notes

Lindsay Bird Mpetyane is the nephew of Emily Kame Kngwarreye (see page 102). Born in 1942 at Ungoola or Bushy Park, he is a member of the Eastern Anmatyerre people. After spending his early childhood in the traditional way of life, he worked with his father and brother herding sheep on Bushy Park Station, a pastoral lease that encompassed his birthplace. When drought hit Bushy Park, Lindsay left to work on Waite River. He subsequently spent several years as a cattleman on Woodgreen Station.

In 1975 Lindsay Bird Mpetyane and his family established their own permanent community on their traditional land close to their sacred sites at Ungoola. Nine years later, in 1984, problems with the water at Ungoola forced them to move further west to Ahakeye Soakage, also known as Mulga Bore an excision of land from Atartinga Station, just south of the Utopia land border. Mulga Bore is now a small community that pursues a semi-traditional lifestyle. Earnings from art supplement the members' income from social security payments. Several women at Mulga Bore have had a long association with the batik movement at the Utopia community to the northeast. Lindsay Bird Mpetyane is one of the few men to have also worked in batik, and was one of the first to express an interest in painting on canvas. Throughout the 1990s Lindsay Bird has been responsible for a significant number of large canvases detailing major Ancestral journeys and activities of Anmatyerre men's law. His paintings are strong and formal, denoting his senior leadership role in the community. He occasionally experiments with radical color changes, but prefers traditional earth ocher hues.

His work is held in many public collections, including the National Gallery of Australia; Art Gallery of Western Australia; Queensland Art Gallery; Powerhouse Museum, Sydney; and the Museum of Victoria.

PLATE 28
Lindsay Bird Mpetyane, b. 1942
Ilkatjera and Atapila at Arimala Soak, 1993
150 x 90 cm (59 x 35.5 in.)
Acrylic on canvas

Freddy Kngwarreye Jones

Big Old Man Kangaroo

This is a painting of the ground design for the sacred ceremony of the Old Man Kangaroo (Alyawarre: "Aherre kngjinye"), and is exceptional in its strength of design and care in execution. These designs are prepared on the earth's surface during lengthy song cycles marking the journey of the Ancestors whose design is depicted. During these ceremonies, men's bodies are covered in down, paint, and ocher, and the significant dances are accompanied by chanting and rhythmic clapping.

This particular design is used on a ceremonial ground near Theleye outstation, one of the many centers on Utopia. Utopia, a former cattle station on Anmatyerre land, is now an Aboriginal community comprising a large number of separate outstations, each of which houses several family groups.

The central motif of the painting is the Old Man Kangaroo's spiritual center. Seated beside him are a number of younger kangaroo men. The small roundels with arcs attached represent the testicular pouches of the male kangaroos, and the small arcs are the pouches in which the females carry their young.

The Old Man Kangaroo story is a major Ancestral route traversing Central Australia, commencing at Theleye and traveling southwest towards Alice Springs through Heavy Tree Gap, which the Ancestors helped form. Heading south, the Kangaroo Ancestors then formed many other landscape features through the eastern MacDonnell Ranges and on to Ayers Rock, before returning to the country they came from via the western MacDonnell Ranges. Freddy Kngwarreye Jones has executed this work in fine detail with great care because of the seriousness and importance of the subject matter.

PLATE 29
Freddy Kngwarreye Jones, b. 1948
Big Old Man Kangaroo, 1990
150 x 121 cm (59 x 47.5 in.)
Acrylic on canvas

Biographical Notes

Freddy Kngwarreye Jones was born in 1948 on Old MacDonald Station. His father, Jacob Jones, was an authoritative Alyawarre man who traveled extensively as a young camel boy, working and mixing with European and Afghan men during the period when camel trains carried goods in the Australian desert.

Freddy Jones lives at Theleye outstation within the Utopia community and speaks the Alyawarre language. The Alyawarre and Anmatyerre peoples are closely related. Alyawarre people's traditional country lies to the east of Anmatyerre country, and many members of the two groups are related by kinship and marriage. Several men from these communities have achieved prominence for their art, including Dave Ross, Lindsay Bird, and Cowboy Pwerle. Most maintain the "classic" geometric circles and parallel lines of men's designs, marking out Ancestral Tjukurrpa routes.

Freddy Kngwarreye Jones is concerned with the Caterpillar Tjukurrpa (Altyerre) or Dreaming, the central Dreaming for the town of Alice Springs. He is also the principal song leader in ceremonies for the meat ant, pink-crested cockatoo, sulfur-crested cockatoo, snake, spider, and kangaroo.

He has exhibited in Melbourne, Sydney, Brisbane, and Perth, and his work has been acquired by several institutions, including the National Gallery of Victoria and Art Bank Australia.

PLATE 29, (detail)
Freddy Kngwarreye Jones, b. 1948
Big Old Man Kangaroo, 1990
150 x 121 cm (59 x 47.5 in.)
Acrylic on canvas

Mary Kemarre and Family

Camp Scene and Women's Body Designs

This episodic work shows family groups traveling in various vehicles on expeditions to gather food and look after country. Abstracted representations of plant forms, like florets, are juxtaposed against a range of cars, the prized possessions of desert people. Today many people use vehicles, preferably four-wheel-drive Toyotas, to travel from place to place and community to community, making connections, gathering food, and caring for their country through ceremony.

The artists have also intentionally given the scene a metaphysical component. Women's body paintings are represented as series of parallel white and red ocher lines abstracted from the body and laid on the ground, as though the earth itself were the body. The horizontal bands are normally made across the chest, while the vertical lines mark the breasts and upper arms. The painting thus represents the people's deep connection to the country they pass through in the course of their everyday activities.

Biographical Notes

Tracts of land are jointly owned among Anmatyerre and other desert families. Expressing the Tjukurrpa or Altyerre journeys and law associated with these lands is both a privilege and a responsibility. Paintings may be individual works or, as here, conceived by one owner and painted with the help of kin.

Mary Kemarre, born in 1925, is one of the four senior women "bosses" on Utopia. She takes responsibility for painting body designs on young women initiates, and sings Awelye songs to encourage their fertility. Her paintings, which might be called "lifestyle narratives," encourage much discussion and humor about the "old-time" ways. Her country is Andaringya (Atarraringya), on the northern end of Utopia, and she has custodial responsibility for the kurrajong tree seed. She is married to Billy Petyarre Morton, a renowned sculptor, and they have a large family. A passionate advocate of preserving traditional practices that ensure social cohesion, Mary is involved in maintaining traditional birth practices and is active in land rights issues.

This painting was executed as part of a month-long project in which canvases were handed to artists at Mulga Bore in Anmatyerre country, northeast of Alice Springs. The work was commissioned by Rodney Gooch, a curator who has worked extensively with artists from Utopia, especially Emily Kame Kngwarreye and Gloria Petyarre.

PLATE 30
Mary Kemarre, b. 1925, and Family
Camp Scene and Women's Body Designs, 1986
113 x 90 cm (44.5 x 35.5 in.)
Acrylic on canvas

Gloria Petyarre

Mountain Devil Lizard

This painting is a close-up sectioning of traditional body painting. The patterning represents the small reptile commonly known as the "thorny devil," but referred to by Gloria Petyarre and other Anmatyerre people as "mountain devil lizard."

The thorny devil (*Moloch horridus*) is an unnerving but beautifully patterned dragon-like creature with barbs and humps across its back and large, bulging protuberances on its head, camouflaging its eyes. Surviving on small insects, it inhabits the dune areas of Anmatyerre country and can be found across much of the Western Desert. As a keeper of this Dreaming or Tjukurrpa, Gloria Petyarre has made it a key theme in her work. Like the thorny devil itself, which has a chameleon-like ability to change its color, Gloria Petyarre's paintings verge on the spectacular in their color changes and stylistic variations.

Biographical Notes

Born about 1945, Gloria Petyarre is a prominent Anmatyerre artist who has been at the forefront of contemporary Australian painting for some years. She lives and works in her own community at Utopia, combining this with visits to major cities for exhibitions and to paint.

A close associate of the major artist Emily Kame Kngwarreye, Gloria Petyarre has exhibited widely since 1977. From 1977 to 1987 she participated in numerous group exhibitions with other women artists from Utopia. In 1989 her paintings were included in *Art from Utopia* at the Austral Gallery, St. Louis, and in 1993, with her husband Ronnie Price, she designed and executed a mural for the Kansas City Zoo.

While she works within the bounds of traditional knowledge and often expresses Tjukurrpa themes and traditional women's body designs, Gloria Petyarre remains a contemporary individualist, exhibiting a number of clear stylistic innovations, both sequential and concurrent. At the same time, the forms or structures that can be discerned underlying much of her work are reminiscent of the forms of other kin, in particular Emily Kame Kngwarreye and her sister Ada Bird.

PLATE 31
Gloria Petyarre, b. c. 1945
Mountain Devil Lizard, 1996
91 x 61 cm (36 x 24 in.)
Acrylic on canvas

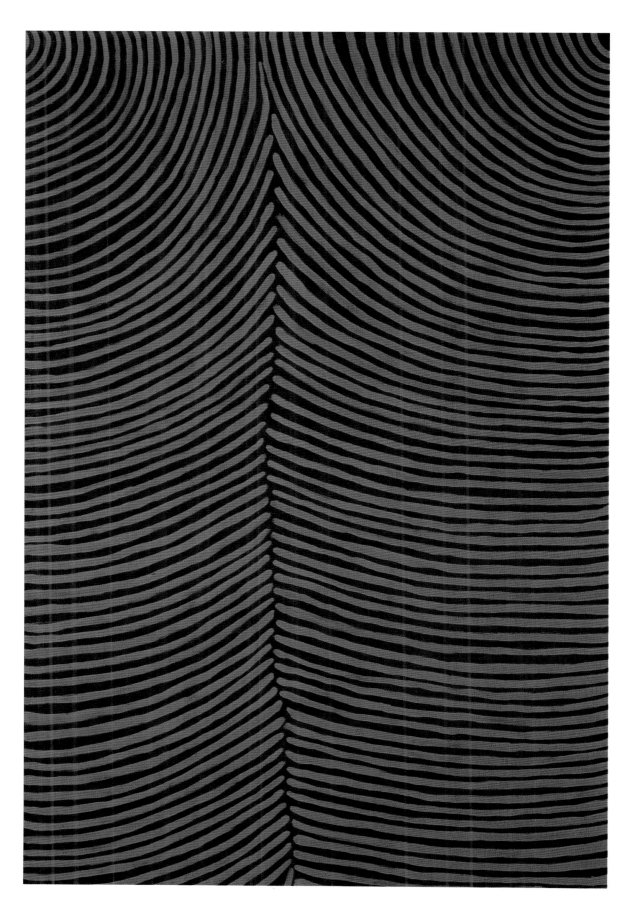

Leaves Being Blown by the Wind

The gently laid brush strokes represent desert litter, the leaves beneath mulga trees, being gently lifted and swirled by the wind.

When painting this work Gloria Petyarre spent days in contemplative peace, thinking of her country and the stillness. "You look … see / in my mind … quiet place my country. This one leaf … plenty wind coming."

PLATE 32 (below, detail opposite)
Gloria Petyarre, b. 1945
Leaves Being Blown by the Wind, 1996
91 x 61 cm (36 x 24 in.)
Acrylic on canvas

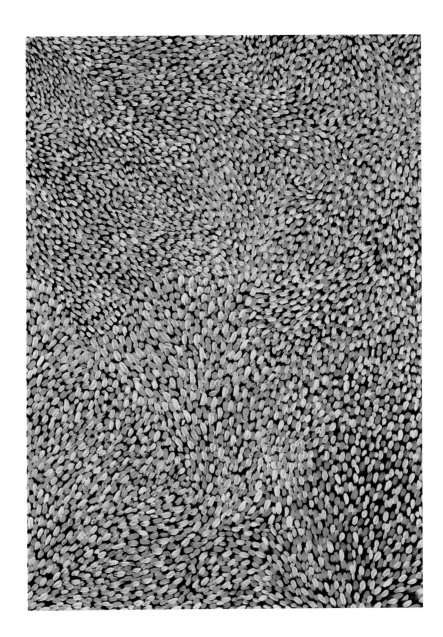

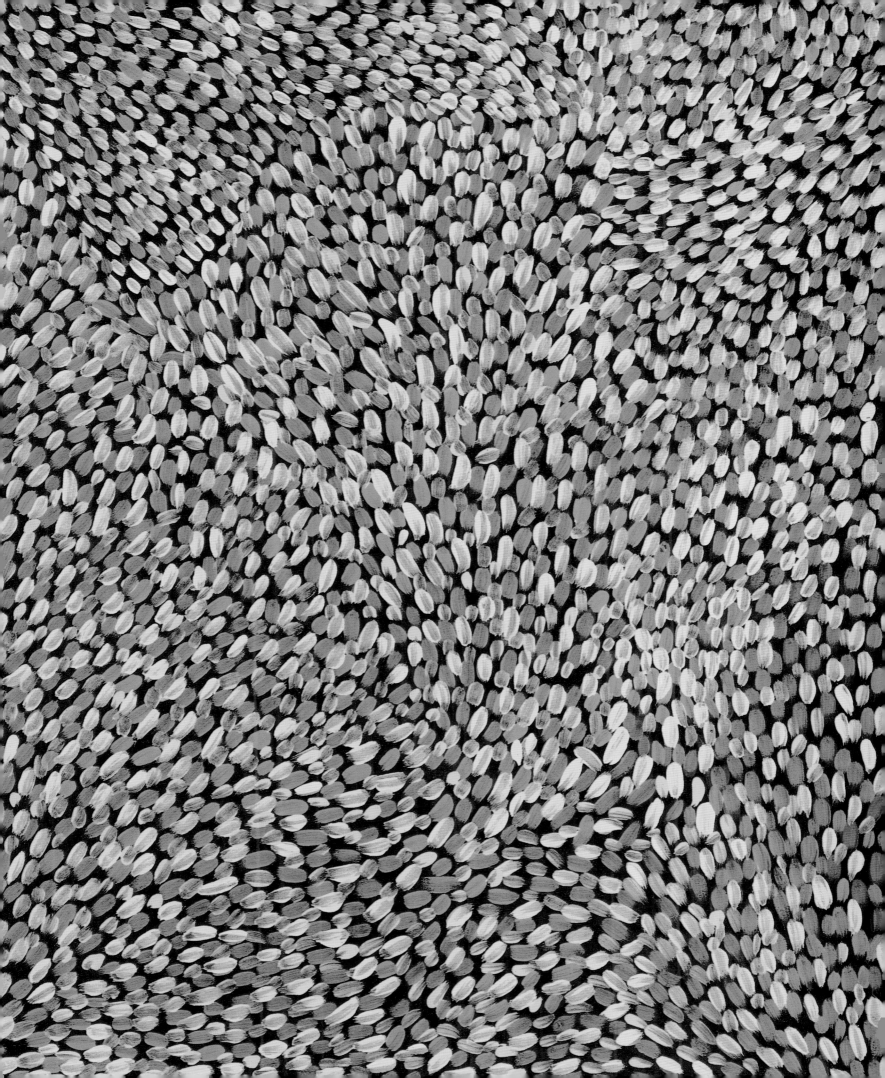

Emily Kame Kngwarreye

Arlatyeye

Arlatyeye *(Vigna lanceolata)* are a type of yam particular to Emily Kngwarreye's country of Alhalkare. She was the "boss woman" responsible for maintaining Awelye (women's ceremonies) for this yam, and her name, "Kame," literally means "seed." In explaining her work she once famously said, "Whole lot, that's whole lot. Awelye is Arlatyeye … Kame [yam seed]. That's what I paint; whole lot."[8]

Although Emily's early paintings showed the track marks and grid lines of emu journeys in search of the kame yam seed, after 1991 these lines and patterns disappeared or were submerged in finely dotted clouds of color. Colors are significant: yellow, for example, often denotes the full ripening time when seeds burst forth and the desert earth begins to dry up.

Just discernible are the arm movements of the artist as she sat at the edge of the painting, reaching in and out, making dots on the flat canvas on the ground before her. This painting can be compared to the plant growth across her whole country, each color denoting different plants and seeds — grass seeds, munyeroo (a pink portulaca flower), acacia (wattle), and desert raisins (small purple-flowering bushes, the fruits of which can be eaten fresh or dried and are stored by desert women over long periods).

Biographical Notes

A senior member of the Anmatyerre community of Utopia, northeast of Alice Springs, Emily Kame Kngwarreye had a prolific and highly successful career as an artist and is widely regarded as one of the most notable Australian artists of recent times.

She was born about 1910 at a small soak known as Alhalkare, and knew a life before the appearance of white men in the desert. Cattle and sheep stations occupied much of her tribal country during her childhood, and she grew up working with stock on these stations, and also as a domestic help.

In the late 1970s and 1980s Emily Kame Kngwarreye, along with other artists from Utopia, took up batik as a means of expressing traditional stories and designs on cloth. Her earliest art works are painted dyed fabrics using the batik technique. She began painting on canvas in the summer of 1988/89. She developed distinctive skeletal linear formations, which were then overlaid with dots to form highly abstracted works. The lines disappeared during the early 1990s, when she began to use color fields of dots raining across the canvas to signify "merne" or everything — the plants and flowers of her desert country. From about 1994 she began more gestural work, using broad, dumped color lines and brush marks evoking Awelye, body designs from women's ceremonies.

Occasionally she produced minimal monochrome works of vertical lines. In the period to 1996 she often used intertwining, meandering strokes as a stylistic device. Her final months were given to sweeping, gestural works.

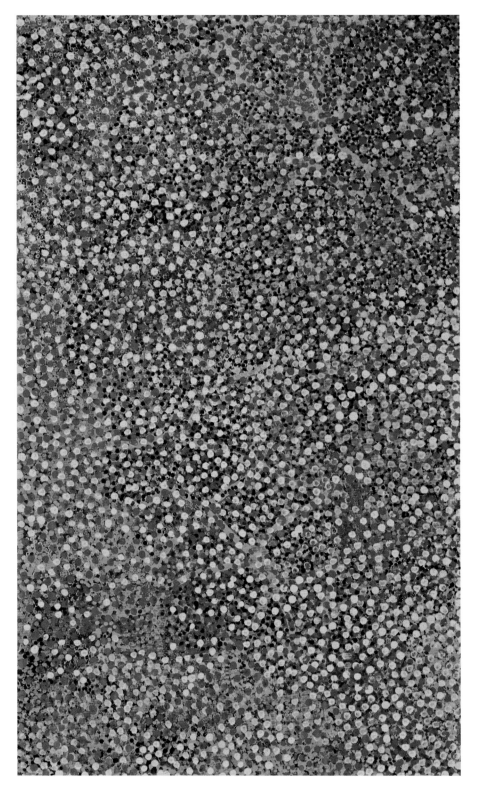

PLATE 33
Emily Kame Kngwarreye, c. 1910–1996
Arlatyeye, 1991
227 x 130 cm (89.5 x 51 in.)
Acrylic on canvas

The principal theme of most of her paintings is the growth cycle of the yam. This staple desert tuber swells under the surface of the earth and is dug mostly by women after the vine has withered and died. Cracks in the surface signify places to dig. In her paintings the yam's underground growth patterns are sometimes marked out, just visible within the dotted vegetation.

Relatively late in her life, Emily Kngwarreye's success as an artist gave her the opportunity to move freely across her country and to maintain her economic status as an elder. She continued to perform Awelye throughout her life, and the sacred body patterns used in these ceremonies as ocher marks on the torsos of women participants underpinned much of her art.

Her artistic legacy has been significant, among both Aboriginal artists and the wider community. Her paintings are held in the collections of all the State galleries in Australia, the National Gallery of Australia, and significant international collections of contemporary art in the USA, Europe, and Britain. In 1995 she was awarded a Creative Arts Fellowship by the Australian government in recognition of her stature as an artist and community mentor. In 1997, the year after her death, her work represented Australia at the Venice Biennale. A major touring retrospective exhibition of her paintings was mounted by the Queensland Art Gallery in 1998.

PLATE 34
Emily Kame Kngwarreye, c. 1910–1996
Untitled, 1996
213 x 122 cm (84 x 48 in.)
Acrylic on linen

Untitled

Emily Kngwarreye's paintings are drawn from her knowledge and status as senior Anmatyerre custodian of the yam. In these abstract paintings she is exploring the plants, especially the yam, and the cycle of nature in her own country of Alhalkare. This is one of her final works, and was completed during the phase of intense activity that she kept up for several months before her death in September 1996.

These sweeping gestural paintings give the appearance of being executed very quickly, but were in fact measured and thoughtful in application. Seated on the ground beside the canvas, she has stretched forward and back, working her elbow and spreading color — pink, yellow, and white — to the length of her arm's reach. Having completed each side, she is left with a void in the center, which she has filled, bending forward in an act of completion.

The underlying template of this work is repeated in numerous paintings by Emily Kame Kngwarreye, including the clouded dot painting of the early 1990s, *Arlatyeye* (see Plate 33).

Lorna Napurrurla Fencer

Seeds, Yarla Dreaming

The yarla or bush potato, *Ipomoea* species, is one of the staple root foods of Warlpiri and other desert people. Collected largely by women, it grows in defined areas, regenerating itself through seeds and division of subterranean tubers. Women dig the potato with small wooden coolamon dishes, or with mulga digging sticks. When a quantity has been gathered, the yams are rubbed clean of dirt, placed in the coals of the fire or in a small depression under the ashes, and baked until soft. Songs that recount the journeys of Bush Potato Ancestors are central to women's ceremonial performances.

This work is a wildly expressive vision of the patterning made by the bush potato both above and beneath the earth, showing the interlinking tubers under the ground as well as the seeds above. Beneath the luxuriously textured white paint is an underlying design of women's body paint for the bush potato. The painting was included in Lorna Napurrurla Fencer's first solo exhibition, which was held in Melbourne in 1996. She named the exhibition *me, Warlpiri* as a statement about identity.

Biographical Notes

Lorna Napurrurla Fencer was born about 1925 at Yartulu Yartulu, and is custodian of inherited land, Yurnurrpa, situated near the Granites Mine area of the Tanami Desert. Her father's country is Wapurtarli. In 1949 many Warlpiri, including Napurrurla, were forcibly transported to the government settlement at Lajamanu (originally called Hooker Creek), situated in the country of the Gurindji people on the edge of the Tanami Desert, 250 miles to the north of their own country around Yuendumu. Napurrurla nevertheless maintained and strengthened her cultural identity through ceremonial activity and art. A prominent woman in the community, she has played an increasingly significant role as an educator.

The travels of Napurrurla and Nakamarra kinship or "skin" groups are the inspiration for Napurrurla's work, and she is custodian of the Dreamings associated with bush potato (yarla), caterpillar (luju), and also bush tomato, bush plum, many seeds, and water for the Napurrurla, Nakamarra, Japarrurla, and Jakamarra skin groups. She has been painting since the early 1980s. Before she began painting on canvas, she painted on traditional women's coolamons and digging sticks for ceremony and for sale. Her works are held in many major public collections, including the National Gallery of Victoria; the Museum and Art Gallery of the Northern Territory; and Artbank, Sydney.

PLATE 35
Lorna Napurrurla Fencer, b. c. 1925
Seeds, Yarla Dreaming, 1996
201 x 117 cm (79 x 46 in.)
Acrylic on cotton

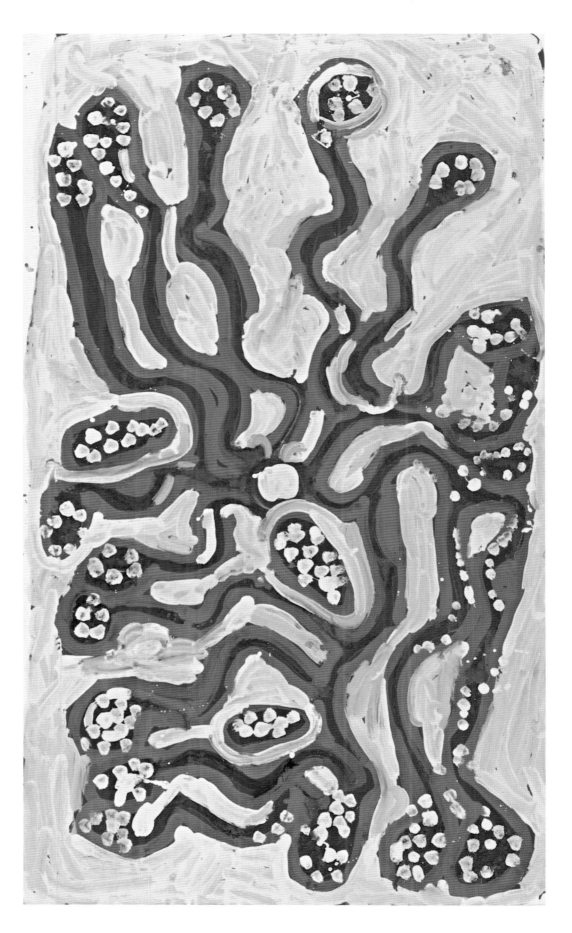

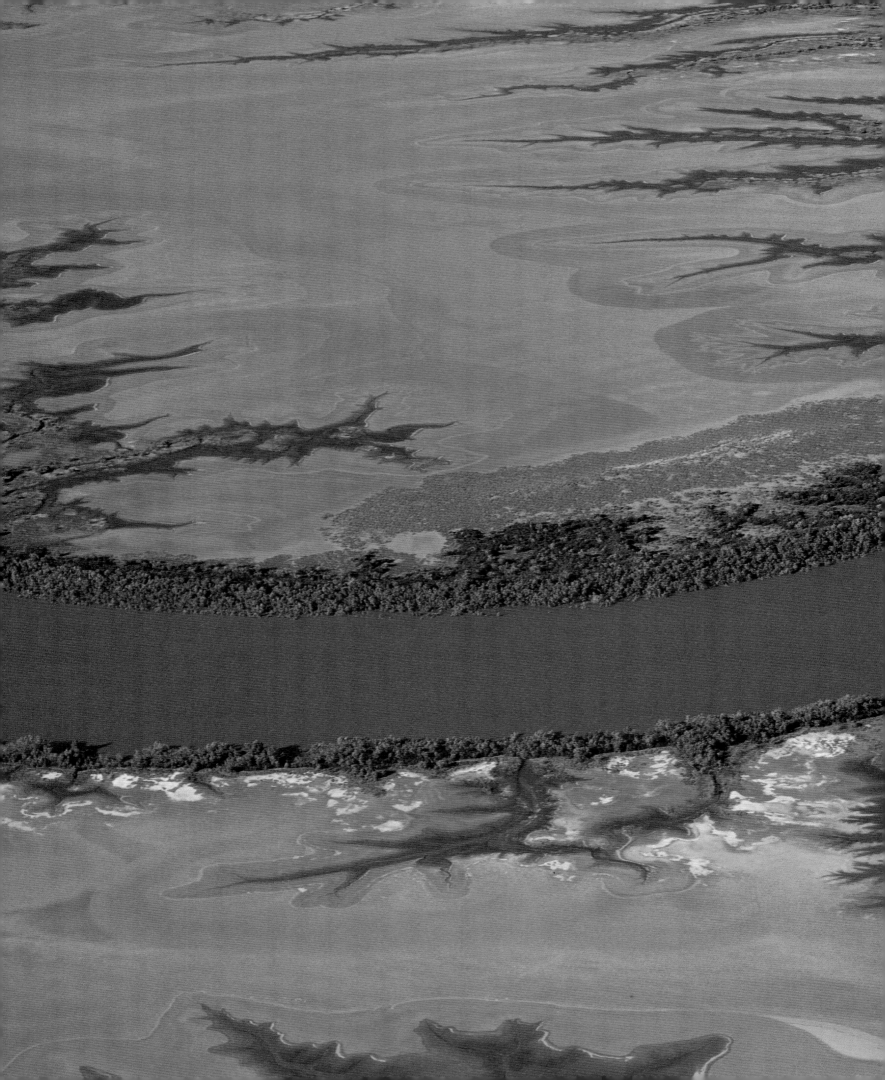

THE KIMBERLEY

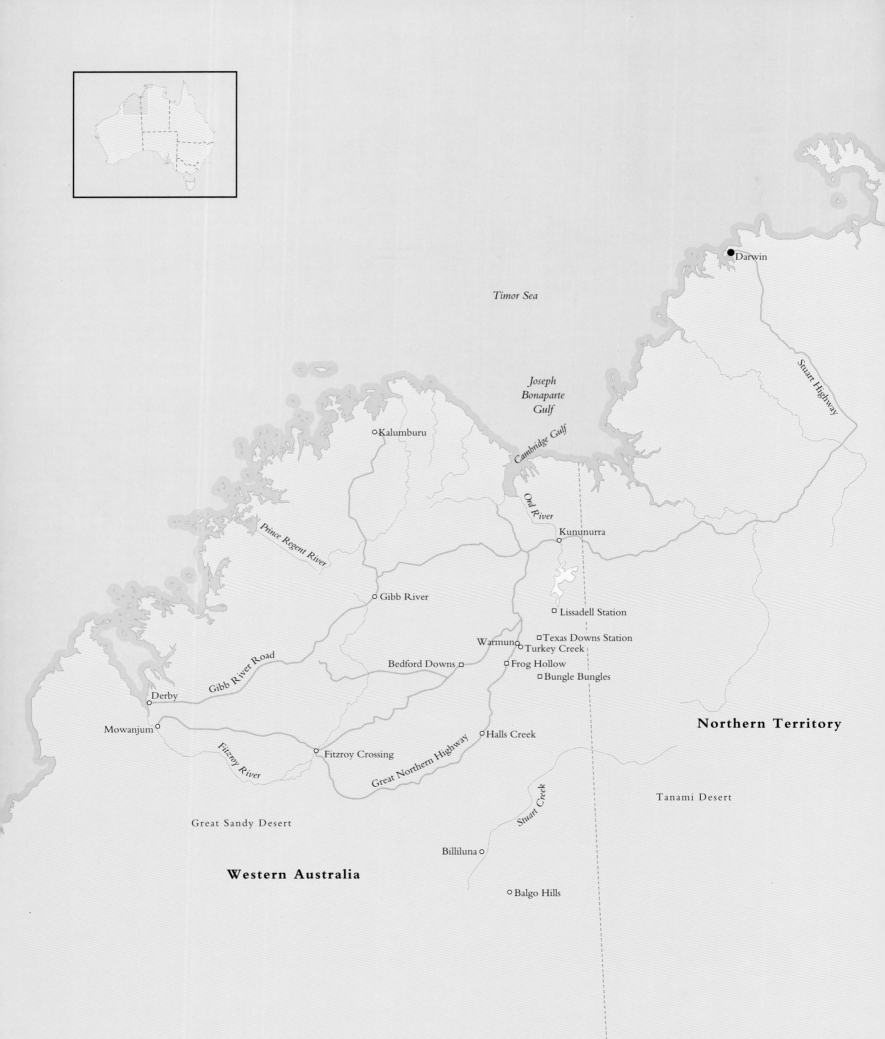

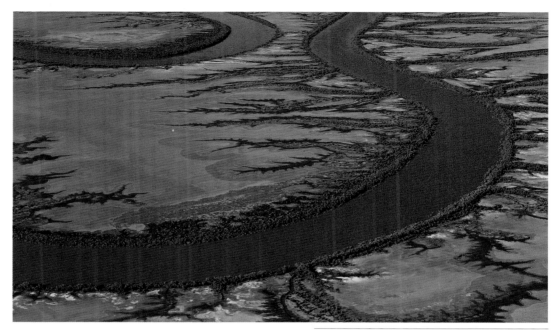

Immense river system of the Kimberley area
PHOTOGRAPH: Richard Woldendorp

The Kimberley

The Kimberley is a rugged region of Australia that extends along the northwestern coast in an arc from Broome to the Cambridge Gulf, bounded on the inland by the matching arc of the Great Northern Highway from Broome to Darwin via Kununurra. Roughly 150,000 square miles in area, the region is known for its deep gorges, dry, forested plains, domed hills and strangely shaped rock formations. The Ord is the major river that cuts its way through this dramatic landscape. To the south and east lies the desert.

The northwest Kimberley is Wandjina country. The Wandjina, who soar across the sky bringing rain and lightning, are harbingers of the annual wet season that transforms the north of Australia in the space of a week, when dry, parched earth gives way to torrential rivers, swamps, and dripping foliage.

The Kimberley houses numerous remote rock-art galleries, which archaeologists consider to be some of the finest paleolithic art in the world. To Aboriginal custodians, the images of giant staring faces speak of their own life source and the religious truths they

*Paintings by Kimberley artists at Waringarri Arts
in Kununurra, Western Australia*
PHOTOGRAPH: Jennifer Isaacs

have upheld over millennia. These galleries, which were periodically repainted, are linked directly to the current art practices of the nations of the region. The Worora and Ngarrinyin peoples, for example, claim direct descent from these spirit beings.

The Wandjina figures painted on rock and bark surfaces and in the modern works of artists such as Jarinyanu David Downs are the watching faces of eternal knowledge — the great Ancestor Spirits themselves, observing the observer with a direct gaze and powerful presence. The radiating arcs around their heads are storm clouds and rain, worn like giant headdresses. Theirs is an all-encompassing spiritual presence in land, sky, and sea, affecting all those with whom the Wandjina come in contact, whether at the sacred places, the rock-art sites where they transformed themselves, or simply by viewing a painting. As David Mowaljarlai has described it:

> [The Wandjina] travelled across the country … His deeds are Yorro Yorro, everything on earth brand new and standing up. Yorro Yorro is continual creation and renewal of nature in all its forms. He installed everything, and he gave it life to continue growing on the back of the Snake.[1]

The history of outsiders' interaction with the Aboriginal people in the Kimberley area is immensely brutal. The overland pastoralists of the 1890s were first to arrive, followed by government agents, pearl fishermen, and police. Their arrival marked a huge change for the indigenous people of the region. Many different language groups were displaced. Aboriginal people were massacred in unprovoked shootings and reprisal raids. In the language of the era, the land was "cleared" for the pastoralists. Sometimes waterholes were poisoned or ration flour distributed laced with arsenic.

The visual expression of the history of this region, as told by Aboriginal people today, reveals the depth of the pain that still exists in their hearts and minds. Some of the beautiful and somber paintings from this area tell tragic tales. They are not only poignant and revelatory, but are also a direct continuation of artistic practice and an expression of sacred belief and law derived from their Spirit Ancestors of the past.

Until 1968, when station owners were compelled to pay Aboriginal workers equal wages, several generations of Kimberley Aboriginal men and women grew up providing labor in return for their keep. Communities lived on the cattle properties, and were thus able to maintain the connection with their country. Both men and women proved adept at managing stock over long journeys or "droves," because they had great physical stamina and could survive in remote areas, knowing the country well. Many Aboriginal women worked around the homesteads, cared for young children, and acted as shepherds. Others, dressed as men, joined white stockmen on the droves.

The introduction of equal wages for Aboriginal station workers heralded the end of the era of Aboriginal labor on such properties. Many Aboriginal people moved to the perimeters of the small towns scattered around the region, or to missions and government settlements. Different language communities were thrown together, and the social dislocation that resulted was severe. With their traditional lands, called the "homelands," sometimes a long way away, men and women began to lose language and culture.

The modern painting movement has coincided with an increase in cultural strength and tenacity as Kimberley Aboriginal communities fight to retain some of their traditional country. Their landmark battles have included a conflict over mining known as the Noonkanbah dispute, significant land claims brought by the Kimberley Aboriginal Land Council, and, in 1998, the Ngarrinyin's fight to have the continuity of their law linked to their ancient cave paintings, up to 60,000 years old,[2] some of which lie within the boundaries of cattle stations.

Aboriginal artists of the region have many different ways of expressing the Kimberley peoples' shared experiences and the concept of religious connection to country. Most of the works have a strong political motivation. The making of modern paintings is the means of achieving a public voice, perhaps fame, and therefore attention to one's cause. The messages from the artists when showing or speaking about art are always similar. In Paddy Neowarra's words, "It should be Aboriginal law in this ground and stay with that law. It started from the beginning … til the end."[3]

Kalumburu

Kalumburu is a former Catholic mission station established in 1908 by Spanish-speaking Benedictine monks. It was initially located on the Drysdale River, but moved to Kalumburu in 1932.

At Kalumburu, encouraged by the missionaries, the Woonambal people began the tradition of painting Wandjina figures on bark as well as making other traditional objects for sale. Some of the earliest examples of Wandjina bark paintings were collected in 1938.[4] The practice of making images of Wandjina directly relating to cave paintings continues to the present in the work of Lily Karedada (see page 118) and other artists.

Wandjina are also carved and painted on other portable objects including engraved nuts from the boab or bottle tree, bark buckets, slices of slate, and bark carrying trays or anggum. Traditional weapons and utensils also included wooden weapons such as boomerangs, spear throwers, shields, and stone and glass spear points (the last-mentioned coming into use after the overland telegraph lines provided a supply of porcelain and glass).

With growing interest in Aboriginal art in the 1970s, the Mowanjum community near Derby became the main center for traditional art, producing Wandjina paintings, carvings, and other works, which were sold through the government center in Perth. The success of contemporary artists has rekindled interest in the earlier "Wandjina painters" of the Kimberley.

Warmun, Turkey Creek, and Kununurra

The Warmun community is close to Turkey Creek, which is the site of the old telegraph station and was once a stop for the camel trains that moved through the northwest carrying provisions to stations and communities. Many Aboriginal people moved to Turkey Creek after the introduction of equal wages on the cattle stations, because the settlement is located on the edge of a number of stations where many of the men and women had worked for most of their lives. Warmun is a significant painting center for the artists of the region.

It was at Warmun in 1975 that Rover Thomas and Paddy Tjamatji began the artistic collaboration that was to become the model for contemporary Kimberley painting. It is significant that the contemporary art of the Warmun people began with a creative dream encounter by Rover Thomas. In 1975 a ceremony was revealed to Rover Thomas through a series of visions or dreams in which he was visited by the spirit of a recently deceased woman he considered his "mother" (a kinship classification), who had been killed in a car accident near the airstrip at Turkey Creek. This spirit recounted her travels after her death. This journey forms the basis of the Kuril

Kuril ceremony, which is a "public" or "open" ceremony that can be performed to any member of the community. One element of the Kuril Kuril is the display of a series of dancing boards on which a simple motif or icon is painted. The first Kuril Kuril boards were painted by Paddy Tjamatji under the direction of Rover Thomas.[5] Their style is simple and uncluttered, with shapes being defined by rows of white dots. The paintings illustrating the Kuril Kuril journey started the modern art movement at Turkey Creek.

Today Warmun artists continue to create maps of particular forms in the landscape on canvas and board. These are painted in both plan and profile, and often include the roads, dams, cattle yards, and creeks of the stations where the artists have worked. They are recording and mapping particular incidents in their recent history; at the same time, rock formations, caves, and hills are given mythological potency. The works thus combine two ways of "seeing": temporal and metaphysical.

Warmun is in Gija country, and Gija artists resident there have followed the example of Rover Thomas and Paddy Tjamatji in depicting topographical maps in broad ocher areas. All of the art from this region uses natural ocher mixed with various forms of fixative, including locally gathered gum from eucalyptus trees called "bloodwoods." The hard dark-red gum exudate is ground and mixed with water, then combined with the ochers. The early paintings were done on strips of Masonite or board, but today most are on canvas.

Some artists work in new media, including paper, for dealers and private galleries. Freddie Timms, for example, periodically exhibits series of canvases using modern acrylic paint in bright color; he also continues to work in natural ochers.

The work of the Warmun artists draws on the Ngarrangkarni or Creation period, a concept referred to in many areas of Australia as the Dreaming (see page 4). The paintings often detail oral histories that blend relatively recent events with Aboriginal understanding of the spiritual forces in nature — cataclysms in which kangaroos mysteriously disappeared, synchronicities between spirits and humans that explain events that happened in parents' or grandparents' memories. Some of the artists, notably Queenie McKenzie and Rover Thomas, also record early conflicts with police and the massacres that local people call "the killing times."

The Warmun artists whose work is represented here are Paddy Tjamatji, Rover Thomas, Queenie McKenzie, Henry Wambini, and Freddie Timms. Other Kimberley artists who are or were once based at Turkey Creek include Madigan Thomas, Hector Jandiny, Jack Britten, Biribi Mungari, Churchill Khan, and Shirley Purdey.

The Warmun community now operates an artists' co-operative to provide artists with materials and sell their work. Until recently they also received services from Waringarri Arts, the Aboriginal-owned arts organization in the town of Kununurra. Among the other artists who have been connected with Waringarri Arts is Billy Thomas (see page 136).

Fitzroy Crossing

The artists currently resident at Fitzroy Crossing reflect a large diversity of language groups and cultural backgrounds. The original owners of the area were displaced in the 1890s. Groups of desert people from further east, including the Walmajarri and Wangkajunga, began entering the region, taking up residence on the new pastoral stations. Others followed, bringing cultural change and a form of syncretic religion that has many Christian themes.

This has been described as a "two-way" religion.[6] A United Aboriginal Mission was established in the 1950s, and many resident Aboriginal people converted, in particular Jarinyanu David Downs (page 122) and Peter Skipper (page 142). Skipper, a Walmajarri man, continues to use strong traditional patterning in his contemporary art and always

Billy Thomas at Waringarri Arts,
Kununurra, Western Australia
PHOTOGRAPH: Carrillo Gantner

Tjumpo Tjapanangka with his work Maryuwar, Great Sandy Desert
in the Warlayirti Artists Centre at Balgo
PHOTOGRAPH: Baillieu Myer

represents Dreaming or Ngarrangkarni events.
Contact with religious concepts and the arts of
outsiders, both Aboriginals and others, has
strengthened these artists' understanding of the
importance of ritual law and encouraged them to
develop its expression through art.

A group of senior men and women at Fitzroy
Crossing has worked since the late 1980s, painting for
the artists' company, Mangkaja Arts. This company
grew out of a literacy class in which the women
learned to read and write English through drawing
and recording personal histories. Art production at
Mangkaja has a strong communal emphasis, similar
to that of Warlukurlangu at Yuendumu (see page 84).

Composite paintings on huge banners have been
displayed at major academic and political gatherings
to represent artists' land rights and sovereignty.

Balgo

The southeastern edge of the Kimberley is a moon-
like landscape of flat plateaus, descending plains, and
clearly outlined lone desert hills and ridges. Here, on
the edge of the Tanami and Great Sandy Deserts, 200
miles from the nearest town of Hall's Creek, lies the
small former mission station of Balgo Hills. The style
and themes of a number of significant artists of this
Aboriginal-controlled community relate closely to
desert works from the Tanami and Western Desert

peoples. Balgo is the center for nine distinct language groupings, and the artists' paintings reflect the codes of mark-making and mapping from their homelands. There are also clear visual links with the southern Kimberley art practice of Fitzroy Crossing.

Painting began at Balgo in 1981. The artists at that time were mostly young men in their early twenties who joined an adult education center. They used figurative and decorative elements that reflected the lessons of the mission schoolroom. The artists depicted Christian traditions in a uniquely Aboriginal way, applying Aboriginal ideas of journey paths and sites to Christian stories.

Later the older men became involved in painting, and easily made the transition to acrylic paint on canvas in 1984. Access to the new, colorful, exciting media triggered a frenzy of painting activity. When canvas ran short, people painted on whatever they could find — roller blinds, scraps of wood, and paper. The women also became involved in painting as a communal exercise, with the older women singing and dancing while others painted.

The principal myth lines associated with Balgo Hills and the surrounding country are those of the Tingari and the Wati Kutjara. The Tingari Dreaming (see page 24) concerns the mythological journeys of a number of initiated Dreaming heroes and ceremonial novices. The Wati Kutjara tells of the travels of two goanna men, both of whom are clever-men or sorcerers (marpan). Their magical acts become the themes of their world-creating story as they travel about the country.

The Balgo artists included in this collection are Tjumpo Tjapanangka, Eubena Nampitjin, and Helicopter Tjungurrayi. The first solo exhibition of Balgo work was held at the Art Gallery of Western Australia in 1986 to wide critical acclaim. Balgo artists market their work through Warlayirti Artists, one of the first community painting centers to develop after Papunya Tula. In style, Balgo paintings have a surface texture of thick paint, dots that coalesce into trails, and a vibrancy of color that is prized by these artists as an expression of the spiritual strength they derive from Ancestral power.

Lily Karedada

Wandjina

The Wandjina figures are powerful visual representations of spirit creatures of the sky who are associated with rain, thunderstorms, and the coming of the wet season. Their images are found on rock shelters and in caves throughout the Kimberley region. The Woonambal people trace their own descent from these Spirit Ancestors, and from the process of their interaction with other creatures of the earth in the Creation era.

This carefully executed Wandjina image by Lily Karedada has utilized a range of techniques. Broad areas are painted using a frayed bark brush, and the headdress and background have been engraved through the ocher to produce serrated patterns. This technique is also used to decorate utensils, weapons, and boab nuts.

The prominent, staring eyes and the absence of the mouth are features of Wandjina imagery, and suggest the features of an owl. The story of another Creation Ancestor, Dumbi the owl, is connected to a Wandjina story of the nearby Ngarrinyin people. Daisy Utemorrah has said, "He has no need of a mouth, he sends his thoughts."[7] Others say that if Wandjinas were given mouths it would never stop raining.

Biographical Notes

A noted painter of themes relating to the great Wandjina spirits, Lily Karedada or Mindindil was born around 1937 and came to prominence as a bark painter from Kalumburu in the Kimberley region. The small mission station at Kalumburu was extensively bombed by Japanese aircraft during World War II, and she recalls that when the missionaries left the area she lived off the land, hiding in caves lest the bombs get her.

Lily Karedada is a senior Woonambal woman from her father's country, Woomban-go-wangoorr, near the Prince Regent River. Her traditional name, Mindindil, means "bubbles" and refers to her totemic spirit — the spirit that notified her father that her mother was pregnant. At the time of the quickening, her father found Lily's spirit coming out of the water in the form of bubbles.[8]

With her husband, Jack Karedada, she produced many images of Wandjina figures throughout the 1980s. She gathered natural ochers from creek beds and rocky deposits, particularly the dark brown ocher mixed with white that gives her work its strength. Ochers are mixed with a gum called goorim, which is made by boiling the exudates from a particular tree. Her works are included in major Australian collections, including the National Gallery of Australia.

PLATE 36
Lily Karedada, b. c. 1937
Wandjina, 1985
53 x 26 cm (21 x 10 in.)
Natural ochers on bark

Artist Unknown

Carrying Vessel

This carrying container made of gathered and pleated bark is an example of traditional artifact production in the Kimberley region. The bark basket has been painted with an overall design of the Wandjina Spirit Ancestors, images of which abound in cave paintings throughout the region. The vessel is an example of the ingenious way in which the nomadic peoples of the region used containers made of natural materials to carry food and personal possessions for vast distances.

PLATE 37 (detail below)
Artist Unknown
Carrying Vessel
22 x 80 x 41 cm (8.5 x 31.5 x 16 in.)
Natural earth pigments on eucalyptus bark

PLATE 37
Artist Unknown
Carrying Vessel
22 x 80 x 41 cm (8.5 x 31.5 x 16 in.)
Natural earth pigments on eucalyptus bark

To make the handles at either end, the bark is cut through and half its thickness is removed; then, after soaking, the bark is bent and gathered into handles, which are bound and braced with hand-spun bark string. The compacted resin that packs both ends is made of a mixture of beeswax and gum extracted from eucalyptus trees.

Carrying baskets such as these were used to transport food and water as well as to cradle infants. From a period in the 1960s these items were painted with Wandjina images and sold through missions and stores in the region.

Jarinyanu David Downs

Kurtal

Kurtal, one of the Creation Ancestors frequently depicted by this Walmajarri artist, is responsible for bringing rain and storms. Kurtal soars over the ocean as a cyclone, collecting barramundi and pearl shells before appearing in the northwest Kimberley area. After moving down the coast, he turns inland and passes through various clan lands. This powerful painting captures and explains the force of the cyclones that appear along the coast, following this same route every year during the pre-monsoon period in November/December. The radiating headdress and dots, reminiscent of the form of looming thunder clouds, give a transforming power to the image.

Throughout the Kimberley and desert regions, particular men are thought to have the power to bring on rain in times of drought through magic songs and the use of sorcery. The rainmakers' power is closely associated with the iridescence of pearl shells, which are worn in the Kimberley region and also used as totemic rain-making devices.

Biographical Notes

Jarinyanu David Downs was born about 1925 near Lake Gregory in northwestern Australia. He was a unique individual who often worked outside the bounds of community organizations. After his conversion to Christianity, he began to express a complex metaphysical relationship with his land that was a blend of Christian biblical teachings and traditional Aboriginal thought concerning Spirit Ancestors and sacred places in the land.

Jarinyanu David Downs was a fully initiated man of the Wangkajunga people. He spent much of his youth working on cattle stations throughout the Hall's Creek area, for a period droving cattle over vast distances. He began practicing art by carving traditional artifacts such as shields, boomerangs, and coolamons and decorating them with ocher.

In the early 1980s he began painting, initially using ocher and bush gum fixative and later moving to acrylic paint, occasionally turning to decorate shields in the same fashion (see page 124). Most of these early works show images of Ancestral characters, particularly Kurtal the rain man. At times the artist mixed painting materials, combining ocher with acrylic and building up the canvas or paper to achieve texture. His works are included in major Australian collections, including the National Gallery of Australia; Art Gallery of South Australia; and National Gallery of Victoria.

PLATE 38
Jarinyanu David Downs, c. 1925–1995
Kurtal, c. 1980s
112 x 66 cm (44 x 26 in.)
Synthetic polymer paint, natural earth pigments, and PVA on canvas

Two shields: Body Design and Kurtal

The shield below reveals the image of Kurtal, the rain man, in ceremonial body decorations, wearing a large headdress, and carrying a sacred twined emblem. These emblems, known as waninga, are huge, elaborate fiber constructions worn on the head and shoulders or carried above the head during dances and ceremonies. Lit by fires at night, dancers holding such emblems are a spectacular presence, and are imbued with the power of the Ngarrangkarni (Dreaming). The companion shield (right) is a simple, minimalist rendition of the strong marks painted on men's bodies during such ceremonies.

Jarinyanu David Downs's early career was spent making small objects for sale such as wood carvings, weapons, and utensils. Although he became a well-known artist when he turned to paint on canvas, these works show that he continued to enjoy working in more traditional media, carving beanwood into shields and painting them with traditional designs.

PLATE 39 (far left)
Jarinyanu David Downs, c. 1925–1995
Kurtal, c. 1986
71 cm (28 in.)
Synthetic polymer paint on
carved beanwood shield

PLATE 40 (left)
Jarinyanu David Downs, c. 1925–1995
Body Design, 1986
69 cm (27 in.)
Synthetic polymer paint on
carved beanwood shield

PLATE 38 (detail opposite)
Jarinyanu David Downs, c. 1925–1995
Kurtal, c. 1980s
112 x 66 cm (44 x 26 in.)
Synthetic polymer paint, natural earth
pigments, and PVA on canvas

Paddy Tjamatji

Bedford Downs Station

Bedford Downs Station is a cattle station on which many of the contemporary Kimberley artists worked as stockmen. It is set in a landscape of grassy plains scattered among massive ridges and sculpted hills. In this work, an organic boab tree form is horizontally suspended (at right) above an undulating ridge. While some paintings of Bedford Downs Station simply depict the topography, many recall the "killing times" of the 1920s, when there were major punitive raids on Aboriginal people in the region.

This is one of the first large landscape paintings that Paddy Tjamatji produced directly for sale to a major collector. From 1984 to the present, the Kimberley artists have developed this pioneering technique of applying natural ochers to canvas and board and delineating the dramatic forms of the Kimberley landscape with white dots.

Although not all the elements are shown, or visible, this painting represents the Dreaming or Creation story of a kangaroo, marlu, at a place named Sugar Bag Hill. A dingo (native dog) chased the kangaroo and killed him in the bed of the Bow River. The kangaroo metamorphosed into a stone form, which can still be seen on the hill near the highway at the turn-off to the Argyle diamond mine. A rock in the river near the Bow River bridge is also the body of marlu.[9]

Biographical Notes

Paddy Tjamatji was born in 1912 and spent his life on cattle stations in the Kimberleys. He began painting in 1975 as a result of a spiritual collaboration with his nephew, Rover Thomas, who experienced a visitation from the spirit of a deceased woman (see page 114). The current paintings produced by the Kimberley artists of this region have flowed from this beginning. During Rover Thomas's dream visitation, the spirit described her journeys from the Kimberleys across vast stretches of the country through to Darwin, and told him of the events along the way. In recounting this sequence of events, the spirit also gave song and dance to Rover Thomas. He discussed this with Paddy Tjamatji, and a ceremony was born in which a series of paintings dreamed or designed by Rover Thomas was actually executed by Paddy Tjamatji and held aloft above the heads of the dancers during the ceremony, named the Kuril Kuril.

Paddy Tjamatji went on to paint large and dramatic boards using a free, rough technique to show the cattle country of the region in schematic form, and portray aspects of the history of the country. He died in 1996. His works are included in most major Australian collections, including the National Gallery of Australia; National Gallery of Victoria; Art Gallery of South Australia; and National Museum of Australia.

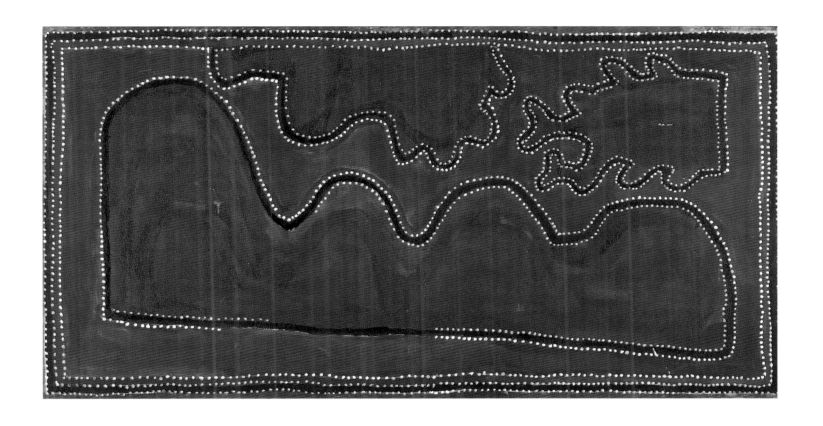

PLATE 41
Paddy Tjamatji, 1912–1996
Bedford Downs Station, 1984–85
181 x 96 cm (72.5 x 38 in.)
Ochers on canvas

Rover Thomas

Gulgoodji

Various sites in the Kimberley are home to snakes, many of which are thought to be physical manifestations of the Rainbow Snake or Rainbow Serpent (see page 174). Sometimes they are at rest in the landscape; on other occasions, they rise and destroy people. The dream sequence that provided the source of many of Rover Thomas's paintings recounts how a woman who was killed at the road crossing near Turkey Creek appears and journeys across the country to Darwin, led by another spirit guide, encountering certain snakes along the journey.

In this, one of Rover Thomas's most lyrical paintings, the spirit figure has a mournful, evocative face. With painterly skill, Thomas has worked the ocher to create emotional resonance. Near by a snake rests under a tree. The square dotted framework maps the country where this incident occurred.

Biographical Notes

Widely considered the pre-eminent Kimberley artist, Rover Thomas was born about 1926, and worked on cattle stations in the Kimberley region for much of his life. He then lived for a considerable time at Warmun community, south of the township of Kununurra. In the mid-1970s he was responsible for the commencement of the modern ocher painting movement, now widespread through the region. He had a dream in which he was visited by the spirit of a deceased relative. He later recounted the songs and dances he had learned in this process to his mother's brother, the artist Paddy Tjamatji. These songs and dances were subsequently enacted in a new ceremony known as the Kuril Kuril, in which painted boards were held aloft by the dancers.

In 1981 Rover Thomas began painting the Kuril Kuril emblems himself, initiating a vigorous painting career that continued until his death in 1998. His sparse, somber ocher paintings combine dreams, mythic map-making, and the symbolic communication of actual events. As a result of his poetic and visual inspiration, many Kimberley artists have maintained and developed his tradition of expressing events of recent history and the creative past, using an extraordinary array of delicate and beautiful natural earth pigments on a range of surfaces, including paper, board, and canvas. Rover Thomas was also responsible for guiding the career of the artist Queenie McKenzie, a lifelong friend who had once saved his life after a riding accident. Queenie McKenzie's painting in the Gantner Myer Aboriginal Art Collection (see page 130), records this incident, in which she stitched his wound under a bough shelter far from any settlement.

In 1990 Rover Thomas represented Australia at the Venice Biennale. His works are included in many major Australian collections, including the Art Gallery of Western Australia; Art Gallery of South Australia; National Gallery of Victoria; and National Gallery of Australia.

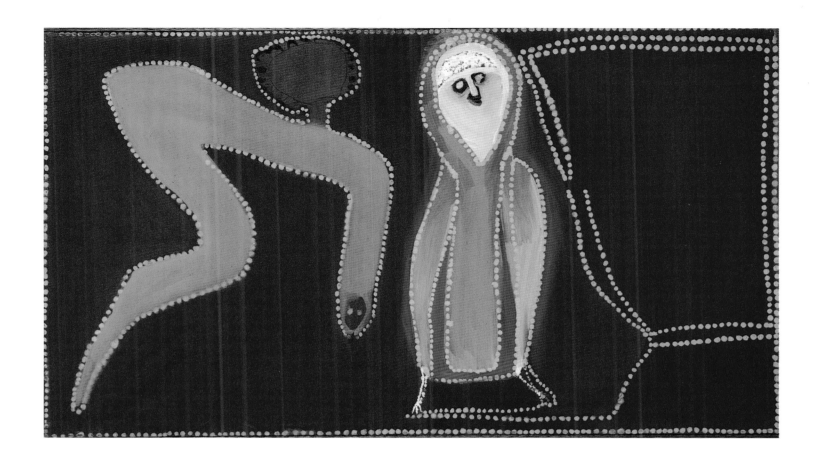

PLATE 42
Rover Thomas, c. 1926–1998
Gulgoodji, 1988
60.5 x 105.5 cm (24 x 41.5 in.)
Natural earth pigments and bush gum on canvas

Queenie McKenzie

Massacre and Rover Thomas Story — Texas Downs Country

This work places on record two important incidents in Kimberley Aboriginal history, both of which occurred on Texas Downs Station. The two events appear on either side of a diagonal dividing line that represents Lajibany (Horseshoe Creek). Above is a massacre that took place early this century and is now part of Aboriginal oral history, although it does not appear in the official records. Queenie McKenzie has illustrated the story as it was told to her. A group of Aboriginal men who had killed a bullock were pursued and shot by white men (shown in white hats) who then burned the bodies to disguise the incident.

The lower side of the painting depicts an event during the artist's working life on cattle stations. While mustering in a remote area, Rover Thomas (see page 128) was thrown from his horse and scalped when his horse trod on his head. Without medical help, Queenie McKenzie boiled a needle and sewed his scalp back on. Rover Thomas went on to become the most significant artist from the Kimberley region. Also to be seen are another woman watching, the fire, a table, pack-saddles, and a traditional bough shelter typical of those used in mustering camps. The hills of Lajibany country show the distinctive landscape forms of the Kimberleys.

PLATE 43
Queenie McKenzie, c. 1915–1998
Massacre and Rover Thomas Story — Texas Downs Country, 1996
140 x 100 cm (55 x 39.5 in.)
Ocher and clay on canvas

Biographical Notes

Born about 1915 on Old Texas Downs Station, east of Turkey Creek, Queenie McKenzie was the daughter of a Malngin/Gurindji woman and a white man. Under the government's system of classification she was therefore a "half-caste," and would normally have been removed from her family at an early age by the authorities under the strict and iniquitous practice of the day. She escaped this fate thanks to the ingenuity of her mother, who rubbed her with charcoal.

Queenie McKenzie's language was Gija but, having spent most of her youth working on cattle stations, she also spoke the colorful and distinctive Aboriginal English of the region, termed Kriol. A respected elder, she taught the Gija language to children and continued to record oral history and uphold traditional songs and ceremonies until her death in 1998.

Queenie McKenzie's painting career was relatively short. She was encouraged to begin painting in the early 1990s by her friend Rover Thomas after she observed his growing success and fame. Following Thomas's style, she began mapping country in natural ochers, blending landscape with witnessed or remembered events, family anecdotes, and mythological information.

Queenie McKenzie participated with other Warmun artists in group exhibitions throughout Australia, and was also an active printmaker. She held solo exhibitions in Sydney and Melbourne. Her paintings are held in the collections of the National Gallery of Australia and all Australian State art galleries.

PLATE 43 (detail)
Queenie McKenzie, c. 1915–1998
Massacre and Rover Thomas Story — Texas Downs Country, 1996
140 x 100 cm (55 x 39.5 in.)
Ocher and clay on canvas

Henry Wambini

Mungadabun

Mungadabun is a tract of land on the old cattle station of Tickalara, just south of Turkey Creek and west of the Bungle Bungles. Situated close to the intersection of the Bungle Bungles road and the old Hall's Creek road, the area abounds with bush tucker. Although it has no permanent waterhole, it was always possible to find ample supplies of nawunji (bush carrot), minjawara (bush plum), and many other wild foods.

Henry Wambini has mapped the area from an aerial aspect, with Mungadabun as the central dark space surrounded by kwali-wali, the small hills that dot the landscape. It is a favorite area for getting craft materials, especially soft wood from the jallaroon tree for carving coolamons (wooden dishes).

Biographical Notes

Henry Wambini was born in about 1923 in a cave that the family sometimes used on old Tickalara Station. He learned stock work on Tickalara and became an adept horseman. As a young man he worked the cattle for a contract musterer on many of the East Kimberley pastoral leases, including Spring Creek, Mabel Downs, Bow River, Texas Downs, and Lissadell. Then he contracted leprosy and was sent to the leprosarium at Derby, where he did gardening and odd jobs. Five years later, when he had no visible lesions, he returned to Bow River.

While Henry was away from Warmun, his wife had married Rover Thomas, so Henry immersed himself in stock work. Some years later his right arm was paralyzed in a truck accident, leaving him unable to cope with the physical demands of working with stock. He moved to Turkey Creek and with a lifelong friend, Jack Britten, helped to establish the tiny community at Frog Hollow.

Henry Wambini is a quiet person. His early paintings were delicate filigree dots with multi-colored patterns. For all their beauty, they often contained distressing sub-plots concerning massacres and painful loss, part of the often violent history of Kimberley black–white relations.

In the past three years, he has adapted well to painting with his left hand. Gone are the pretty colored areas. His work is now hard, spare, and simple, with broad expanses of ocher giving a sense of powerful tension. They are confident works; no longer a second-stringer to major artists such as Rover Thomas, he has developed a presence and profile of his own among Australian artists. After participating widely in group exhibitions with other Warmun artists, he held his first solo exhibition in Melbourne in mid-1999. His works are held in the National Gallery of Victoria and other collections.

PLATE 44
Henry Wambini, b. c. 1923
Mungadabun, 1997
90 x 120 cm (35.5 x 47 in.)
Ocher on canvas

HENRY WAMBINI   135

Billy Thomas

Death of a Black Snake

This painting records an event that occurred in the artist's country, Billiluna, in the Great Sandy Desert, during the Creation time, when the land was formed by the actions of Ancestral beings. This painting shows the great fight that took place between Gunamboorlayi, the black snake, and Joongoorra, the yellow snake. Gunamboorlayi was wandering far from her own country, searching for her children, when she came upon Joongoorra. In the tumultuous fight that ensued, Gunamboorlayi was killed. As the snakes writhed and thrashed, they formed the hills and valleys of the area.

Biographical Notes

A senior man who has come to prominence as an artist in recent years, Billy Thomas was born near Billiluna and now lives at Mud Springs near the small town of Kununurra, Western Australia. He speaks Wangkajunga language and is of the Joongoorra skin or kinship group.

He is concerned with the textural qualities of clays and ochers, and with developing a symbolic repertoire to represent the creative activities of the Ancestors who formed the landmarks and waterholes in the country of his birth. Billy Thomas has had several successful exhibitions in leading Australian contemporary art spaces in both Sydney and Melbourne.

PLATE 45 (below, detail opposite)
Billy Thomas, b. c. 1920
Death of a Black Snake, 1997
80 x 160 cm (31.5 x 63 in.)
Clay and ocher pigment and fixative on canvas

Young Women's Corroboree

The curved lines of this work mark out the furrows in the sand made by women's feet during ceremonial dancing, which the artist calls their "corroboree."[10] In Creation times, groups of women Ancestors gathered and formed themselves into lines according to kinship groupings; they then began to dance with a characteristic short, jumpy movement, knees bent one behind the other. One group moved clockwise, the other anticlockwise within the circuit of the first. Then, bending to the other side, they circled off again. The trails their feet left in the sand are shown by the yellow ocher markings. It was this action that formed certain waterholes near Billiluna in the artist's country. The "corroboree" is performed annually.

Moondooroo

This is an archetypal image developed by the artist to represent a deep waterhole called Moondooroo, where two good camping areas are situated very close together. Here these are represented by the curving, back-to-back U-shaped ocher markings.

PLATE 46 (left)
Billy Thomas, b. c. 1920
Young Women's Corroboree, 1997
50 x 40 cm (19.5 x 15.5 in.)
Clay and ocher pigment and
fixative on canvas

PLATE 47 (opposite)
Billy Thomas, b. c. 1920
Moondooroo, 1997
61 x 40 cm (24 x 15.5 in.)
Clay and ocher pigment and
fixative on canvas

Freddie Timms

Police Hole, Bedford Downs

Police Hole, where Freddie Timms was born, is shown as the small black lozenge at lower left. Two creeks wind through the flat grasslands of Bedford Downs Station (the yellow and white areas).

Low hills surround the creeks. This abstracted plan-painting style is characteristic of the artist's maps of the cattle country where he lived as a child. Freddie Timms' totem is the dingo, marranyi, one of the key Dreamings of this area.

Biographical Notes

Freddie Timms was born about 1946 at Police Hole, southwest of the present Turkey Creek community. He was named Ngarrmaliny after the country of his birth in his own language, Gija. He has worked at many different jobs in the cattle industry, starting when he was only twelve years old. His work and travels have taken him to numerous stations in the Northern Territory and Western Australia. In recent years he has combined community health work with painting.

After a period helping Rover Thomas (see page 128), Freddie Timms began producing his own works using only natural ocher. A visit to Melbourne and the stimulation and support of private galleries allowed him to begin to paint in brightly colored acrylic paint. He now alternates between the two media.

Freddie Timms has successfully moved into the world of mainstream art culture, and is now a pre-eminent contemporary artist. He exhibits with the eminent Watters Gallery in Sydney, but lives in his own Kimberley country. His works are included in major Australian public galleries, including the National Gallery of Australia and the National Gallery of Victoria.

PLATE 48
Freddie Timms, b. c. 1946
Police Hole, Bedford Downs, 1996
100 x 80 cm (39.5 x 31.5 in.)
Casein paint on marine ply

Pijaju Peter Skipper

Nganpayijarra

This painting vibrates with the squared meander reminiscent of the pearl-shell patterns engraved over millennia to denote journeys and track marks for Western Australian nomadic peoples. These circle and encompass two figures shown among various U-forms indicating marks in the ground where they camped. The artist simply stated, "These Nganpayijarra [men] travelled around the Ngarrangkarni [Dreaming] making the country as they went."

Biographical Notes

Pijaju Peter Skipper was born around 1929. He is a Jangkarti man from Japingka country, on the western side of the Great Sandy Desert. Forced to leave his home country as a young man, he ventured into a cattle station. He recalls being scared, because he had never seen white men, cattle, or cars before. His life changed markedly when he began working with horses and cattle on the stations. After moving into Fitzroy Crossing, he also became active in translating the Bible into Walmajarri language.

Pijaju Peter Skipper is an individual artist of great imagination. His paintings resonate with ancient symbolic references connected to Aboriginal religion in the land of his youth, but many also have illustrative and pictorial narratives. He is a committee member of Mangkaja Arts Resource Agency, based in Fitzroy Crossing. His works are held by major Australian institutions, including the National Gallery of Australia; Art Gallery of Western Australia; and National Gallery of Victoria.

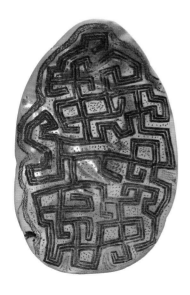

PLATE 49
Pijaju Peter Skipper, b. c. 1929
Nganpayijarra, 1996
122 x 92 cm (48 x 36 in.)
Acrylic on cotton duck canvas

(left)
Unknown Kimberley Artist
Engraved pearl shell with ocher, early 20th century
19 cm (7.5 in.) high
M. H. de Young Museum, San Francisco
Gift of David and June Major, and
Blossom and Dwight Strong

Tjumpo Tjapanangka

Maryuwar, Great Sandy Desert

According to Warlayirti Artists, the artists' corporation in the Balgo Hills, this work depicts important events and places in the artist's own country. It shows a number of women, represented as straight lines, camped near fires, which appear as black circles. The women have built windbreaks to protect themselves. The dominant key pattern of squared meandering lines in the bottom of the painting marks the journeys of a small wallaby (marla), feral cats, and rabbits. The artist stated that he had shown the tracks of these animals in an abstracted form. Also shown are spindles used for making hair string, which is traditionally spun from a mix of human hair and marla fur, and more recently has included the fur of feral animals.

The wallaby tracks pass close to an important red ocher site, which is shown, lower right, as a small red painted area. Red ocher, and the journeys of sacred animals associated with the formation of such ocher deposits in the Creation period, play a very important part in men's sacred ceremonies. The gathering and use of red ocher remains sacred men's business.

Although the extended story line of this painting was not communicated by the artist, the presence of spindles and a number of women's camps indicates collective activities of both men and women in the Creation time or Tjukurrpa. Spindles are frequently associated with women's love-magic.

PLATE 50
Tjumpo Tjapanangka, b. c. 1925
Maryuwar, Great Sandy Desert, 1997
150 x 100 cm (59 x 39.5 in.)
Acrylic on linen

Biographical Notes

For much of his life, Tjumpo Tjapanangka lived a mobile existence across Western Australia in the area known as the Great Sandy Desert. Born about 1925, he is now resident at Balgo Hills, but has also lived at Kiwirrkura and Kintore. He speaks Kukatja language.

Tjumpo Tjapanangka paints many Creation or Tjukurrpa themes, including water, snakes, bandicoots, kangaroos, flying ants, and rain-making. He has exhibited through Warlayirti Artists at Balgo since 1987. Among the notable exhibitions in which his paintings were included are *Mythscapes, Aboriginal Art of the Desert* (National Gallery of Victoria, Melbourne, 1989), *Songlines, Paintings from Balgo Hills* (Rebecca Hossack Gallery, London, 1990), *Aboriginal Paintings from the Desert* (Union of Soviet Artists Gallery, Moscow, and Museum of Ethnographic Art, St. Petersburg, Russia, 1991), and *Tjukurrpa Desert Dreamings, Aboriginal Art from Central Australia* (1971–1993) (Art Gallery of Western Australia, Perth, 1993). His paintings are in the collections of several State art galleries, including the Art Gallery of Western Australia and the National Gallery of Victoria.

PLATE 50 (detail)
Tjumpo Tjapanangka, b. c. 1925
Maryuwar, Great Sandy Desert, 1997
150 x 100 cm (59 x 39.5 in.)
Acrylic on linen

Eubena Nampitjin

Kalarmindi

Eubena Nampitjin grew up at the site of this painting — a waterhole named Kalarmindi, which is situated near Punmu. This was once a frequent watering stop for drovers and their cattle on the Canning Stock Route, which until recently was the major Western Australian overland droving route. The co-use of fragile waterholes resulted in the destruction of the environment belonging to many Aboriginal peoples, so that in times of drought they were forced to seek refuge in communities with permanent water and access to food supplies.

Parallel sand dunes occur throughout this region. Eubena Nampitjin has shown them extending from two watercourses. In one of these the Kalarmindi waterholes are represented as three small circles beside the watercourse.

Biographical Notes

Eubena Nampitjin was born about 1924 at Yalantjirri, in the remote desert south of Balgo. As a child she traveled on foot across large tracts of desert, from one soak or waterhole to another. With her mother and other kin, she gathered desert foods, particularly reptiles such as goannas and lizards, and collected fruits and root vegetables. She participated fully in ceremonies connected to the travels of the Tingari women Ancestors, and is now a senior law woman and custodian of all women's law for the area called Kinyu on the Canning Stock Route. She lives at Balgo Hills in the Great Sandy Desert with her husband, Wimmitji Tjapangarti, who is also a prominent painter. She speaks Kukatja and Wangkajunga languages.

Eubena Nampitjin works for the community artists' company, Warlayirti Artists, through which her work has appeared in numerous group exhibitions from 1986 to the present, including *Mythscapes, Aboriginal Art of the Desert* (National Gallery of Victoria, 1989), *Contemporary Aboriginal Art 1990 from Australia* (Third Eye Centre, Scotland, 1990), *Flash Art* (Australian National Gallery, Canberra, 1992), and *Power of the Land, Masterpieces of Aboriginal Art* (National Gallery of Victoria, 1994). Until her eyesight failed recently, she also exhibited regularly in Melbourne with her husband, Wimmitji Tjapangarti. Paintings by Eubena Nampitjin are held in the collections of the National Gallery of Australia; National Gallery of Victoria; and notable private collections. In 1998 she won the open painting award at the National Aboriginal and Torres Strait Islander Art Award in Darwin.

PLATE 51
Eubena Nampitjin, b. c. 1924
Kalarmindi, 1997
120 x 80 cm (47 x 31.5 in.)
Acrylic on linen

Helicopter Tjungurrayi

Sarnpilgo Soak

The central black circle is a water soak near Jupiter Well, Western Australia. Jupiter Well was an important meeting place for Aboriginal peoples. The natural waterhole has now been replaced by a bore, a few small houses, and a grove of trees.

During nomadic times such soaks were periodically maintained to prevent them from being spoiled or silting up. Some soaks were dug out to a considerable depth and were maintained as permanent wells, the sides shored up with sticks and brushes. These wells were covered from the heat of the day or dug in a slanting direction to prevent the water from evaporating. Other soaks were semi-permanent but required digging out to maintain the water levels.

The small black circles connected by lines represent the small black stones that are a feature of the landscape around Sarnpilgo. Beyond the stone country, the sand dunes are marked as radiating lines.

Biographical Notes

Helicopter Tjungurrayi, who is in his early fifties, is one of the younger generation of artists at Balgo Hills. He speaks Kukatja language and grew up near Jupiter Well in the Gibson and Great Sandy Deserts. This country lies about halfway between Kiwirrkura and "Well 33" along the Canning Stock Route.

Helicopter was given his name as a result of an incident in the 1960s, when he fell seriously ill and was collected by a flying doctor in the first helicopter seen in the area. Now a marpan or medicine man himself, Helicopter practices as a traditional healer in the Balgo community. Recently the name Helicopter became kumanjayi, meaning that it cannot be spoken aloud because the prefix "Hel" sounds like the name of someone else who has died, and if spoken would call up their spirit. As a result, Helicopter has been renamed "Chopper." He is married to the artist Lucy Yukenbarri and they live in a small annex to the extended family house at Balgo.

Helicopter began painting in about 1995. He has participated with other artists from Warlayirti Arts in exhibitions in Australian capital cities, in the Netherlands, Germany, and Sweden. His paintings are held in the collection of the Art Gallery of New South Wales and featured on the cover of the journal *Revue du Louvre,* Paris, in 1998. He has become a much-sought-after artist, known for his use of brilliant blue, red, black, and white striping zigzag vertical meanders.

PLATE 52
Helicopter Tjungurrayi, b. c. 1946
Sarnpilgo Soak, 1997
120 x 80 cm (47 x 31.5 in.)
Acrylic on linen

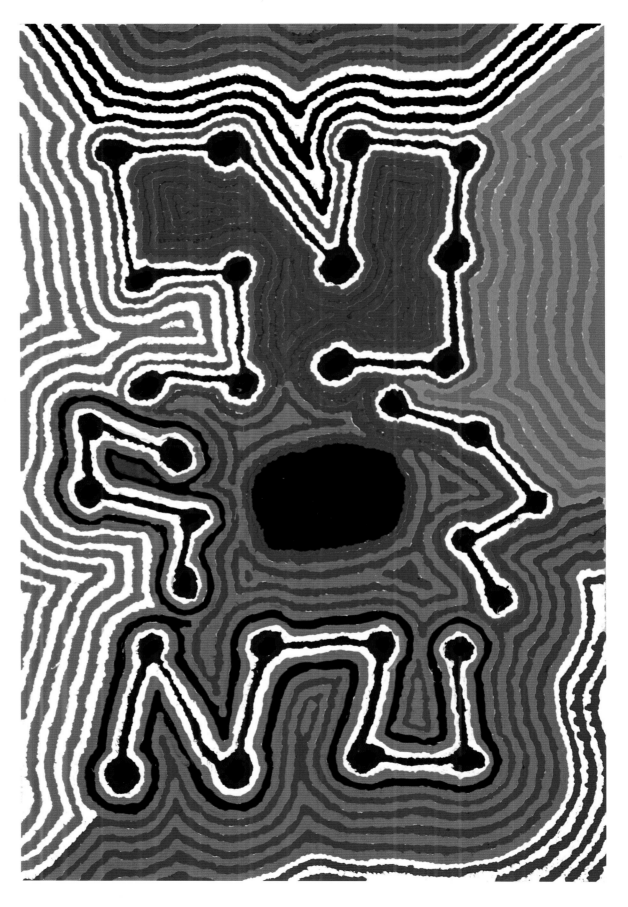

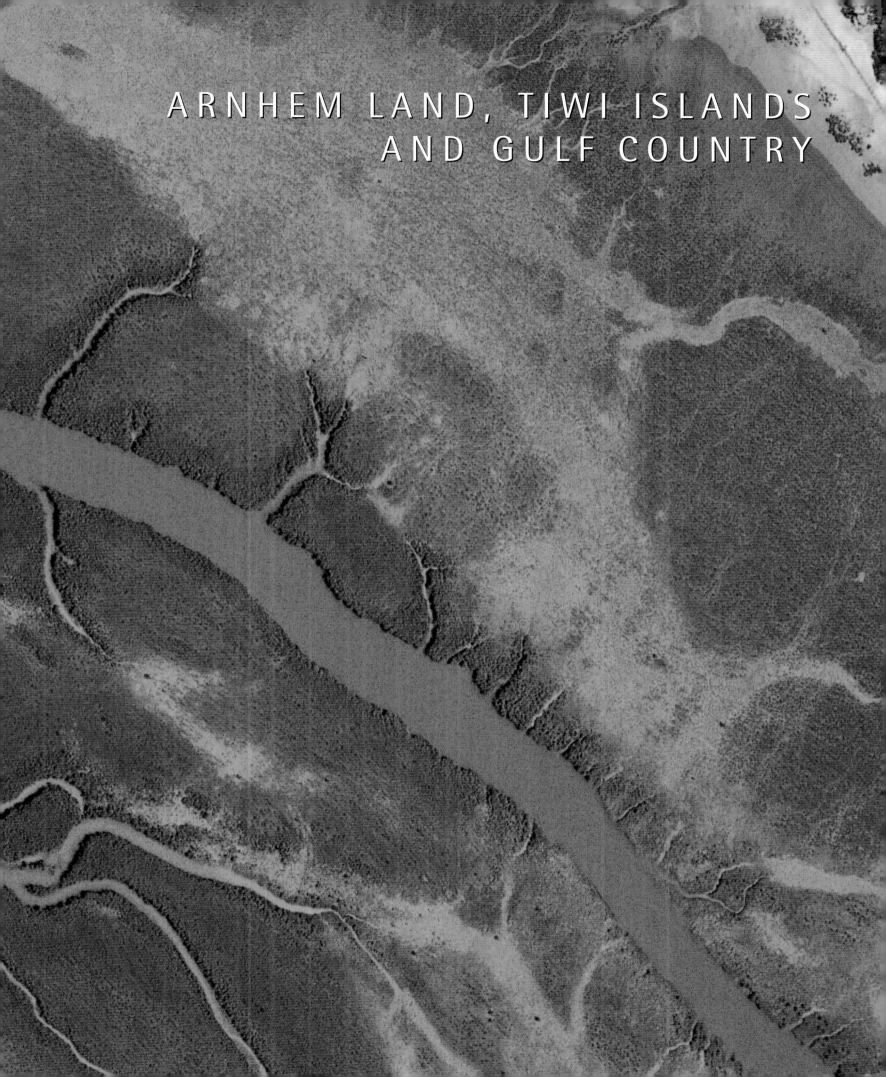

ARNHEM LAND, TIWI ISLANDS
AND GULF COUNTRY

Croker Island

Arafura Sea

Tiwi Islands   Melville Island

Elcho Island
(Galiwinku)

Munupi ○   ○ Milikapiti

Melville B

Western Region

○ Maningrida   ○ Milingimbi

○ Nguiu

*Van Diemen
Gulf*

○ Oenpelli (Gunbalanya)

Ramingining ○

○ Yi

Bathurst Island

● Darwin

Kakadu
National
Park

South Alligator River

East Alligator River

Liverpool River

○ Kubumi

Goyder River

Clyde River

Caledon Ba

Baniyala
○

Arnhem Land

Woodah Island

Mann River

Groote
Island

Roper River

○ Ngukurr

Limmen Bight

Limmen Bight River

Northern Territory

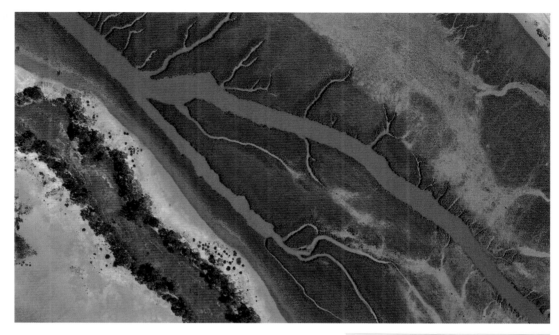

Arnhem Land coastine, Northern Territory
PHOTOGRAPH: Richard Woldendorp

Arnhem Land, Tiwi Islands, and Gulf Country

Arnhem Land

The coast of Arnhem Land was first named by Dutch explorers who viewed it from a vessel called the *Arnhem* in 1623. It is a region of sparse dry sclerophyll forests,[1] rugged escarpments, lagoons, flood plains, and coastal mangroves, extending from approximately 100 miles east of Darwin to the coast of the Gulf of Carpentaria. The northern coast is dissected by a number of huge rivers that swell in the wet season, making parts of the country inaccessible by land.

The peoples of Arnhem Land lived a relatively trouble-free existence until quite recently. The Arnhem Land area was declared a reserve for Aboriginal people in 1931, and the entry of outsiders was expressly forbidden in an attempt to protect the clans of the region from a range of "undesirable" contacts, including Japanese and Malay fishermen as well as cattle station personnel. More recent threats to the traditional lifestyle include mining, disputes over fishing rights, and, within Aboriginal communities, differing opinions about the most beneficial direction for change in the years to come.

Today, thousands of Aboriginal families live in rural outstations as well as in the sizable towns that have grown from the original government and mission settlements. The religion of the land remains immensely strong throughout the region, despite the pragmatic absorption of the themes, concepts, and theories taught by Christian missions. People continue their traditional seasonal activities, hunting, fishing, and using their encyclopedic knowledge of the environment to provide their families with a range of bush foods to supplement the widely available store-bought European foods. As Wandjuk Marika, a clan leader of eastern Arnhem Land, put it in 1985, "We're operating on old ways."

The peoples of Arnhem Land have a long tradition of painting on bodies, on objects, and on bark as a means of exchanging information and revealing knowledge of sacred law in relation to the Creation Ancestors and their land. At the base of the rocky Arnhem Land escarpment lie extensive plains interspersed with billabongs and swamps formed by huge river systems. This is a perfect habitat for a wide variety of birds, particularly waterfowl, as well as fish and game, including kangaroos, wallabies, possums, fruit bats, echidnas, and goannas. All of these images are depicted in the widespread wealth of rock art in the region and appear in the great art traditions of the Kunwinjku people of western Arnhem Land.

The World Heritage Area of the Kakadu National Park abuts the western edge of Arnhem Land. It is not only an important natural history zone, but also houses some of the most magnificent rock-art sequences in the world, notably the sites at Nourlangie and Ubirr. Some rock overhangs contain hundreds of individual paintings, which together form massive galleries recording the art and thoughts of the people over millennia. The antecedents of today's bark painting tradition can be readily seen in these rock-art images of Rainbow Serpents, Lightning Spirits, hunters, kangaroos, and the prized fish, the barramundi. The oldest of the paintings depict fine, red-ochered figures called mimih, delicate,

thin spirit creatures who are believed to have first taught humans the skills of hunting kangaroos. Frail and sometimes mischievous, the mimih can abduct children if they wander too far from the camp at night. Mimih figures also appear in many of the contemporary bark paintings of western Arnhem Land.

Elsewhere in Arnhem Land, beyond the escarpment and to the east, the journeys of great Creation Ancestors link disparate communities hundreds of miles apart. The peoples of eastern and central Arnhem Land, the Yolngu — the name literally means "we people" — are united by a common kinship system that divides all the peoples into two halves, or moieties,[2] the Dhuwa and Yirritja, within which are a range of language groups. The principal Spirit Ancestors of the Dhuwa moiety are Djankawu and Wawilak, while those of the Yirritja are Barama and Laindtjang.

As these Ancestors traveled they hunted, gathered food, and observed animal species, naming them as they went. On their journey across the land they gave birth to the people, and in each different area a new language was spoken. They are not only the original progenitors of modern-day people in this region, but also the source of language, design, and art. The sacred designs of Arnhem Land are imbued with power and authority because they were given to Yolngu by the Ancestors.

In eastern Arnhem Land, ownership of particular designs is strictly kept within kinship lines from generation to generation, but innovation in execution by the rightful owner is permitted and indeed applauded if it gives the design greater power or resonance. As in other areas of Australia, songs were exchanged during lengthy ceremonial gatherings throughout Arnhem Land. Over millennia, ceremonies have connected people across vast distances for trade, political activity, marriages, and the exchange of sacred knowledge, which included designs.

Bark paintings

Throughout the extensive northern region, people built simple shelters made of strips of eucalyptus bark, and the inside surface of these shelters was often painted with figures of kangaroos and other animals. Early travelers mainly reported seeing these shelters in western Arnhem Land communities. In his *Wanderings in Wild Australia,* the ethnographer Baldwin Spencer observed:

> *They are very fond of drawing both on rocks and the sheets of bark of which their Mia Mias are made… Today I found a native who, apparently, had nothing better to do than sit quietly in the camp, evidently enjoying himself, drawing a fish on a piece of stringy bark.*[3]

The traditional technology for stripping the trunks of eucalypts for these shelters is exactly the same as that used for making bark paintings today. In the past, stone axes were the only tools available, but today steel axes and tomahawks are used. The back of the bark is placed over a fire until the sheet uncurls, then it is stripped of extraneous fiber and burnt material. Finally, sandpaper is used to smooth the inner surface. In some communities bark paintings are then given stretcher sticks, which are tied at either end or sewn through the bark to prevent it from returning to the curved shape of the tree trunk. It is normal, however, for the bark sheets to be somewhat irregular, and to change shape with atmospheric moisture.

The fine cross-hatching characteristic of many Arnhem Land bark paintings is achieved with brushes made of a few strands of human hair, sometimes up to four inches long. These were standard across Arnhem Land, but in recent times store-bought brushes have come into use. Slivers of grass and reeds are also occasionally used for the fine outlines, and chewed twigs for the background.

The traditional colors are natural ochers from the earth's surface itself. Deposits of particularly strong white, yellow, red, and black ocher were traded

David Malangi working on a bark painting of pythons, part of the Wawilak Creation story
PHOTOGRAPH: Jennifer Isaacs

Stripping eucalyptus bark for painting or making tunga (containers) on Bathurst Island
PHOTOGRAPH: Reg Morrison

between peoples and are frequently associated with the actions of Dreaming Ancestors. A certain kind of yellow ocher, for example, is found where the Dreaming turtle left a deposit of his fat, white ocher may be the feces of the Rainbow Serpent, and a dark brown or red ocher is frequently associated with places where blood was spilt. Black is generally extracted from the charcoal of fired tree bark or campfires, but a beautiful brown-black pigment with a low sheen also occurs in various deposits of manganese in eastern Arnhem Land and Groote Eyelandt.

Individual communities and artists have their own supplies of the colors needed for the paintings, and these vary in subtle ways, so that paintings by particular artists may be distinguished by their use of characteristic colors or ochers. The ochers are ground on a stone palette, then mixed with water. A small amount of fixative is also added. Until very recently, the natural fixative from a bush orchid (*Dendrobium* species) was rubbed on the stone palette before the ocher was ground. Today commercially made wood glues provide an effective substitute, although the older paintings are notable for the softness of their color and their powdery pastel surfaces.

Art institutions and collectors have shown increasing interest in bark paintings over the past decade, but the fragility of the materials has led to concern about their conservation and care over time.[4] A number of art communities, including those at Oenpelli, Ramingining, and Elcho Island, have responded by introducing ocher painting on paper. The designs and content remain the same as if they had been painted on bark. On several occasions, however, key curators of Aboriginal art have publicly stated their preference for bark paintings as an art form because of the three-dimensional nature of the works, their references to and continuity with the past, and the aesthetic appeal of their colors and surface texture.

The Collection of Arnhem Land Art

Although Aboriginal people painted with ocher on the interior surface of their bark houses, the practice of painting on strips of stringy bark has become much more widespread over the past fifty years. The earliest paintings that found their way into Australian museums are images of birds and animals collected in 1878 from Port Essington, the site of the first attempt at European habitation on the northern coast of Australia. The first recorded move to commission paintings from Aboriginal artists was by Baldwin Spencer at Oenpelli in 1912. Spencer specifically intended these to be portable expressions of the cave art. Mostly the paintings depict animals in profile, sometimes being hunted by figures with spears and other weapons. The fine cross-hatched lines known as rarrk that are a feature of many contemporary Arnhem Land paintings only appeared on bark much later, as a transference from body-painting and ceremonial life.

The Australian–American Scientific Expedition to Arnhem Land in 1948 proved immensely important in establishing the breadth of stylistic tradition and artistic practice in the far north of Australia. The group traveled from Yirrkala to western Arnhem Land, camping in each area for several weeks. On their return the collection they made was divided between various State art galleries. Apart from Spencer's collection, this was the first time that large numbers of bark paintings had entered Australian art galleries. They caught the imagination of white artists and designers seeking a distinctively Australian visual idiom, and soon images taken straight from these bark paintings were being widely used in graphic arts, interior furnishings, ceramics, and other domestic items. Images of X-ray kangaroos and dancing mimih figures thus entered the Australian psyche through magazines and the world of design.

By the 1960s the Church Missionary Society in Oenpelli was actively encouraging artists to paint small works for sale through the mission's shop in Sydney. Mission art helpers, however, were somewhat prudish and resistant to "pagan" religious themes, particularly those that depicted sacred ceremonies in which sexual activities had a role. Censorious attitudes produced self-censorship from the artists, who, after all, wanted to sell their paintings. Spirit figures who might previously have exhibited large genitalia were now modestly covered with grass skirts or "nagas," the handkerchief-tied cloth coverings widely used as clothing in Arnhem Land. Nevertheless the mission's support and promotion of art ensured that Oenpelli remained a vital art-producing area.

A Methodist mission was set up by Wilbur Chaseling at Yirrkala in 1935, and the local artists were also encouraged to make bark paintings. Here, without the background of cave art, the artists were transferring their religious body paintings and designs for bark coffins directly onto the flattened bark strips.

Partly in response to the proliferation of commercialized designs in the graphic arts, major Australian galleries had shown little further interest in collecting Aboriginal art works, though important collections were made by the anthropologists Charles Mountford, Donald Thompson, and Ronald and Catherine Berndt. A significant change occurred in 1959 when Tony Tuckson, a gifted abstract painter and deputy director of the Art Gallery of New South Wales, became enamored of the strong visual impact of Aboriginal art. Tuckson mounted an expedition in conjunction with art patron Dr. Stuart Scougall and Scougall's secretary Dorothy Bennett, resulting in a remarkable collection of bark paintings from Yirrkala. These were large, episodic myths depicted in separate squares on the barks.

Encouraged by the responses of missionaries and visitors, the clan artists of Arnhem Land stepped up production, and art works soon became a significant source of cash. This was reinforced in the 1970s with the development of government subsidies and the establishment of art centers and galleries set up specifically to exhibit Aboriginal art in each Australian State. In line with federal government policy and the 1976 Northern Territory Aboriginal Land Rights Act, the former Arnhem Land reserve became Aboriginal land, administered by the Northern Land Council under a series of trusts. Independent councils were appointed in each community. These councils, their art centers, and art advisers continue the active work of encouraging the collection, marketing, and promotion of bark paintings of the region.

At present, Aboriginal art centers in the communities receive government support for staff and running costs, but the marketing is often placed in the hands of prominent private galleries. The principal art-producing communities represented in this collection are Oenpelli, Maningrida, Ramingining, and Yirrkala. Many other individual Aboriginal artists in the communities and in towns, stimulated by the contemporary painting movement, are involved in recovering their culture through art.

Oenpelli

The community at Gunbalanya or Oenpelli now numbers about 750 people. The houses are clustered around a spectacularly beautiful billabong and face the rock formation known as Inyalak, which contains many cave paintings recording the animals and creatures of the surrounding country. The Kunwinjku residents' visual culture thus draws on a tradition that can be dated back some 20,000 years.

Some of the cave paintings also record Aboriginal reactions to offshore visitors and subsequent incursions onto their land by outsiders. There are men in uniforms wearing hats, and images of boats with sails, some obviously European, others more Indonesian in design. Horses, guns, and axes are also to be seen in the rock art of western Arnhem Land, evidence of the fear these powerful newcomers inspired.

In the early part of the nineteenth century several attempts were made to form European settlements on the northern coast of Australia. During one of these ventures a small herd of buffalo went feral and rampaged throughout Arnhem Land to the coast of the Gulf of Carpentaria. In the 1890s Paddy Cahill moved to present-day Oenpelli to hunt these buffalo, and it was Cahill who made the first collection of bark paintings, in conjunction with Baldwin Spencer. Spencer called these works "drawings."[5] This is a useful term to differentiate the art of this region, which features animated figurative compositions depicting mythological creatures, spirits both benign and malevolent, and men and women going about their daily business of hunting.

The Anglican Church Missionary Society managed the community at Oenpelli from the 1930s. In the 1950s the mission began a program of capital works, and by the 1960s it had established a bilingual literature program. The mission purchased and sold bark paintings to help fund its programs.

Today the community at Gunbalanya is independent and runs a very active arts center, Inyalak Arts and Crafts, which benefits from daily visitors from Kakadu National Park. Bark painting is still the predominant art of the region, but the introduction of painting on paper has proved successful commercially, and has the added benefit of allowing gifted artists to keep working, regardless of the seasonal availability of bark. The art of western Arnhem Land is represented in this collection by a number of early works by unknown artists.

Maningrida

Maningrida, situated at the mouth of the Liverpool River in central Arnhem Land, is the largest of the Arnhem Land communities. The settlement was set up in 1949 by the Northern Territory administration in order to provide a refuge for the numerous Aboriginal groups of the region, who were gravitating in large numbers to regional centers such as Darwin and Katherine.

At first Maningrida was called a "trading post" and was set up by "patrol officers," both terms straight out of frontier thought. Within a decade, the community was a well-established center for people from many language groups. Training in various skills was offered under the government "assimilation" program. A bakery and a workshop were set up, and a large building program was instituted. Soon the bark shelters and traditional homes gave way to simple community houses made of fiber-cement sheeting and timber. As the population increased, hundreds moved to the center semi-permanently.

The missions' activities in other parts of Arnhem Land had proved the economic worth of Aboriginal art, so at Maningrida bark painting, weaving, and carving were encouraged. They soon became a means of trade for the people of the surrounding countryside, who were able to exchange the cash they earned from making art works to buy goods at the store.

Maningrida Arts and Culture, the local arts center that markets the work from the region, was established in the early 1970s. This was a volatile time. The official policy of assimilation was abandoned in favor of encouraging people to retain their traditional values and connections to their remote spirit country. An arts center was established at Maningrida and the federal government's galleries in each State promoted the work of Maningrida artists, so that during this period it became the most highly regarded and exhibited community in Arnhem Land.

Maningrida Arts and Culture provides services to more than 200 bark painters, weavers, and carvers, most of whom live on small outstations that span a region covering 4000 square miles. The cultures of the region include Yolngu communities east of Maningrida and Kunwinjku, Rembarrnga, and others to the west and south.

In association with Maningrida Arts and Culture, a community museum, Djomi Museum, was set up as a keeping place for the most important works. A large collection is now displayed to a high conservation

James Iyuna painting at Maningrida with his brother John Mawurndjul
PHOTOGRAPH: Jennifer Isaacs

standard. The center organizes workshops and cultural programs involving different Aboriginal groups, and a program of training and employment for young, enthusiastic workers in the Maningrida region is in place. This collection features the work of artists associated with Maningrida: Peter Marralwanga, Bruce Wardungku, Timothy Wulanjbirr, Mick Kubarkku, Owen Yalandja, James Iyuna, Sally Garromara, Mirigunbala, Nguminala, and Terry Ngamadara.

Ramingining

Ramingining is an Aboriginal community of 900 Yolngu that lies approximately 250 miles east of Darwin, inland from the coast opposite Milingimbi, an island in the Crocodile Islands group. The clans are from a radiating area north, west, east, and south of the community. The community includes many language groups, and most people are multilingual.

The distinctive form of bark painting and visual arts that has developed here emphasizes strongly drawn figures, bold patterning, and contrasting bright ochers. Although Yolngu in central Arnhem Land have expressed their Dreaming designs and Ancestral patterns on many different surfaces for millennia, the trade in bark paintings from this community is relatively recent. Previously, small bark paintings were made at the behest of the Methodist mission that was established in the mid-1920s on the nearby island of Milingimbi. Some of the more significant older Ramingining artists, including David Malangi (see page 196), sold their first paintings through this art center at Milingimbi. Other Ramingining artists represented here are Philip Guthayguthay, Joe Djembungu, and Jimmy Wululu.

Yirrkala

The tall, rangy Yolngu of eastern Arnhem Land were left relatively undisturbed until 1933–34, when there was a series of killings at Caledon Bay and on Woodah Island. The Northern Territory administration and the Anglican Church Missionary Society mounted a joint expedition into the area to apprehend the perpetrators. Three men were subsequently tried and imprisoned. In humanitarian circles, it was thought that "the natives" needed support and succor rather than punishment, and soon a mission was set up at the community now called Yirrkala, a central meeting point for clans from the northern and eastern coasts.

The Methodist mission was established in 1935 to initiate the conversion of Yolngu to Christianity. There was also a shift to education in English, and ever-increasing interaction with the wider world. During World War II the north coast of Australia was considered particularly vulnerable to Japanese invasion, and Yolngu and other Aboriginal groups were trained in coastal surveillance. The Australian army and air force established a base at Yirrkala, interacting with Yolngu on a daily basis. This was the Yolngu people's first experience of interacting with whites on an equal footing; previously they had only dealt with government agents, missionaries, and others in authority. The presence of military personnel also led to an expansion of the trade in bark paintings.

From the earliest times Yolngu paintings have been used as both religious and political tracts. They employ a symbolic language to record the meaning and geography of their traditional country in episodes across the bark. The designs are derived from body paintings, in the same manner as those in central Arnhem Land (Ramingining and Maningrida), but they are taken to elaborate lengths. These works are not designed to be viewed as elegant patterns or decorative works of art, but are imbued with religious power. The patterning and composition of the elements is owned by particular families or linked kinship groups, who also own the land being discussed on the painting. Aesthetics are based on the correct representation of land in the designs according to patterns and symbols owned by that clan or language group. Individual skill is appreciated, however, and the introduction of an added component of line-making that gives the work greater power is much admired.

From at least the 1960s, Yolngu have used their bark paintings as a means of demonstrating their ownership of these lands. Because their territory was so remote, Yolngu were completely unaware that Australia had been annexed by England, and that the Northern Territory had been designated as a territory of South Australia in 1863. Today Yolngu continue to maintain their inalienable sovereignty over their own land, and express this in their paintings.

In 1962 the Methodist mission encouraged the Yirritja and Dhuwa moieties to complete two large plywood panels, each depicting the moiety's own designs, to be displayed on either side of the altar in the local church. The results were spectacular. After much consultation, the elders of each language group chose the patterns and images that marked out the journeys of Ancestral Spirits who created the very land itself. Their journeys were marked across the land, indicating the descent lines of the present Yolngu community. This was the first of many occasions on which Yolngu have gently but forcefully stated their claim to independence through painting.

The same approach animated the subsequent political fights in which Yolngu attempted to confirm their land ownership through the Australian courts. In 1971 Yolngu from Yirrkala brought the first Aboriginal land rights case in Australia.[6] The case began with a petition in the form of a letter and a bark painting detailing the claims of the clans of the region, who were attempting to stop the Australian government from allowing a large bauxite mine to be established on their land. Sacred objects and bark paintings were also tendered as evidence in court.

Although the case was lost and the bauxite mine went ahead, the strength of the evidence given in court established an opening for further landmark cases. The 1970s and 1980s saw the emergence of a strong Aboriginal land rights movement, which culminated in the handing back of the Arnhem Land Reserve to Aboriginal people and the establishment of the very powerful Northern Land Council. In 1976 the Northern Territory Land Rights Act was passed, establishing the legal framework through which Aboriginal communities could lay claim to land.

Yolngu continue to make magnificent bark paintings both small and large, although recently artists have returned to episodic depictions of their Creation beliefs in a form reminiscent of the original church panels. Among the artists who have explored this form are Galuma Maymaru and Dhukal Wirrpanda, whose work is represented here. A large exhibition of these episodic works, called *Title Deeds*, was held at the Museum of Contemporary Art in Sydney in 1998.

Tiwi Islands

Bathurst and Melville Islands are the traditional home of the Tiwi people. The islands lie close together, separated by a strait about 700 yards wide. Although they are only 60 miles from Darwin, it appears the Tiwi had very little contact with mainland indigenous peoples before the arrival of outsiders.

The first Catholic mission was founded at Nguiu on Bathurst Island in 1911, and Herbert Basedow and Baldwin Spencer, the first ethnographers to visit the area, arrived on the islands soon afterwards. They observed and published photographs of the beautiful burial poles known as Pukumani, or Tutini, which are only made by the Tiwi people. But by far the most elaborate art reported from the earliest times was the spectacular body decorations, facial paintings, armlets, mourning rings, and headdresses that were worn during the dancing at major Tiwi occasions such as the Pukumani burial ceremony and the Kulama or yam ceremony.

All aspects of individual creativity are highly valued among Tiwis — song, dance, and visual art.

A bark painter's stone palette with earth ochers,
fixatives and brushes
PHOTOGRAPH: Reg Morrison

Pukumani dancers wear full face and body paint, feathered headdresses, and false beards, and carry ornate multi-flanged spears to disguise themselves from the spirits of the dead who might cause them harm.

As anthropological interest in the Tiwi grew, Australian museums began to collect or commission Pukumani poles for their permanent collections. A particularly significant group of decorated Pukumani poles, which includes some that are two feet in diameter, was made for the Art Gallery of New South Wales through the deputy director, Tony Tuckson, in the 1950s.

Tiwi themselves continue to commission poles for use at funerals. The number erected around the grave depends upon the wealth of the family and the status of the deceased. Although nearly all Tiwi regard themselves as Catholics, the Pukumani and Kulama ceremonies remain an integral part of cultural practice. Tiwi designs are universally abstract and geometric, and have altered little over the decades since they were first illustrated by Spencer in 1914.[7]

Three small towns on the islands now have art advisers employed by the local Tiwi councils or artists' companies. At Nguiu, on Bathurst Island, a number of art and design enterprises have been established, beginning in the early 1970s, with particular success in textiles. This community has sold and exhibited Pukumani poles, carved and painted figures, birds, and other Tiwi fiber arts. The two communities on Melville Island at Munupi and Milikapiti also encourage artists, co-ordinate major commissions, and arrange exhibitions in private galleries in Australia and other countries.

For Tiwi, their art is a means of celebrating their own identity through distinctive and instantly recognizable patterns, grids, circles, and bold decorations. Tiwi buildings, cars, schools, and clothing provide surfaces that are an extension of the body — and all offer potential for designs. The Tiwi artists included here are Leon Puruntatameri, Mathew Freddy Puruntatameri, Andrew Freddy Puruntatameri, Pedro Wonaeamirri, Enraeld Djulabinyanna, Freda Warlipini, Declan Apuatimi, Concepta Kantilla, Therese Ann Pilakui, Marie E. Pautjimi, and John Wilson.

The Gulf Country

Ngukurr, an Aboriginal community on the Roper River, is the home of a remarkable art community whose adventurous colors and pictorial qualities set them apart. It is a former Anglican mission, bordered by cattle country. Its residents come from many language groups, including Mara, Alawa, and Ngalakan, on whose lands the community was situated. As in other parts of Aboriginal Australia, the people communicate with each other in a mixture of languages, and most are multilingual. They also speak the distinctive and idiosyncratic Aboriginal English termed Kriol.

Many community members have been making traditional arts and crafts for sale for decades. Field officers from Mimi Arts and Crafts in Katherine, the nearest large town, collected these items and marketed them in the 1980s. It was not until 1986, however, that Ngukurr people began to engage in printmaking and painting using canvas and acrylics, encouraged by the Northern Territory Open College of Technical and Further Education. Willy Gudabi (see page 220), who had previously painted on bark, produced works divided into segments like episodic myths, similar to those from Yirrkala which recounted the journeys of Ancestral beings in vignettes. The early paintings of both Ginger Riley Munduwalawala (see page 224) and Djambu Barra Barra were partly cross-hatched. What marked these paintings out as a complete departure was the pictorial qualities, the story-telling, and the artists' spectacular use of color — Ginger Riley's luminescent lawn greens, pinks, and yellows, and Willy Gudabi's range of blues. The depictions of birds, scorpions, and other creatures set out to illustrate stories were also unique.

By 1987, major collectors had become interested in the work and had purchased paintings entered in the National Aboriginal Art Awards in Darwin. Group exhibitions followed in Melbourne. These overwhelmingly colorful paintings have links to the very beginnings of Aboriginal contemporary art. Ginger Riley encountered the color of Albert Namatjira's paintings on a trip to Alice Springs in the 1950s. This had a profound influence on him, just as the work of Ginger Riley has influenced both Aboriginal and non-Aboriginal artists today.

Artists Unknown

Fish

This early bark painting of a barramundi was probably made by a Kunwinjku artist from western Arnhem Land. The artist has used the stylistic device of revealing the internal organs of the fish. Here the backbone is represented diagrammatically, with the disks marked as stripes. The body is covered in cross-hatching or rarrk. This was a technique introduced on bark from body painting, where cross-hatched patterns were painted on the chest; it was little used in the early cave art. The rough-cut piece of bark pre-dates the use of stick binders as stretchers at either end, a practice introduced by the missionaries.

The barramundi is a very important Kunwinjku Creation Ancestor believed to have formed the bends and meanders in the river system. Multiple images of barramundi fill the cave wall at the World Heritage site of Ubirr in Kakadu National Park, and appear in numerous other rock-art friezes.

PLATE 53
Artist Unknown
Fish, c. 1963
25.5 x 59 cm (10 x 23 in.)
Earth ochers on bark

Fish

This freely painted image of a barramundi is typical of early western Arnhem Land bark paintings. In style, it resembles the early cave paintings of the escarpment country of western Arnhem Land. The bark has been rubbed with charcoal, then painted with a chewed bark brush using white earth pigment, possibly kaolin. The veil of yellow dots across the body of the fish is unusual.

The roughly cut piece of bark pre-dates the introduction of bracing sticks. As this practice was common at Oenpelli in the 1960s, this bark may have originated at Croker Island, a Kunwinjku community off the coast of Arnhem Land.

PLATE 54
Artist Unknown
Fish, c. 1963
24.5 x 52.5 cm (9.5 x 20.5 in.)
Earth ochers on bark

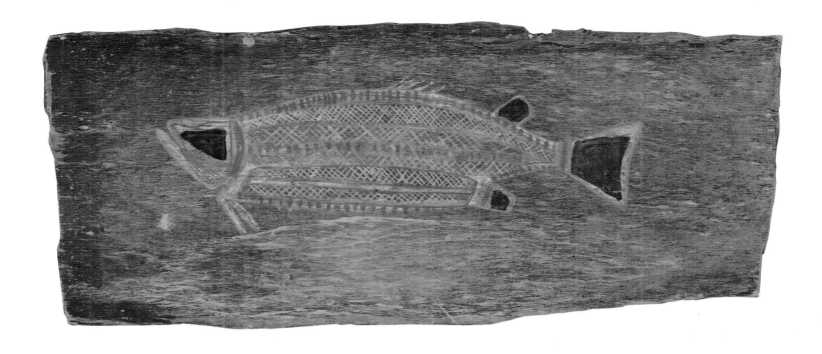

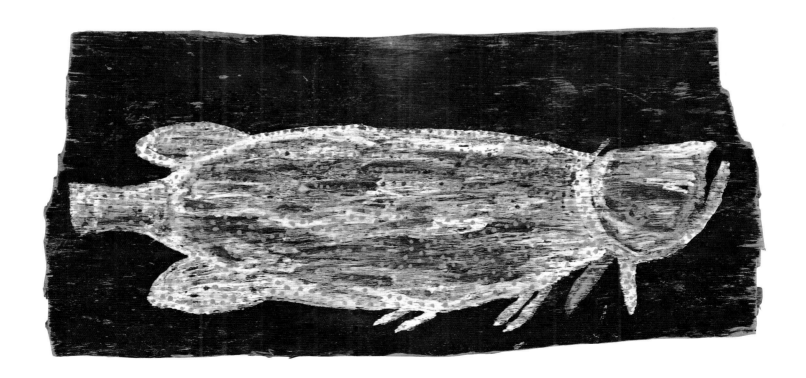

Unknown Kunwinjku artist

Kangaroo

Images of kangaroos are the subjects of many early cave drawings in the extensive rock-art galleries of the escarpment country of the Kunwinjku people. The kangaroo is a major Creative Being, and is celebrated in the sacred songs and performances of the Ubarr ceremony of western Arnhem Land. Kangaroos are also a food source. Hunting these marsupials was men's work, as was the prescribed ritual division and distribution of the meat. Kunwinjku people still follow strict rules for dividing and distributing kangaroo portions. It is thought that these were first practiced by the mimih spirits and taught to man.

The figure is shown in profile with internal organs visible — a device termed X-ray art. The painter has revealed the lungs, liver, spinal column, and part of the gut — body parts that are also handed to specific kin under the laws of distribution.

Biographical Notes

Many Kunwinjku prefer to retain their old way of life as hunters and gatherers on their own lands. Some bark artists, such as this unknown artist, retain close stylistic links to the form of depicting animal and spirit images in rock art.

When this painting was done, it was common practice for the mission at Oenpelli to sell paintings without details of the artist or the subject. Numerous "X-ray kangaroos" were produced by Kunwinjku artists for sale to the mission. For decades these popular images were erroneously regarded as the most "authentic" Aboriginal art.

PLATE 55
Unknown Kunwinjku Artist
Kangaroo, c. 1960
86 x 57 cm (34 x 22.5 in.)
Earth ochers on bark

Peter Marralwanga

Namaynwarreh, the Salt Water Crocodile

This bark painting shows a crocodile enveloping the smaller figure of a kangaroo or wallaby. Both the crocodile and kangaroo are the subject of major Creation stories that account for the formation of the landscape in western Arnhem Land.

Biographical Notes

Peter Marralwanga was born in 1916 and died in 1987. He lived in the small community of Marrkolidjban in the Liverpool River district. Marralwanga was one of the most significant Kunwinjku artists of western Arnhem Land, painting animals, spirit figures, and the Ancestral Rainbow Serpent throughout his adult life. Along with Yirawala, he is credited with being the first artist to introduce particular striped cross-hatching designs for the sacred Mardayin ceremony into bark painting, a technique he passed on to the brothers John Mawurndjul and James Iyuna (see page 178).

Marralwanga was one of the first Kunwinjku artists to explore the full possibilities of enlarging his subject to fill the bark ground. In time, his surface patterning became increasingly complex and hypnotic, with the use of subdivided areas, finely detailed rarrk (cross-hatching) and the delineation of patterned areas with white dots on black lines. His works are held in the Art Gallery of South Australia; National Gallery of Victoria; National Gallery of Australia: Museum and Art Gallery of the Northern Territory; Australian Museum, Sydney; Museum of Victoria; and National Museum of Australia, Canberra.

PLATE 56
Peter Marralwanga, 1916–1987
Namaynwarreh, the Salt Water Crocodile, 1983
92 x 47 cm (36 x 18.5 in.)
Earth ochers on bark

Bruce Wardungku

The divided body of Karndakidj the Antilopine Kangaroo

Karndakidj the antilopine kangaroo lives in the western Arnhem Land forests. It is hunted as game, and has Ancestral and ceremonial importance. This work shows the animal after it has been speared by a mimih spirit, shown with two spears, a womerah or spear-thrower, and woven dilly bag (a conical hunting bag). The mimih are hunters par excellence, and taught Kunwinjku these skills as well as the correct method of cutting up the carcass.

Each section of the animal may correlate to a particular landscape feature such as a rock, which is also embodied in or represented by ritual objects. The shimmer of the finely cross-hatched patterns on the surface of the work adds Creative Ancestral power and resonance.

Biographical Notes

Bruce Wardungku was born in 1971 and is an eastern Kunwinjku artist. He lives at the community of Marrkolidjban, one of the satellite communities of Maningrida in western Arnhem Land.

PLATE 57 (left, detail opposite)
Bruce Wardungku, b. 1971
The divided body of Karndakidj the Antilopine Kangaroo, 1997
131 x 57 cm (51.5 x 22.5 in.)
Earth ochers on bark

Timothy Wulanjbirr

Ngalyod, the Rainbow Serpent

Throughout Australia the Rainbow Serpent is a powerful, pervasive, and important Creative Ancestor figure associated with generative ceremonies ensuring the fertility of species. Yet the Rainbow Serpent can also be destructive, bringing on violent thunderstorms if sacred laws are transgressed. The Rainbow Spirit may be male or female in different parts of the country. It is the most powerful Ancestral Spirit. Associated with water, the monsoon season, and wild storms, the Rainbow Spirit arcs across the sky in the form of a rainbow at the end of a storm. Its voice is that of thunder, and it is also associated with the Lightning Spirit.

The Rainbow Spirit has a number of manifestations for the Kunwinjku. One of them is Ngalyod, who lives beneath the water at specific waterholes in western Arnhem Land. Law governs people's behavior at these places lest Ngalyod be angered and cause sickness or cyclones. The painting shows the leaves and corm of the waterlily, which is closely associated with this figure. The serpent can metamorphose into other animal forms or become a blend of several — snake, fish, crocodile, buffalo, and kangaroo. Ngalyod's transformational character becomes a metaphor for the actual transformation of the forests of Arnhem Land with the coming of the wet season, when dry waterholes become swamps teeming with fish and bird life.

Biographical Notes

Timothy Wulanjbirr is an eastern Kunwinjku artist who lives at Mumeka in the Mann River district of western Arnhem Land. This painting was made while he was living in Maningrida in the wet season of 1994–95. An accomplished bark artist, Timothy is known for his finely executed cross-hatched rarrk patterns, which appear to embody the power of "the shimmer," a feature of Kunwinjku art that is regarded as having spiritual resonance. Depending on the subject, it echoes the vibrating patterns of death adders or the light reflecting on the surface of the water.

PLATE 58
Timothy Wulanjbirr
Ngalyod, the Rainbow Serpent, 1994
139 x 65 cm (54.5 x 25.5 in.)
Earth ochers on bark

Mick Kubarkku

Dibdib Spirit

The Dibdib is a malevolent female spirit who inhabits the bush country near Barrodjowkkeng outstation. In this painting she is carrying numerous dilly bags, which she uses to carry bush foods. Dibdib spirits walk around in the bush, calling out to confuse people and make them lose their way.

Ngalyod, Rainbow Serpent, from the Rock-holes at Kubumi

In the Kunwinjku country of western Arnhem Land, Ngalyod the Rainbow Serpent can appear as part snake, part crocodile, part buffalo, or part fish. This representation shows Ngalyod in the form of three metamorphosed snake figures, each with the horns of a buffalo, a snake's body, and a fish's tail.

The Rainbow Serpent is closely connected to water, to the wet monsoon season, and to the waterlily-covered swamps and billabongs that occur throughout the country. Here Ngalyod is shown at the Kubumi rock-holes. These rock depressions, visible only in the dry season, are represented by the circular dotted designs. The highly prized pure white pigment used for the fine cross-hatching in this work is mined and traded from a sacred site, and is said to be the feces of the Rainbow Serpent.

Biographical Notes

Mick Kubarkku was born about 1925 and has spent his life on small outstations close to waterholes and billabongs, sometimes moving camp to hunt seasonally. He speaks eastern Kunwinjku, and is of the Kulmarru clan, Dhuwa moiety. In recent years he has remained at Kubumi, a community near Mumeka outstation.

Kubarkku has painted for most of his adult life, initially learning from his father Ngindjalakku and making paintings for sacred ceremonies, then later beginning to sell his works through the government settlement of Maningrida. He is one of the few men who remember the old artists of the caves and can give detailed interpretations of the figures and content of the cave paintings. His subject matter and stories are a direct continuation of the cave-art tradition, although his style of image-making is distinctive, particularly the rendition of his figures and rarrk (cross-hatching). His work has a raw, rough, and direct quality, in which the use of white dotted areas on black is a stylistic marker. His cross-hatching is open and unlabored. Kubarkku is one of the great living Kunwinjku artists, and is part of the flourishing group of artists that also includes John Mawurndjul and James Iyuna (page 178). His works are held in most of the major Australian public galleries and museums, and the Kelton Foundation, Los Angeles.

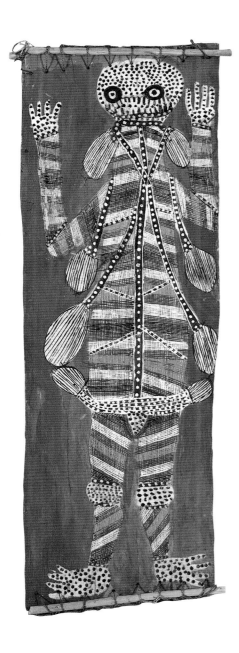

PLATE 59 (above)
Mick Kubarkku, b. c. 1925
Dibdib Spirit, 1997
138 x 46 cm (54.5 x 18 in.)
Earth ochers on bark

PLATE 60 (right)
Mick Kubarkku, b. c. 1925
*Ngalyod, Rainbow Serpent,
from the Rock-holes at Kubumi*, 1995
190 x 67 cm (75 x 23.5 in.)
Earth ochers on bark

James Iyuna

Mandjabu, Conical Fish-trap with Barramundi

Until recently, conical fish-traps were important items of equipment, used daily throughout central and western Arnhem Land. These traps, called mandjabu, are made of the flexible canes of the milmil vine, *Malasia scandens*, and are laid horizontally in tidal inlets and streams. The traps have a "neck" or entrance that is set to face the receding tide. Often a fence is used to guide the fish to the mouth of the trap. When the water is high, the fish swim inside; then, as the water recedes, the fish remain within the belly of the conical trap, unable to swim out of the neck. The technology of these traps is part of Kunwinjku law. The traps are associated with a specific geographical site where the mandjabu became "djang," or spirit.

Using the finest hair brushes and cross-hatched lines, Iyuna has simultaneously shown the trap and disguised it under the reeds. Namarrkol, the great barramundi of the northern Australian waters, is just visible caught within, facing the conical mouth of the trap.

Biographical Notes

An eastern Kunwinjku painter, James Iyuna is part of a long tradition of exceptionally fine bark painters whose themes reflect the Ancestral Spirits and religious beliefs of the escarpment people of eastern Arnhem Land. He explores the formation of natural phenomena and particular relic marks left by the Creation Ancestors, including the barramundi (Namarrkol), mimih spirits, and the Rainbow Serpent (Ngalyod).

James Iyuna's father, Anchor Galumba, was known as an expert fish-trap craftsman. James and his brother John Mawurndjul have been leading bark painters since the early 1980s. They are among the most highly regarded of the artists who work through Maningrida Arts and Crafts in central Arnhem Land. The brothers live in the outstation community of Mumeka, south of Maningrida on the Liverpool River. James Iyuna's work has been included in numerous collections, including those of the National Gallery of Australia, National Gallery of Victoria, the Art Gallery of Western Australia, and the National Maritime Museum, Sydney.

PLATE 61
James Iyuna, b. 1959
Mandjabu, Conical Fish-trap with Barramundi, 1990
225 x 77 cm (88.5 x 30.5 in.)
Earth ochers on bark

Sally Garromara

Fish-trap

The sculptural shapes of conical fish-traps are depicted both in abstract and in highly representational forms in many bark paintings from western Arnhem Land. Parts of the landscape west of Maningrida are said to be the metamorphosed forms of fish-traps left by the Creation Ancestors. Deeper meanings connect these everyday objects with their function of replenishing and renewing the human species. In song and ceremony, the entry of fish to and from the neck-like opening is compared with the sexual act, the process of birth, and the renewal of life itself.

These fiber sculptures are part of a tradition that extends back millennia, and are one of the few important fiber utensils still made today and sometimes used for their original purpose. They are one of the oldest forms of art that have retained their original function and are in use.

Biographical Notes

Sally Garromara speaks Nakkara language and is one of many artists and craftspeople who sell their work through the Maningrida Arts and Culture Centre. She is proficient at spinning bark and other fiber strings, twining and weaving dilly bags, and making coiled baskets of pandanus fiber. In 1997 her weaving was exhibited in the Netherlands.

PLATE 62 (below)
Sally Garromara
Fish-trap, c. 1994
165 cm (65 in.) long
Weaving

PLATE 61 (detail opposite)
James Iyuna, b. 1959
*Mandjabu, Conical Fish-trap
with Barramundi*, 1990
225 x 77 cm (88.5 x 30.5 in.)
Earth ochers on bark

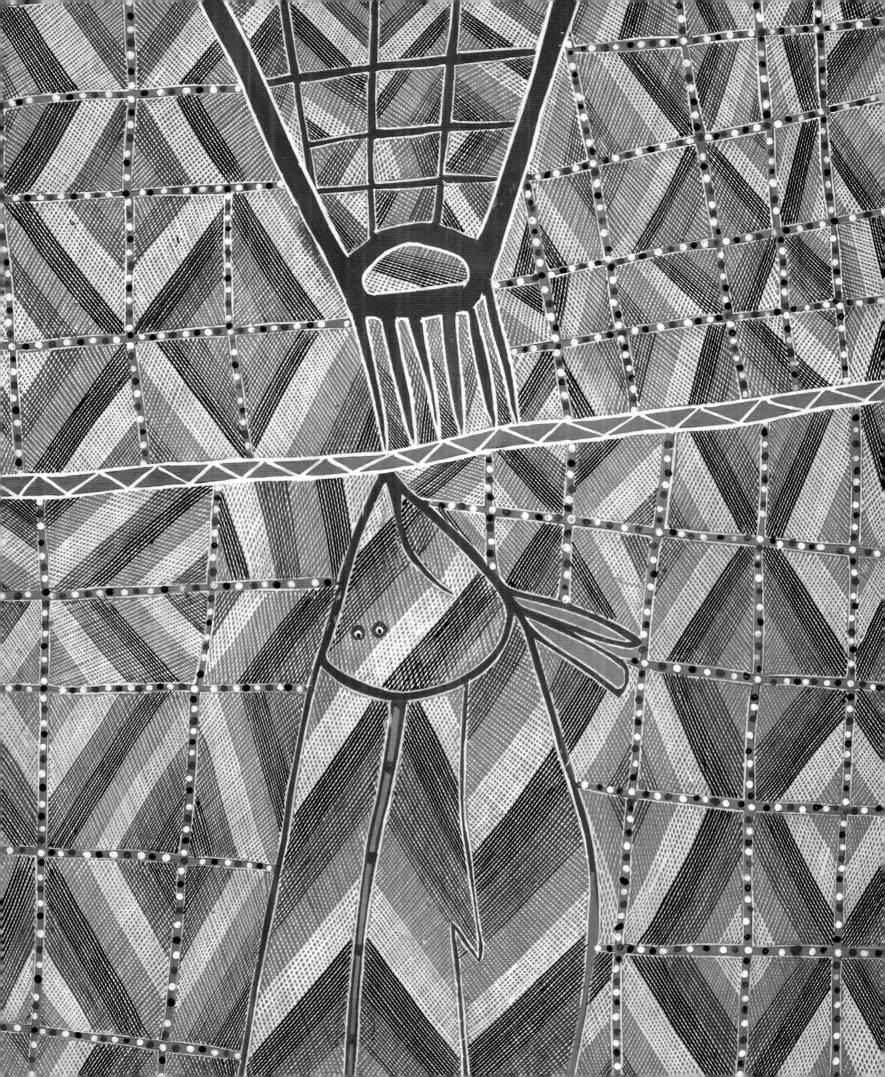

Owen Yalandja

Yawk Yawk Spirits

Yawk yawk are female water spirits that in appearance and habit closely resemble the European notion of mermaids. Half spirits and half fish, they entice unwary fishermen beneath the water of the lagoons in Arnhem Land that are their domain. They also have an association with sorcery and occasionally show a malevolent tendency, like the mimih, who are dry-land spirits of the rocky escarpment country.

Yawk yawk are closely associated with Ngalyod, the Rainbow Serpent. They may have long hair like reeds of trailing water weed, and can take on the features of fish or the bodies of snakes. Specific sites are regarded as the remains of yawk yawk transformed into rock or waterhole features during the Creation era (Dreaming or Wongar time). One such place, known as the "Dreaming Lady," is now the permanent home of the Dangkorlo clan, to which the artist, Owen Yalandja, belongs.

Biographical Notes

Born about 1957, Owen Yalandja has lived all his life on his tribal lands in western Arnhem Land, apart from a well-remembered trip to London to perform traditional dances. His usual residence is Barrodjowkkeng, but, along with his family and other Kunwinjku, he may move camp seasonally to different rivers and swamp areas to hunt, fish and enjoy bush foods. He is known for his carved and painted sculptures as well as bark paintings of mimih and yawk yawk. He continues to perform as a key singer at traditional ceremonies.

PLATE 63
Owen Yalandja, b. c. 1957
Yawk Yawk Spirits, 1997
130 x 14 cm (51 x 5.5 in.) 105 x 12 cm (41.5 x 4.5 in.)
Earth ocher on carved wood

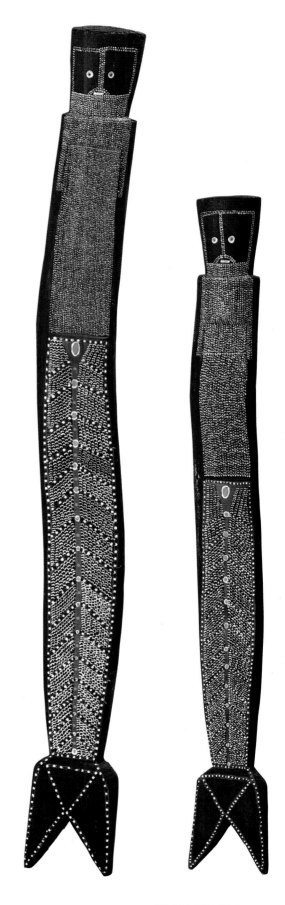

Mirigunbala

Untitled

This is an abstract depiction of plant forms showing three trees associated with food. Such paintings are elaborately and hypnotically painted on the chests of dancers at particular ceremonial occasions — initiations, funerals, and nature "increase" or renewal ceremonies. At another level of interpretation the design is a map of country and a reference to the artist's clan ownership of that country.

Biographical Notes

Mirigunbala has principally concentrated on art for ceremonial or traditional purposes, but for short periods produced works on bark for sale through Maningrida Arts and Culture. This work was completed in 1978 at Bureda, a remote outstation where a few families lived in bark shelters, continuing their seasonal hunting practices in the forests and at the waterholes of western Arnhem Land. The families supplemented their wild foods by selling art works to make occasional purchases from the Maningrida store, which sent supply trucks to the satellite communities.

PLATE 64 (left, detail opposite)
Mirigunbala
Untitled, 1978
90 x 55 cm (35.5 x 21.5 in.)
Earth ochers on bark

Terry Ngamandara

Gulach (Spike Rush) at Barlparnarra

The painting is the detailed clan design used in sacred ceremonies for owners of the gulach or spike rush, *Eleocharis dulcis*, which covers much of the swamp area at Barlparnarra, western Arnhem Land. The slender, light-green spiky reeds form a thickly woven carpet across the water, their corms descending into the mud beneath. Groups of women move through the swamp, gathering the sweet, nutty corms and removing the rough outer layer. Sometimes these corms are ground and made into a paste, then formed into cakes. The corms are also an important food of magpie geese.

This design is painted on the chests of ceremonial initiates at circumcisions and during other rituals.

Biographical Notes

Terry Ngamandara was born outside Darwin in a bush camp where his mother and father were living. Shortly thereafter, his family returned to their clan country near the Cadell River in western Arnhem Land, close to the large swamp, Barlparnarra. Here, Terry Ngamandara became immersed in the religion and culture of his own people, the Girnimba and Garramirra, and was fully trained under traditional men's law in the designs for totems, including gulach (spike rush) and water goanna.

The community forms part of the Gochan Jiny-jirra outstation associated with the Djankawu Creation sisters (ancestors of the Dhuwa moiety, at Barlparnarra termed Murlurlu). The journey route of the two women arrives at the Barlparnarra swamp.

Before taking up painting on bark, Ngamandara spent time in the nearby Aboriginal community of Maningrida, where he did construction and forestry work, as well as laboring in fishing enterprises. This technical training assisted him when he later turned to art under the tutelage of the senior artist England Banggala. His bark paintings are held in the collections of the Art Gallery of New South Wales, Art Gallery of South Australia, National Gallery of Victoria, and National Gallery of Australia.

PLATE 65
Terry Ngamandara, b. 1950
Gulach (Spike Rush) at Barlparnarra, 1996
168 x 85 cm (66 x 33.5 in.)
Earth ochers on bark

Nguminala

Clan Country

The design refers to particular waterholes in the artist's clan estate in the escarpment area of western Arnhem Land. The waterholes are shown as circles in the center of the work. On either side are water weeds and plants that rest on the surface of the water.

Another interpretation was given by the artist in 1972: that the leaf shapes that look like surface daphnia, swimming with whip-tailed flagella, also represent waterlily seed-cases. These are all subjects explored by artists from this area and are closely connected to the Rainbow Serpent. Such full-frame designs of closely hatched patterns or rarrk are imbued with creative power, and are also painted on the bodies of ceremonial participants.

Biographical Notes

Nguminala is an occasional artist who in 1972 lived a traditional hunting lifestyle in the escarpment country of western Arnhem Land. His paintings were collected by community staff at Maningrida.

PLATE 66 (left, detail opposite)
Nguminala
Clan Country, 1972
59.5 x 31 cm (23.5 x 12 in.)
Earth ochers on bark

Philip Guthayguthay

Spirit Figures

This painting shows two Ancestral women known as the Wagilak sisters with their sacred digging sticks (the elongated shapes on either side). The Wagilak story extends across Arnhem Land, beginning in the far east and continuing through Ramingining, the artist's country. The Sisters are primary creative figures who gave birth to all the clans of the Dhuwa moiety and formed many features of the landscape, particularly the waterholes, which they made by inserting their digging sticks into the earth. Their journey finished at a sacred waterhole, where they were swallowed by the giant python, who was angered that one of the sisters had polluted his watery home.

Biographical Notes

Philip Guthayguthay was born in 1935 in the bush at Lirrabambitj, about six miles from the present location of Ramingining. At the time, his clan, the Liyagalawumirri, lived in bark houses known as galawu. His painting subjects reflect personal totems associated with the Wagilak story, especially the native cat or quoll from which he gets his nickname "Pussycat."

At different times he has been a stockman, a construction worker, and a crocodile shooter, selling hides to the mission at Milingimbi. He has been a bark painter since the 1960s, first at Milingimbi and later on the mainland.

In 1983 Guthayguthay held a solo exhibition of his clan patterns in a prominent Sydney gallery, becoming the first bark artist to have his work accepted as contemporary abstract paintings. Djon Mundine, the art adviser at Ramingining at the time, has described Guthayguthay as an industrious and enthusiastic artist who worked long hours into the night, cradling a torch on his neck in order to keep painting, because his house had no electricity. His paintings are held in the collections of many public galleries, including the National Gallery of Australia, National Gallery of Victoria, and Museum of Contemporary Art, Sydney.

PLATE 67
Philip Guthayguthay, b. 1935
Spirit Figures, 1996
125 x 65 cm (49 x 25.5 in.)
Earth ocher on bark

Joe Djembungu

Niwuda Honey

This is a ritually important image of three sacred objects or rangga, which symbolize bush honey. The rangga are constructions made of rolled wads of paperbark tightly bound with hand-spun string. A long string tassel hangs from the rounded end. The string surface is painted with ocher in diamond patterns, which are the Yirritja moiety's honey design. In Arnhem Land there are several species of native bee. These insects are classified according to the same kinship system applied to human beings, some being Yirritja, some from the opposite moiety, the Dhuwa. The designs for each are distinctive.

The cells of the hive are shown empty (red), with pollen and bee eggs (black) and full of honey (white). The ovoid black shapes are the entrances to the hive, where the bees can be spotted by honey-gatherers as they fly to and from the tree.

The Niwuda honey design is used in sacred dances during a number of ceremonies, including species increase ceremonies and funerary ceremonies. The design may be painted on the bodies of dancers or applied to many other objects. The rangga objects in this painting are thought to embody the power of the honey Ancestor who found or gave the honey to today's people, the Yolngu.

Biographical Notes

Born in central Arnhem Land in 1935, Joe Djembungu is one of the principal songmen at Ramingining. At important initiation ceremonies, when large groups of related families gather, many attend each day's ritual singing and instruction for the initiates. Djon Mundine, the art adviser at Ramingining in the 1980s, has recalled that at the largest and most important ceremonies Joe Djembungu was always there, leading the singing with a beautiful baritone voice. Djembungu's bark paintings are a reflection of his ritual leadership in Yirritja law, and principally his inherited responsibility for the lands associated with honey "business."

PLATE 68
Joe Djembungu, b. 1935
Niwuda Honey, c. 1988
113 x 35 cm (44.5 x 14 in.)
Earth ochers on bark

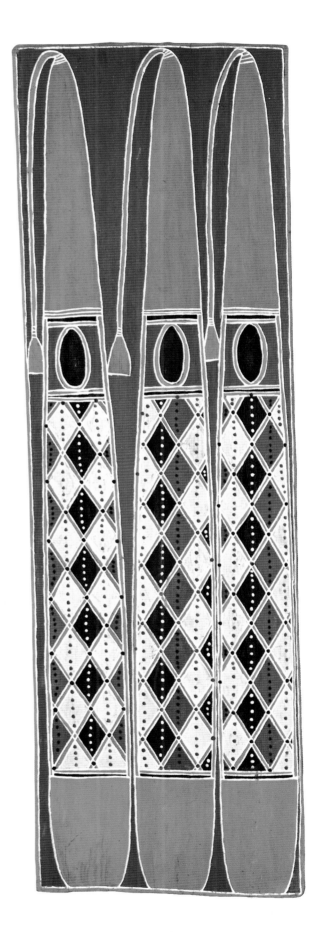

Jimmy Wululu

Yirritja Honey Story

This is a highly contemporary, abstract rendition of the sacred body designs used for dancers and ceremonial participants in Yirritja ceremonies. These ceremonies re-enact aspects of the Creation stories linked to the presence of wild honey. The people of central Arnhem Land distinguish several types of honey according to the type of bee and the honey produced. As with all aspects of the natural world, different species of bees belong either to the Yirritja or to the Dhuwa moieties.

This painting shows the design of Niwuda, the Yirritja honey bee. In the Yirritja Creation beliefs, honey was spread across Arnhem Land from east to west. A fire broke out in the east and spread across the country. Tiny quail-like birds called djirigitj fled before the fire, and are said to have carried honey across the country to central Arnhem Land.

Wululu has refined the totemic representation of honey to this pattern. The diamond design is the insignia of the Yirritja clans and symbolizes the individual cells of the beehive. Various patterns within the cells show them as full, partially full, or empty of honey.

Biographical Notes

Jimmy Wululu was born in the bush in 1936. He lived a traditional life until the establishment of missionary settlements on the central Arnhem Land coast, notably at Milingimbi. A member of the Daygurrgurr clan, he speaks Gupapuyngu language and lives at Ramingining. The art of this area is vigorous, highly stylized, and emphasizes design and draftsmanship in the representation of traditional body-painting patterns, as well as following linear figurative depictions of Creation events in the landscape.

Wululu worked for a time as a builder in the settlement of Ramingining, and his draftsmanship and tight structure have a craftsman-like precision. He is noted for his minimalist work, particularly the catfish design and honey design, for which he is a custodian. His works are included in the National Gallery of Australia; Art Gallery of New South Wales; Art Gallery of South Australia; National Gallery of Victoria; Museum of Contemporary Art, Sydney; and the Kluge-Ruhe Aboriginal Art Collection in Charlottesville, Virginia.

PLATE 69
Jimmy Wululu, b. 1936
Yirritja Honey Story, 1997
77 x 47 cm (30.5 x 18.5 in.)
Earth ochers on bark

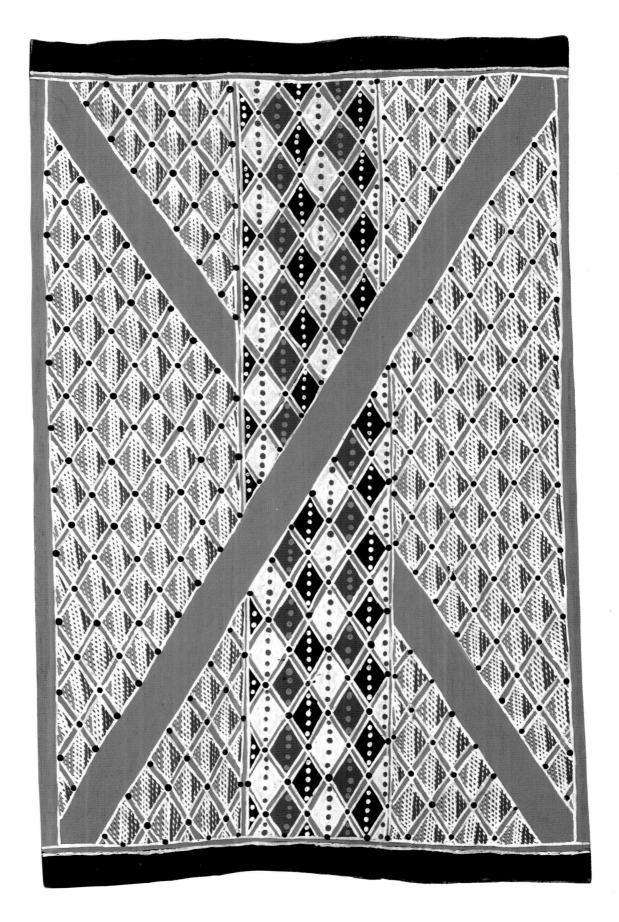

David Malangi

Gunmirringu Mortuary Rites

This is one of many archetypal representations of the story of the great hunter Gunmirringu painted by David Malangi, who concentrated on this theme in the 1960s and 1970s. The story concerns a hunter, a great Creation Ancestor, who moved across Manarrngu country until he encountered a great snake beneath a particular tree and was killed. His death and the ritual that ensued marked the first mortuary ceremony.

The painting shows this ceremony in progress. The body of Gunmirringu is in the center. Around it are two songmen with their clap-sticks and other partial figures, including kangaroos, as well as sacred objects that have significance in the Gunmirringu story, such as the stone axe at lower left. The figure at top (torso only shown) is holding a kangaroo leg. The tree form is that of a sacred white-flowering plum tree.

In 1966, when Australia adopted decimal currency, the central motif of the original dollar note was a direct representation of the Gunmirringu story from one of Malangi's bark paintings. The artist knew nothing of this until he saw the note. In compensation, the Reserve Bank recognized Malangi's copyright, awarded him compensation, and so began the recognition of Aboriginal copyright that continues in Australian public life today.

The copyright infringement hurt Malangi greatly at the time, particularly as part of his most important sacred ritual information was used without consent. In Aboriginal law this type of offense carries the most serious punishment. The designer unwittingly compounded the infringement by intermixing Malangi's imagery with a number of other Aboriginal figures from the cave paintings of western Arnhem Land, an area unrelated to Malangi.

Malangi now recalls the whole event with some pride. The Australian government awarded him a gold medal, which remains one of his proudest possessions in his beautiful bush camp at the waterlily-covered lagoon, Yathalamara.

Biographical Notes

David Malangi was born in 1927, and for most of his life he has lived at Yathalamara with his extended family. He is the head of the Manarrngu clan and is one of the most powerful elders of central Arnhem Land. With the death of clan leaders who owned adjacent lands, Malangi inherited custodianship for vast tracts of land on either side of the Goyder River, and associated responsibilities for caring for sacred sites recounting the journeys of both the Djankawu Creation Ancestors and of the Ancestor Gunmirringu.

Malangi is a prolific artist whose work has been sought after by major international collectors since the 1960s. In style, his bold collection of individual imagery and shapes on a clear red ocher or sometimes black ground has influenced several other central Arnhem Land painters. His strong, graphic images, often thickly outlined in white, return to particular themes, but always in differing formations.

PLATE 70
David Malangi, b. 1927
Gunmirringu Mortuary Rites, 1972
69 x 53 cm (27 x 21 in.)
Natural earth pigments on eucalyptus bark

Henry Nupurra

Feathered Morning Star Pole

The Morning Star pole is used in Morning Star rituals, which are still held in central and eastern Arnhem Land. Tall, thin poles such as this are used in lengthy song ceremonies. The feathered tassels represent the Morning Star moving at dawn. In ceremonies relics of deceased people are occasionally attached to these tassels. Traditionally the timbers are cut and bound with string; when the ceremonial pole is complete, its makers take it to the hosts of the ceremony and receive payment.

Today these poles are also made for specialized exhibition in major art galleries. They are owned by the traditional custodians of the Morning Star ceremony, or Marradjirri ceremony. The string is from the bark of the kurrajong tree. White cockatoo feathers are used to represent the stars. The small orange feathers are from the neck of the northern rainbow lorikeet. No cockatoos are killed during the collecting of these feathers, because they are a sacred bird and a totem of the Marradjirri traditional custodians.

Yolngu believe that when a person dies the spirit returns to Burralku, the home of the dead. The spirit people at Burralku begin the Morning Star ceremony, which goes throughout the night. One old woman keeps Banumbirr, the Morning Star, in her dilly bag. Just before sunrise, when the moon sinks beneath the horizon, the ceremony rises to a climax. There is a dark quiet, then the star appears to herald the morning. Dancers playing didgeridoo and clap-sticks re-enact this ceremony throughout eastern Arnhem Land, recreating the events of the Creation Time when the old lady opened her dilly bag to release the Morning Star, which then traveled across the sky from eastern Arnhem Land to the west.[8]

Biographical Notes

Henry Nupurra was born in 1932 and is a senior artist of the Djambarrpuyngu people of Elcho Island or Galiwinku in northeast Arnhem Land. He is a prominent participant in the ceremonies he calls "memory ceremonies," which are held about one year after a death. At these ceremonies, the spirit of the deceased is sent to the home of the Morning Star in dances and rituals involving these feathered poles.

PLATE 71 (right)
Henry Nupurra, b. 1932
Feathered Morning Star Pole, 1997
153 cm (60 in.) high
Wood, string, ocher, feathers, and beeswax

PLATE 72 (detail opposite)
Galuma Maymuru, b. 1951
Manggalili at Djarrakpi, 1997
257.3 x 110 cm (101.3 x 43.5 in.)
Earth ochers on bark

Galuma Maymuru

Manggalili at Djarrakpi

The full creative history of the Manggalili clan's homeland of Djarrakpi is depicted in episodes in this work. Djarrakpi was founded by Guwark the night bird and Marrngu the possum, and the site is marked today by a sacred tree, the wild cashew, marawili. The central theme is the connection this tree forms between the temporal and spiritual domain. Guwark the bird roosts on this tree. The possum, Marrngu, travels up and down the tree, tending sacred strings of possum fur, which are the connection between Manggalili people's spirits and the afterlife in the sky above. The clan design shown beside Marrngu is the representation of the scratch marks of possum feet on the marawili and on the land.

The mortuary ceremonies observed by Manggalili include the construction of a large, low sand sculpture, the yingapungapu. This area is marked out on the painting as a large lozenge shape, together with significant Ancestors and totemic figures. Crabs' tracks are also associated with this section.

Behind the sand dunes at Djarrakpi is a large lake associated with the female Creation Ancestor, Nyapalyngu. She is shown twice, standing beside her large sacred digging stick. The lake is also shown, edged with dunes and possums. One edge of the lake was created from possum-fur string, which has now formed a shallow dune.

These great paintings are major tracts, documents that in both content and layout reveal Yolngu religious beliefs and land-creation information. They follow, in plan form, the geography of the land and the sacred features that are apparent even today.

Biographical Notes

Galuma Maymuru is the daughter of Narritjin Maymuru, a master artist who was leader of the Manggalili clan during the first Aboriginal land rights case in 1970–71. She is married to Dhukal Wirrpanda (see page 202) and lives in northeast Arnhem Land, sometimes at Baniyala outstation, but mainly on her husband's country at Dhuruputjpi. She paints for the artists' co-operative at Yirrkala, Buku-Larrnggay Mulka Arts. The themes and designs in her paintings follow the wealth of imagery taught to her by her father and uncles.

A qualified schoolteacher, Galuma grew up watching her father paint at a time when he was recognized as among a handful of immensely important eastern Arnhem Land painters. She was one of the first Yolngu women taught full Manggalili clan designs, sacred designs that were previously the domain of men fully trained in song and ritual information.

Galuma's bark paintings have been exhibited at the National Aboriginal Art Awards in Darwin since 1984, and at major exhibitions of Yirrkala bark paintings in Sydney and Brisbane. Her paintings are held at the National Gallery of Australia and by the Kelton Foundation in Los Angeles.

PLATE 72
Galuma Maymuru, b. 1951
Manggalili at Djarrakpi, 1997
257.3 x 110 cm (101.3 x 43.5 in.)
Earth ochers on bark

Dhukal Wirrpanda

Dhalwangu at Dhuruputjpi

This complex work is an episodic depiction of Creation aspects of the land of the Djapu clan and the events that formed the land, particularly at the area now known as Dhuruputjpi. It shows four separate areas of country, signaled by the shark, the tall water birds called brolgas, the sunrise, and honey.

The shark or Bulmandji is a central Creation Ancestor for the Djapu people. Bulmandji was lying in the sun on the sandy shore when the Creation Ancestor Mureiana (or Ganbulabula) came to hunt with his two wives. While the women were gathering oysters, they came upon the shark, and when they reported this to their husband, he rushed to the beach and speared the shark.

The wounded shark traveled on until he came to Djapu country, where he named himself Mana, making his camp in Dhuruputjpi Creek at a beautiful large freshwater lagoon. Various locations in the land are named for the different part of the shark's body: head, fins, back, tail, and gall bladder.

The shark Dreaming intersects with the great Creation story of the Djankawu, the Creation Ancestors of the Dhuwa moiety. The Djankawu traveled to the area close to Dhuruputjpi known as Yalata, a grassy plain with clumps of vegetation fed by freshwater springs created by the sisters' digging sticks. This story is shown in the panel beside that depicting Mana the shark. Here brolgas are walking to and from the water springs in search of food, their footprints visible in the mud. Many brolgas live there today. The background linear design represents leaves floating on the surface of the water.

The third segment of the bark painting shows a simplified and sacred design of one of these wells, and the circle also represents the first sunrise, Walirr.

The fourth segment, which exhibits strong diamond-patterned designs, relates to the sugar-bag design that was painted on Mureiana's chest. The diamonds are the cells of the beehive, shown as empty and full. The lozenge-shape is a sacred emblem associated with this area, and the round-topped emblem is an actual rock in the landscape where the Ancestors were hunting when they first came upon the shark. The small area of land is the traditional country of the clans known as "bottom" Dhalwangu and Warrimirri.

PLATE 73
Dhukal Wirrpanda, b. 1957
Dhalwangu at Dhuruputjpi, 1997
313 x 124 cm (123 x 49 in.)
Earth ochers on bark

Biographical Notes

Dhukal Wirrpanda was born in 1957. His father's name was Djungi, and he is the husband of Galuma Maymuru. With his brother Wuyal, he is the leader of the Dhudi-djapu clan of the Dhuwa moiety. He divides his time between Dhuruputjpi and Baniyala, two outstation communities in northeast Arnhem Land, and works through the art center at Yirrkala, the Buku-Larrnggay Mulka Centre.

Dhukal Wirrpanda is one of the most prominent of the younger artists from the Buku-Larrnggay Mulka Centre. He is also renowned for his carved and painted wooden figures. He has exhibited carvings or paintings since 1984, beginning at a major exhibition of artworks by the clans of Baniyala held by the Crafts Council in Sydney. Some of his large episodic works were featured at the National Aboriginal and Torres Strait Islander Art Awards at the Museum and Art Gallery of the Northern Territory in 1996, 1997, and 1998. His paintings are held in the National Gallery of Australia and the Kluge-Ruhe Aboriginal Art Collection in Charlottesville, Virginia.

Dhukul Wirrpanda completed this painting for the exhibition *Native Title*, which was held at the Museum of Contemporary Art, Sydney, in September–October 1997. A strongly political work, like others from related clans, it tells in episodes the creation of the land by the Spirit Ancestors of the present-day Yolngu peoples of the area. Paintings of this kind have been used as title deeds or visual documents in defending Aboriginal land rights in Australian courts and Parliament.

PLATE 73 (detail)
Dhukal Wirrpanda, b. 1957
Dhalwangu at Dhuruputjpi, 1997
313 x 124 cm (123 x 49 in.)
Earth ochers on bark

The Pukumani Ceremony

Andrew Freddy Puruntatameri, Mathew Freddy Puruntatameri, John Wilson, Leon Puruntatameri and Pedro Wonaeamirri.

The Tiwi Ancestor Purukuparli first decreed that death should come into the world, and made the first Pukumani ceremony. In 1984 Declan Apuatimi (see page 217) and Raphael Apuatimi gave the following version of the Pukumani story to Margie West of the Museum and Art Gallery of the Northern Territory.

The First Death — The Story of Purukuparli

Purukuparli had a wife, Waiji (Bima). His brother the moon-man Tapara did not have a wife; he was a single man. He watched Waiji with her baby Jinani as she went out hunting for bush tucker for her husband. Tapara followed her and took her into the bush with him all day [committed adultery], and brought her back late in the afternoon. She had left Jinani, Purukuparli's son, in the heat all day without food, and he died of hunger. Purukuparli said to Tapara, "You took my wife away all day and then my son died of hunger!" Tapara said, "You'll have to give me that little boy so I can heal him. In three days I can bring him back alive," but Purukuparli said, "No! We have got to follow my son. Nobody returns now, we will all die. We have all got to follow that little boy."

Then Purukuparli and Tapara began to fight with forked clubs, and Purukuparli stabbed his brother in the eye. Tapara went up into the sky and three days later he turned into the full moon. Today you can see the marks that Purukuparli made with his club, Taputaringa, as dark spots on the moon. Purukuparli picked up Jinani's body and walked far into the sea and they both drowned. He left his wife behind in the bush and she turned into a curlew. You can still hear her today crying out in sadness and in shame for what she did. Before he drowned, Purukuparli taught all Tiwi how to do a proper mourning ceremony. Ever since then, when someone dies, people make burial posts, paint themselves and dance. This is the Tiwi custom and everybody has to follow it.[9]

Pukumani Poles

The Tiwi carve these decorated burial poles or Tutini Pukumani for positioning around the grave approximately a year after a person has died. A full Pukumani ceremony then takes place, with associated body painting and sequential dancing and performances to ensure that the soul of the deceased is at rest and to release the living relatives from the taboos associated with their proximity to the deceased (including restrictions on food and social contact). To prepare for the ceremony, specific relatives commission master carvers to make Pukumani poles. When the ceremony is completed, the grave and its stationary sculptures are left to the elements.

The poles represent the assembled figures of relatives and Ancestors. Those with figures on top represent the Ancestral Beings connected to the Pukumani story, in particular Purukuparli, Bima, Tapara, and Jinani. Pukumani poles with forked prongs signify the ensuing fight with clubs, while others show the birds that were present at the first funeral ceremony.

Biographical Notes

Andrew Freddy Puruntatameri

Andrew Freddy Puruntatameri (other names Jarman and Patrick) was born in 1973. A relatively young Tiwi carver, Andrew Freddy is strong and enthusiastic, preferring to make large, dramatic works requiring strength and skill such as this one, depicting Jurrukukuni (the owl) on top of the Pukumani pole.

The son of Paddy Freddy Puruntatameri, a great Tiwi carver, he is one of the most important traditional carvers and painters working at Jilamara Arts and Crafts at Milikapiti on Melville Island. His traditional country is Munupi, to the east of Milikapiti, and his skin or kinship group is pandanus.

Andrew Freddy is a keeper of the owl dance as represented in this carving, and even his house is painted with many owl images. He has contributed to group exhibitions since 1992, and also to Tiwi installations at the Museum of Victoria, National Gallery of Victoria, and National Maritime Museum, Sydney.

Mathew Freddy Puruntatameri

Mathew Freddy Puruntatameri was born in 1972 and lives at Milikapiti on Melville Island. His traditional country is Munupi on Melville Island; his skin or kinship group is pandanus, and, like his brother Andrew, he is the owner of the owl dance. He hunts regularly for enjoyment and as a continuation of Tiwi land use, and is particularly famed for his stingray-spearing forays.

Since 1992 he has worked for Jilamara Arts and Crafts at Milikapiti, making ocher paintings on paper, canvas, and bark, as well as ironwood carvings. Mathew Freddy acts as an assistant in the craft center, helping his disabled sister with art work. He has exhibited extensively throughout Australia.

John Wilson

John Wilson was born in 1955 and presently lives at Milikapiti on Melville Island in the Tiwi homelands, where he is a famous sea hunter. His kinship group or skin group is fire, and his dance is that of the magpie goose. John Wilson staunchly upholds traditional customs and beliefs, particularly the legend of Purukuparli, which he is famous for recounting. A student of the history of Tiwi carving, he sometimes takes six months to complete one work.

John Wilson has worked as a printmaker and is one of the master carvers and painters among the Tiwi today. He has exhibited widely with other Tiwi artists, and his unique figurative representations of Ancestral characters such as Purukuparli, Bima, and Tapara are held in the collections of major Australian museums, including the Museum of Victoria and the National Gallery of Victoria. His work also forms part of a major Tiwi installation at the National Maritime Museum, Sydney.

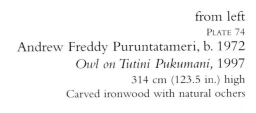

from left
PLATE 74
Andrew Freddy Puruntatameri, b. 1972
Owl on Tutini Pukumani, 1997
314 cm (123.5 in.) high
Carved ironwood with natural ochers

PLATE 75
Mathew Freddy Puruntatameri, b. 1972
Forked Tutini Pukumani, 1997
304 cm (119.5 in.) high
Carved ironwood with natural ochers

PLATE 76
John Wilson, b. 1955
Ancestral Figure, 1997
91 cm (36 in.) high
Carved ironwood with natural ochers

PLATE 77
John Wilson, b. 1955
Ancestral Figure, 1997
93 cm (36.5 in.) high
Carved ironwood with natural ochers

PLATE 78
John Wilson, b. 1955
Ancestral Figure, 1997
93 cm (36.5 in.) high
Carved ironwood with natural ochers

from left

PLATE 79
Leon Puruntatameri, b. 1949
Tokwampini, 1977
73 cm (28.5 in.) high
Carved ironwood with natural ochers

PLATE 80
Leon Puruntatameri, b. 1949
Tokwampini, 1977
93 cm (36.5 in.) high
Carved ironwood with natural ochers

PLATE 81
Leon Puruntatameri, b. 1949
Tutini Pukumani, 1997
313 cm (123 in.) high
Carved ironwood with natural ochers

PLATE 82
Leon Puruntatameri, b. 1949
Bird on Tutini Pukumani, 1997
347 cm (136.5 in.) high
Carved ironwood with natural ochers

PLATE 83
Pedro Wonaeamirri, b. 1974
Jinani on Tutini Pukumani, 1997
295 cm (116 in.) high
Carved ironwood with natural ochers

Leon Puruntatameri

Leon Puruntatameri is a respected traditional carver. He was born in 1949, and has lived in the Tiwi Islands all his life. In the 1950s he attended the small Catholic mission school at Nguiu on Bathurst Island. After this he worked in road and house construction in the small communities on Melville Island. At present he lives at Milikapiti on Melville Island. His traditional lands are further to the east at Munupi. His kinship group is the scaly mullet, and he is owner of the jungle fowl dance.

A proficient and meticulous carver and painter, Leon Puruntatameri has been active in the arts all his life. He is often commissioned to make important Pukumani poles for major funeral ceremonies, and he has executed carved poles for important public art installations, including the Darwin Airport. His carvings form part of the permanent collections of the National Maritime Museum, Sydney; the National Gallery of Victoria; and Campbelltown City Art Gallery, New South Wales.

Pedro Wonaeamirri

Pedro (or Gurrumaiyuwa) Wonaeamirri was born in 1974 and is therefore one of the younger Tiwi artists currently painting on paper and canvas as well as making Pukumani carvings and figures for the Jilamara Arts and Crafts community at Milikapiti on Melville Island. His country is Goose Creek, where he hunts magpie geese; his skin or kinship group is pandanus, and he is owner of the magpie goose dance. He has exhibited with the Tiwi artists from Milikapiti since 1992, and his work is included in installations at the Museum of Victoria, National Gallery of Victoria, and National Maritime Museum, Sydney. In 1996 he was awarded an Australia Council Fellowship.

Pedro Wonaeamirri has traveled extensively in Australia, and is the current president of Jilamara Arts and Crafts. In 1988 he was the Northern Territory's nomination for Young Australian of the Year. A skilled diplomat, he upholds Tiwi culture rigorously, maintaining an earlier, now rare, "old Tiwi" language and painting his artwork only with the traditional wooden comb rather than modern brushes.

from left
PLATE 76 (detail)
John Wilson, b. 1955
Ancestral Figure (detail), 1977
91 cm (36 in.) high
Carved ironwood with natural ochers

PLATE 77 (detail)
John Wilson, b. 1955
Ancestral Figure (detail), 1997
93 cm (36.5 in.) high
Carved ironwood with natural ochers

PLATE 78 (detail)
John Wilson, b. 1955
Ancestral Figure (detail), 1997
93 cm (36.5 in.) high
Carved ironwood with natural ochers

Enraeld Djulabinyanna

Tapara

This sculpture of a male figure depicts Tapara the moon or moon man, who plays a central part in the Purukuparli story, the source of the Tiwi Pukumani ceremony (see page 206). Funeral ceremonies today continue the ancient Tiwi practice of mourning the dead with elaborate dances. Each person comes forward from the group to carry out a spectacular solo dance depicting aspects of the Purukuparli narrative or illustrating their own connection to their country or to animals and sea creatures.

The expressive qualities of this carving echo aspects of Tiwi dance. Soloists lean forward, hunching their shoulders, with their arms extended straight before or beside them away from the body. Strong rhythmic stomping with bent knees is part of the performance. Full body painting gives each participant the appearance of a moving sculpture. Brightly painted geometric patterns camouflage their bodies so that they blend with the Pukumani poles and the other dance participants.

Biographical Notes

Born around 1885, Enraeld Djulabinyanna was a celebrated Tiwi artist who achieved fame in the 1950s and 1960s. His work was collected by Dorothy Bennett (see page 159), who placed it in key Australian collections. Djulabinyanna was renowned for his carvings of Purukuparli and Bima. Two of these are held in the National Gallery of Australia.

PLATE 84
Enraeld Djulabinyanna, c. 1885–1970s
Tapara, c. 1955
55 cm (21.5 in.) high
Natural ochers on ironwood

Freda Warlipini

Body Designs

The design is quintessentially Tiwi — geometric ocher designs that are related to similar patterns applied to three-dimensional objects such as burial poles, tunga (bark baskets), and elaborate and beautiful body and face paintings.

The work of Freda Warlipini is often rugged and excitingly free. She paints with wide, modified brushes, and uses only the rich yellow, red, black, and white ocher colors that occur naturally in the Tiwi islands. The painted designs are specific to the artist, but are also made as a public commitment to Tiwi culture, which is quite distinct from mainland indigenous culture.

Biographical Notes

Freda Warlipini is approximately sixty-five years old and lives at Milikapiti on Melville Island. She lived a fully traditional life on her own Tiwi land, known as Mirrikawuyanga, until a mission removed her from her parents at a young age. She then lived on Melville Island at Garden Point, a community so named because it was the site of the mission's vegetable and fruit gardens. During World War II, the Tiwi community on Garden Point, now called Pulurumpi, was Australia's first line of defense against attack from the north. Many contemporary Aboriginal people tell of Japanese planes roaring overhead during the bombing of Darwin, which continued for two years.

Upon marriage Freda moved to neighboring Bathurst Island, where she lived until her husband passed away. She then returned to Melville Island and began living at Milikapiti, where she became one of the important women participants and dancers during Tiwi Pukumani and Kulama ceremonies. She is adept at making tunga, parmajini (armbands), and other ceremonial regalia. Before becoming a contemporary painter on canvas and paper in the mid-1990s, she employed her typical abstract Tiwi geometric patterns as body decoration and facial ornamentation, as well as decorating small barks and tunga for sale.

Freda has rocketed to prominence in the past three years, with two solo shows in 1999. Although she uses high-quality artist's brushes rather than traditional frayed bark, she drastically modifies these to produce a tool with which to create her characteristically free brushwork.

A quiet, retiring woman, Freda lives with her daughter and family. She is now mainly involved in painting, although she spends a considerable part of the year in traditional bush activities, including fishing, hunting, and food-gathering.

PLATE 85
Freda Warlipini, b. c. 1934
Body Designs, 1997
93 x 84 cm (36.5 x 33 in.)
Earth ochers on canvas

PLATE 86
Freda Warlipini, b. c. 1934
Body Designs, 1997
100 x 104 cm (39.5 x 41 in.)
Earth ochers on paper

Tiwi Spears

Spears

These elaborate multi-pronged, doubled-sided barbed spears are known as arawuningkuri. A Crocodile Ancestor of the Tiwi people of Bathurst and Melville Islands first made this spear and taught the Tiwi how to carve it with stone axes and smooth it with mussel shell. Today spears are made with steel tools, but still retain the traditional ocher paintings and Tiwi designs. They also continue to be used in ceremony, including the Pukumani burial ceremony and the Kulama or yam ceremony, during which they are placed around the ritual yam oven.

Ceremonial spears are commissioned by relatives during the planning phases of the Pukumani ceremony. Among the Tiwi people of Bathurst and Melville Islands, the Pukumani funeral ceremony is an occasion for elaborate body decoration and the wearing and carrying of special decorated objects. Tiwi abstract patterning is similar on all surfaces — bodies, regalia, carved Pukumani poles, spears, and bark baskets. Men use these spears in dances, at which they also wear full body decoration, including feathered headdresses and strong, colorful face and torso paintings. At the close of the ceremony, the spears are sometimes left upright at the grave, their shafts embedded in the soil. Like the Pukumani poles themselves, the spears become a symbol of the transitory nature of life, decomposing slowly in the elements.

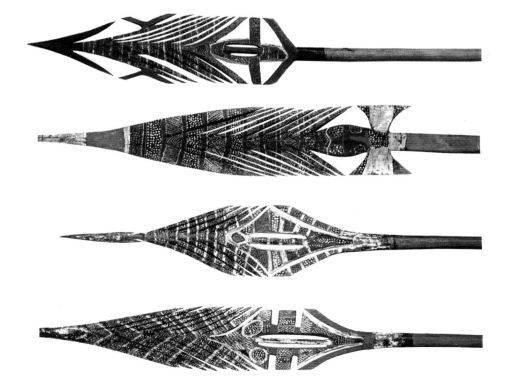

PLATE 87 (detail)
Artist Unknown
Tiwi Ceremonial Spear, c. 1963
117 cm (46 in.) high
Painted wooden carving

PLATE 88 (detail)
Artist Unknown
Tiwi Ceremonial Spear, c. 1963
118 cm (46.5 in.) high
Painted wooden carving

PLATE 89 (detail)
Artist Unknown
Tiwi Ceremonial Spear, c. 1963
122 cm (48 in.) high
Painted wooden carving

PLATE 90 (detail)
Artist Unknown
Tiwi Ceremonial Spear,
c. 1950s–1960s
99 cm (39 in.) high
Painted ironwood

Declan Apuatimi

"Female" Ceremonial Spear

These multi-barbed spears were made in the early 1960s. Decorative techniques include the use of abstract patterning similar to that employed on the carved Pukumani posts and the bark baskets or tunga.

As well as being used for the Pukumani funeral ceremony and Kulama or yam ceremony, ceremonial spears played a part in Tiwi age-grading rituals for young girls. When a girl reached puberty, her father would make a spear and give it to her promised husband, after first holding it beneath the young girl's legs in a symbolic act of defloration. Among the Tiwi the spear is sometimes colloquially referred to as a wife; hence the reference to this spear as being a "female" spear. "Female" spears are fatter than "male" spears, with barbed flanges on both sides rather than only on one.

Biographical Notes

Declan Apuatimi was a famous and significant Tiwi artist. An exceptionally good carver, he was a fully initiated man who took responsibility for masterminding ceremonial activity each year. He was a stickler for tradition, and a great dancer and singer. In traditional Tiwi society, individuality is encouraged and praised within the confines of general Tiwi style. Artists are traditionally commissioned to make objects within the culture, and, since the 1970s, for sale to outsiders. One of many Tiwi who worked with Asian pearl divers and Australian soldiers during World War II, Declan spoke fluent Indonesian and Tiwi all his life, but markedly less English.

Declan Apuatimi was taken under the patronage of Lord Alistair McAlpine in 1984. His works are held by numerous institutions, including the National Gallery of Australia, National Gallery of Victoria, Flinders University Art Museum, National Museum of Australia, the Museum and Art Gallery of the Northern Territory, and the Kelton Foundation, Los Angeles. He died in 1985. In 1987, a retrospective exhibition of his work toured major Australian cities.

PLATE 91 (detail)
Declan Apuatimi, c. 1930–1985
"Female" Ceremonial Spear, c. 1960s
212 cm (83.5 in.) high
Painted ironwood

Concepta Kantilla, Therese Ann Pilakui, Marie E. Pautjimi

Bark Baskets

These baskets are only made by the Tiwi people of Bathurst and Melville Islands. They are carried over the shoulder on a stick placed through a loop made of lawyer cane vine or pandanus fiber, which is also used to stitch the side seams. They are painted with traditional patterns and used in the Pukumani ceremony to hold gifts for the dancers. Today these gifts are often money, but in the past they were natural commodities. Towards the end of the mourning dances, the baskets are emptied and placed on top of a carved pole to "close" the ceremony.

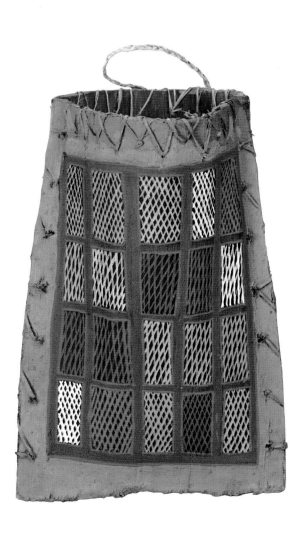

PLATE 92 (below, left)
Concepta Kantilla
Tunga, Bark Basket, 1997
65 x 46 x 30 cm (25.5 x 18 x 12 in.)
Earth ochers on bark

PLATE 93 (opposite, top)
Marie E. Pautjimi
Tunga, Bark Basket, 1997
96 cm x 61 cm x 48 cm (38 x 24 x 19 in.)
Earth ochers on bark

PLATE 94 (opposite, bottom)
Therese Ann Pilakui
Tunga, Bark Basket, 1997
126 cm x 67 cm x 63 cm (49.5 x 26.5 x 25 in.)
Earth ochers on bark

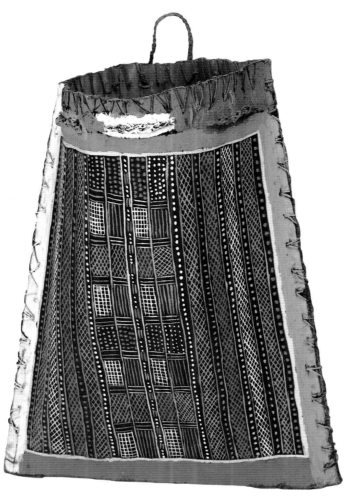

Willy Gudabi

Grandfather's Paintings

The work is divided into segments that reveal small scenes of nature. The subjects relate to the renewal of life and natural species, the totemic life of the artist, and his links to the universe around him.

Willy Gudabi explained this work at Ngukurr in 1995:

> One old man used to walk, from World War I to World War II. "Look son, don't forget this one," [he said.] "You do this one. Singing first, circumcise, men dancing." Today I got shirt, boots, not that old man. He didn't like clothes, he didn't like swags, he used to live in the caves. That's what he taught me to do — this one — before he died. He took me back to a place called Nutwood Downs, he say handing on, "You never see me no more. You come visit me and see what I done in the caves." When you go across the river, you see in the caves all what he done, his paintings. All about, Alawa. You go, right up to Limmen Bight, Hodgsons Downs, his paintings. He left behind for his great-grandchildren, that old man. I was teach by him, because he's my grandfather. I was making paintings, even boomerangs, and bark paintings. I'm never stop, until I die. That's my culture.

Willie Gudabi's grandfather, Gudang, appears in the central left panel. A number of butcher birds that have significance to the artist can be discerned, some in ceremonial body paint. In the lower left and top right are butterflies. Several creatures connected with ceremony are also depicted, including bull-ants and biting insects. Among Alawa, as with other people, the pain of initiation is associated with the pain inflicted by such creatures. The dotted background gives an intensity to the linear overlay of each scene.

The deeper meaning of different aspects of this painting was not conveyed by the artist, because it is exclusive to men's law, which he termed "business."

Biographical Notes

Willy Gudabi was born about 1916 and grew to manhood working on many Northern Territory cattle stations, including Nutwood Downs and Hodgsons Downs. He spent his later life at Ngukurr, the former Roper River mission. He died in 1996.

The colorful work Ngukurr artists was first brought to public notice through the paintings of Willy Gudabi, his wife Moima, and Ginger Riley. Willy Gudabi illustrated totemic plant forms, insects, birds, and fish of his Alawa country on the edge of the Gulf of Carpentaria in the Roper River area. As he reveals in the statement about his work, the theme and imagery are derived from traditional knowledge, from cave paintings, and were taught to him by his grandfather.

The works of Ngukurr artists have been exhibited widely within Australia.

PLATE 95
Willy Gudabi, c. 1916–1996
Grandfather's Paintings, 1995
160 x 122 cm (63 x 48 in.)
Acrylic on board

Gertie Huddlestone

Ngukurr Sunset

Gertie Huddlestone was brought up under the mission system at Ngukurr in southeast Arnhem Land. With her five sisters, she worked in the mission gardens, digging, planting flowers and vegetables, and collecting the flowers for the church. Here she has painted the landscape of the Ngukurr area as a colorful garden planted in rows.

In the foreground is an imaginary garden against the backdrop of the hills and the landscape of Ngukurr at sunset. The natural bush country is also tiered as though landscaped. The central image of the tree called the Jirrilma acts as a marker, a key to seasonal change. When its white flowers fall on the ground below, this signifies that sharks are ready to be hunted. The white butterflies on the tree are another sign that it is shark time. The artist has said:

> *A lot of things tell us like that. Jirrilma flowers falling tell us it's a good time to hunt shark. When the wattle tree flowers then it's good to hunt turtle. When the bloodwood has flowers it's sugarbag time. Always from the flowers.*[10]

Biographical Notes

Gertie Huddlestone was born about 1930 and lives at the community of Ngukurr, formally the Roper River Mission. She belongs to the Mara and Yukul language groups. She has had two solo exhibitions in Melbourne and has exhibited widely throughout Australia with her four sisters, Eva Rogers, Angelina George, Dinah Garadtji, and Bettie Roberts. The sisters are concerned with depicting landscapes that express their nostalgia for the beautifully laid-out gardens that they tended for the Anglican missionaries in their youth, as well as their love for the natural bush, which they perceive as a garden full of signs and meaning.

PLATE 96
Gertie Huddlestone, b. c. 1930
Ngukurr Sunset, 1996
123 x 100 cm (48.5 x 39.5 in.)
Acrylic on canvas

Ginger Riley Munduwalawala

The Four Archers and Garimala

In this work Ginger Riley has painted a grand apocalyptic version of the landscape and Creative beings from his mother's country, the Limmen Bight area of the Gulf of Carpentaria. The painting can be viewed as though from the air, or it can be read vertically in layers. Beside the Limmen Bight River, a group of ridges rises from the flat ground to form idiosyncratic ranges like the backs of ancient creatures. Known as The Four Archers, these formations are central to Ginger Riley's thought, because he is the hereditary custodian and guardian of the area. The Four Archers have been represented several times from different perspectives, first as rounded hills against a sunset sky, then as a turret-like formation above the horizontal lines, an often-used decorative device.

The central image is the great Creation Ancestral Spirit, Garimala. Ginger Riley refers to Garimala as "A taipan who can strike you dead in a minute." A dragon-like Rainbow Serpent figure, Garimala sometimes doubles itself. Two serpents are shown here in the angry form associated with the monsoon season, rising into the sky, spitting fire, with horns on their heads and barbs raised on their backs. The doubling of the sky-serpent images is repeated in nature in the "double rainbow" effect after storms.

At lower left, the Four Archers are shown at sunset, with the red rays of the sun making the rocks glow against a blue sky. In the lower right is a wilder depiction of events in the landscape. Here the powerful snake becomes a singular character, Bulukbun, who is rising out of the sea near Beatrice Island, at the mouth of the Limmen Bight River. Ginger Riley recounts that some boys once misbehaved during ceremonies, and Bulukbun was angered, making it rain. When the boys took shelter in a cave, he rose up high and reached over the island and into the cave, where he breathed fire over them.

In the central panel, beneath the arch formed by the serpents, are two small scenarios in which Ginger Riley focuses on other characters, known as Gorima, from the Creation era. In the center, a Gorima figure and a kangaroo stand beside a raised message stick or ceremonial board used to call people to a gathering. In Creation times the kangaroo, Jatukal, once traveled towards the Limmen Bight River in search of a mate. Beneath this is a small Gorima hunting group, consisting of a man and a smaller figure, perhaps his son, hunting an animal in a tree.

PLATE 97
Ginger Riley Munduwalawala, b. c. 1937
The Four Archers and Garimala, 1989
168 x 168 cm (66 x 66 in.)
Synthetic polymer paint on canvas

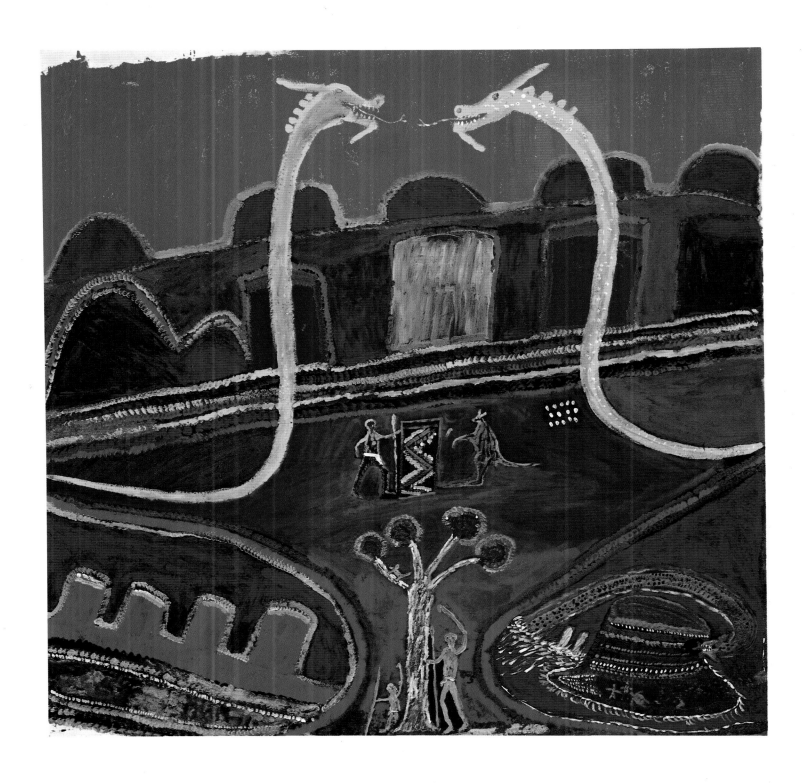

Biographical Notes

Ginger Riley Munduwalawala was born around 1937 in the southeastern corner of Arnhem Land. He comes from the Mara people and regards himself as a "coastal saltwater man." He spent his early life in the bush, intermittently visiting Roper River Mission (now Ngukurr Aboriginal community), where he was exposed to reading, writing, and the stories of the Bible. At the same time he traveled through his own country on foot, hunting and food-gathering. On these "foot walks," he learned a great deal about the Four Archers, their significance for his own community, and his responsibilities as Jungkayi (guardian) for his mother's country. He left the community at about fifteen years of age to seek a different life on cattle stations, where he worked as a drover and mustered cattle, but in the 1970s he returned to Ngukurr.

Ginger Riley first saw contemporary paintings by an Aboriginal artist when he visited Alice Springs as a teenager, droving cattle for the large station owner, Lord Vestey. There he met Albert Namatjira (1902–1959), the first Australian Aboriginal artist to work in non-traditional colors, who painted the beautiful desert ranges and vegetation in bright purples, greens, and blues. This, according to Riley "stayed in his mind." With the provision of paints in his own community, he began painting at Ngukurr in 1987.

Today Ginger Riley paints only the country for which he is responsible. He won the Alice Prize in 1992, followed by the National Australian Heritage Commission Art Award in 1993. In 1997 he was awarded an Australia Council Fellowship, and became the first Aboriginal artist to be honored with a one-man retrospective exhibition at the National Gallery of Victoria.

In 1992 he took a lease on a cattle station of 200 hectares at Wamungu, in his own country near the Limmen Bight River. He lives there in relative seclusion; he sometimes paints, but mostly he rests, preferring to paint "down south" in Melbourne, where paints and a studio are provided by his friend and representative Beverly Knight. His work is represented in all Australian State art galleries and the National Gallery of Australia.[11]

PLATE 97 (detail)
Ginger Riley Munduwalawala, b. c. 1937
The Four Archers and Garimala, 1989
168 x 168 cm (66 x 66 in.)
Synthetic polymer paint on canvas

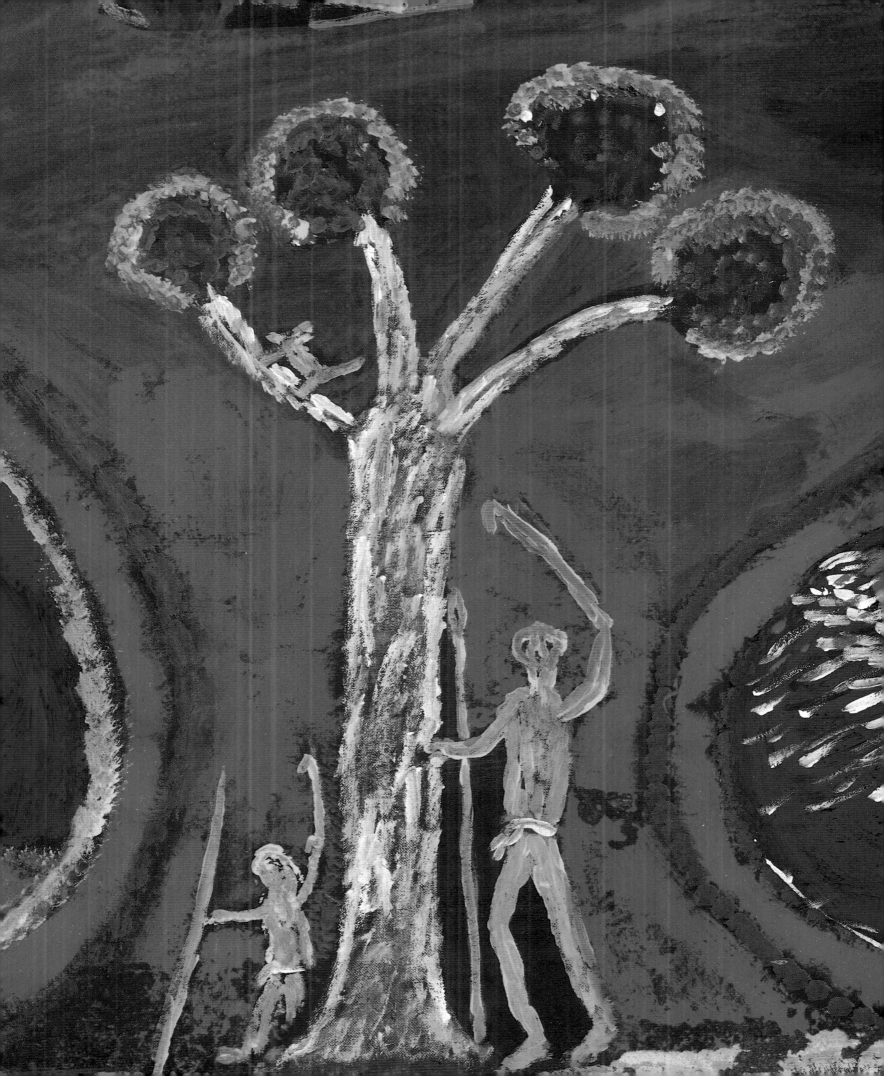

Notes

Spirit Country

1. The story of the first people who came to the shores of eastern Arnhem Land at Yelangbara has components that reflect real social history. The Yolngu peoples of eastern Arnhem Land had continuous contact with the Macassans of Indonesia for several centuries before Europeans arrived.

2. A discussion of this and other aspects of Aboriginal philosophy is contained in Nancy M. Williams, "Intellectual Property and Aboriginal Environmental Knowledge," *CINCRM, discussion paper no. 1* (Darwin: Centre for Indigenous Natural and Cultural Resource Management, 1998).

3. Williams, "Intellectual Property," 5.

4. Dhayirra Yunupingu, "Waarga ga rumbal ngilimurru," *Yan* (Yirrkala), no. 3, 1992, 16–21, quoted in Williams, "Intellectual Property," 6.

5. Songs and designs were sung and shown, but the "ownership" remained with the giver.

6. Williams, "Intellectual Property," 17.

7. Marcel Mauss, *The Gift: Forms and Functions of Exchange in Archaic Societies*, translated by I. Cunnison (New York: Norton, 1967), 9–10.

8. Douglas Fraser, *Primitive Art* (London: Thames and Hudson, 1962),123.

9. Fraser, *Primitive Art*, 126.

10. Barbara Glowczewski, *YAPA, Peintres Aborigenes des Balgo et Lajamanu* (Paris: Baudoin Lebon Editeur, 1991), 121.

11. Sebastian Smee, "The Galleries," *Sydney Morning Herald,* 10 November 1998.

12. Terry Smith, "Kngwarreye Woman Abstract Painter," in J. Isaacs, T. Smith, J. Ryan, and D. and J. Holt, *Emily Kngwarreye Paintings* (Sydney: Craftsman House, 1997).

13. A useful discussion of this "fecundity" is contained in Barbara Glowczewski, *YAPA* 118–123.

14. Miriam-Rose Ungunmerr, "Dadirri," *Compass Theology Review,* nos. 1–2 (1988): 9–10.

15. Wandjuk Marika, *Wandjuk Marika: Life Story as Told to Jennifer Isaacs* (St. Lucia: University of Queensland Press, 1995), 125.

The Desert

1. Baldwin Spencer and F. J. Gillen, *The Native Tribes of Central Australia* (London: Macmillan, 1899).

2. Discriminatory laws in relation to alcohol have altered, but there are still conflicts between the legal assumptions and imperatives of Aboriginal traditional law and the Australian legal system. This particularly affects painters, who sell their works then immediately are required to redistribute the proceeds. Others have allowed appropriate relatives to paint and sell works on their behalf, and have then faced challenges over "authorship" and attribution.

3. Geoff Bardon, "The Gift that Time Gave: Papunya Early and Late, 1971–1972 and 1980," in J. Ryan, *Mythscapes. Aboriginal Art of the Desert* (Melbourne: National Gallery of Victoria, n.d.), 13.

4. Geoff Bardon, *Aboriginal Art of the Western Desert* (Adelaide: Rigby, 1979), 64.

5. Marina Strocchi, *Ikuntji, Paintings from Haasts Bluff 1992–1994* (Alice Springs, NT: IAD Press, 1995), 106.

6. Strocchi, *Ikuntji*, 105.

7. Strocchi, *Ikuntji*, 11.

8. J. Green, translation of statement by Emily Kngwarreye, cited in M. Boulter, Foreword, *The Art of Utopia; A New Direction in Contemporary Aboriginal Art*, ed. M. Boulter (Sydney: Craftsman House, 1991), 9.

The Kimberley

1. David Mowaljarlai and Jutta Malnic, *Yorro Yorro Spirit of the Kimberley* (Broome: Magabala Books, 1993), 133.

2. In June 1998 the Ngarrinyin, led by David Mowarljarlai, were invited to UNESCO in Paris to present visual and oral assessments of their own connections to the paintings.

3. Quoted from the Pathway Project, as reported in *Sydney Morning Herald*, 21 June 1997.

4. Ian M. Crawford, *The Art of the Wandjina* (Melbourne: Oxford University Press, 1968), 36.

5. Wally Caruana, *Roads Cross: The Paintings of Rover Thomas* (Canberra: National Gallery of Australia, 1994), 25.

6. Judith Ryan, *Images of Power. Aboriginal Art of the Kimberley* (Melbourne: National Gallery of Victoria, n.d.), 64.

7. Quoted in Mowaljarlai and Malnic, *Yorro Yorro*, 133.

8. Cited in Ryan, *Images of Power*, 18.

9. Story told to Don Macleod, 12 February 1985; records courtesy Mary Macha, Perth.

10. The term "corroboree" was taken from a New South Wales Aboriginal dialect in the nineteenth century, but became a generic English word for Aboriginal dance. It is retained in some areas in current Aboriginal English usage.

Arnhem Land, Tiwi Islands, and Gulf Country

1. Dry sclerophyll forests are dominated by small-leaved native species that have evolved over millennia to minimize moisture loss in the dry Australian climate. In Arnhem Land they have an understorey of food plants, including yam vines and fruits.

2. "Moiety" is an anthropological term that literally means "half," and in this case is used to identify the two sets of opposite but interrelated kin groupings into which Yolngu are divided. The same concept of moieties is applied to the natural world.

3. Baldwin Spencer, *Wanderings in Wild Australia* (London: Macmillan, 1928), 2: 792.

4. By their nature bark paintings are three-dimensional objects, and the basic ground always tends to return to the shape of the tree. The bark also takes up atmospheric moisture, altering its shape, a property that some curators find alarming. This can be eliminated by storing and displaying the paintings in controlled humidity and temperature conditions, and by the use of binding sticks to brace the paintings. Many conservators prefer to allow the bark to move to some extent within any framing device.

5. Spencer, *Wanderings in Wild Australia*, 2: 792.

6. *Milirrpum and others v. Nabalco and the Commonwealth of Australia*, 1971.

7. Baldwin Spencer, *Native Tribes of the Northern Territory of Australia* (London: Macmillan, 1914).

8. Courtesy Bula'bula Arts, Ramingining, Northern Territory.

9. Documented by Margie West of the Museum and Art Gallery of the Northern Territory, as told to her by Declan and Raphael Apuatimi, Nguiu, 1984.

10. Gertie Huddlestone interview, quoted in J. Isaacs, "Bush Gardens," *Art and Australia*, 35, no. 4 (1998): 157.

11. Information from Judith Ryan, *Ginger Riley* (Melbourne: National Gallery of Victoria, 1997) and discussion with Beverly Knight.

Glossary

acacia	Small trees found widely in the drier regions of Australia and Southern Africa. Seeds of many species formed the staple diet of desert Aboriginal people. Edible grubs are found in the roots of some acacias, including *Acacia witjiana*.
Altyerre	Term used by the Anmatyerre people for the Dreaming or Creation era (q.v.).
anggum	Carrying vessel made from bark in the Kimberley region.
Awelye	Anmatyerre women's songs and dances; women's ceremony and law.
bandicoot	Small, furry, burrowing marsupial.
barramundi	Large fish similar to the American snook; both freshwater and saltwater varieties are hunted by coastal indigenous communities.
bilby	Small, long-eared marsupial, once prevalent in the Australian desert; digs burrows similar to rabbit burrows'.
billabong	Freshwater lagoon, still-water pool.
billy	Small tin bucket with wire handle used for boiling water on an open fire or for collecting food.
boab tree	Bulbous-trunked tree of the Kimberley region of Australia.
bore	Water pipe drilled and sunk to the level of the subterranean water table from which water can be pumped.
bush tucker	Wild Australian foods, both plant and animal.
cameleers	Immigrants from the Punjab, Pakistan, and Afghanistan, collectively known in Australia as Afghans, who used their camels to transport goods through the dry Australian interior.
clap-sticks	Pairs of carved hardwood sticks, usually 1–1.5 feet in length and up to 2 inches in cross section, which are struck together to make a rhythmic musical accompaniment to songs.
coolamons	Curved. oval wooden bowls and dishes of various sizes and shapes carried by women of the Central and Western Desert regions.
corroboree	This term was taken from a New South Wales Aboriginal dialect in the nineteenth century, but became a generic English word for Aboriginal dance. It is retained in some areas in current Aboriginal English usage.
Creation Ancestors	Primary spiritual beings, creators of landscape, ancestors of Aboriginal people, and givers of indigenous law.
Creation era	The period in which Creation Ancestors journeyed across the Australian landscape, shaping its features, naming plants and animals, and handing ritual knowledge on to humans.
curlew	A migratory wading bird that gives an eerie call at dusk.
damper	Unleavened bread baked in the ashes of the campfire.
daphnia	A tiny surface-dwelling water insect.
Dhuwa	One of the two moieties of the Yolngu people (q.v.).
digging stick	Thick hardwood stick sharpened at one end. The basic utensil used by Aboriginal women to dig for roots and burrowing animals.
dilly bag	A woven conical bag used to carry food in Arnhem Land; also of sacred and ceremonial significance.
dingo	Native dog.
Dreaming	The most common English translation of the complex, multi-leveled concept that in Aboriginal religious philosophy encompasses the journeys and actions of spiritual beings during the Creation era, the system of religious law they laid down, and the ways in which humankind and all living things connect to that creative power in the present day. Indigenous terms for this concept include Tjukurrpa (among the Pitjantjatjara), Altyerre (among the Anmatyerre), and Ngarrangkarni (among the peoples of the Kimberley).
droves	Journeys in which herds of cattle or sheep are required to walk overland, sometimes for hundreds of miles, tended by drovers (q.v.) on horseback.
drovers	Specialized workers employed to oversee movements of cattle and sheep in the Australian inland; similar to American cowboys.
echidna	Spiny anteater.
euro	Small member of kangaroo family, adept in rocky terrain.
gulach (spike rush)	Water reed with edible corm that grows in freshwater pools along the northern Australian coast.
hair string	String or twine made from human hair and animal fur with the aid of a hand-held spindle of crossed sticks.
kartilka	*See* kuniya
kinship	Connections between family members. Among Aboriginal groups this term covers relationships both within and between generations, and through both mothers' and fathers' lines of descent across many generations. People also have kinship with certain animals and plants through common descent from or relationship to a particular Creation Ancestor.

Kriol	Hybrid but distinct language, widely used among Aboriginal peoples of northern Australia, blending English with Aboriginal languages.
kuniya	Carpet snake (a non-venomous python); also known as kartilka.
Kuril Kuril	Ceremony performed by Kimberley people. Known as the context in which Paddy Tjamatji first displayed painted boards.
kurrajong tree	A large tree (*Brachychiton* species) that has multiple uses. The seeds are edible, and it is a source of both timber and bark.
kuruwarri	The design pathway of Creation Ancestors marked out on a painting, usually consisting of lines connecting circles. The main journey that maps the country.
kurdungurlu	Guardian, supervisor, protector, or "policeman" whose responsibility is to ensure that the owners of particular sites are accurately carrying out ritual designs or law, for the protection of both the owners and the sites.
Lightning Spirit	Male Creation Ancestor of western Arnhem Land. Associated with female Rainbow Serpent and wet-season thunderstorms.
liwirringki	Small burrowing lizard or skink that lives under spinifex grass in the desert country northwest of Alice Springs.
mamu	Spirit or ghost.
mardayin ceremonies	A major sequence of sacred ceremonies practiced in Arnhem Land.
marla fur	The fur of a small kangaroo or wallaby.
mimih	Small, thin, mischievous spirit creatures inhabiting the rocky escarpment of western Arnhem Land. They are not Creation Ancestors, but taught humans how to hunt and butcher the kangaroo and how to use the spear and womerah. Sometimes also spelt "mimi."
moieties	Anthropological term used to describe the two sets of opposite but interrelated kin groupings into which peoples such as the Yolngu of eastern Arnhem Land are divided. The same concept of moieties is applied to the natural world.
mulga	*Acacia aneura*, a type of desert tree with exceptionally hard wood, used for . clusters of long, flat, strap-like leaves.
rarrk	Term used in Arnhem Land for sacred patterns created by cross-hatched painted lines.
rock-hole	Water source contained by rocks; may be a sheltered pool (large or small), or a subterranean soak (q.v.).
sclerophyll forest	Dry, open forest of trees with small, leathery leaves adapted to minimize moisture loss (literally, "hard-leafed").
soak or soakage	Desert water source; usually applied to residual water along river beds or rocky pathways. The water may remain visible, or may appear as a damp patch, which must be dug out and let settle, or it may not be visible at all. Foreknowledge is required to locate hidden soaks by careful digging under apparently dry sand.
songlines	Series of songs sung during ceremonies, recounting the journeys of Creation Ancestors from place to place.
spinifex	A clumped, spiky desert grass. Exudes a type of gum, which can be pounded and heated to make block resin for affixing ax heads and womerah handles and for sealing cracks in weapons and utensils.
sultana	Small dried fruit.
swag	A thin mattress inside a canvas covering; can be rolled up and carried on the back.
taipan	An extremely venomous snake.
Tingari	Generic name for a group of Creation Era men and women Ancestors of the Pintupi people.
Tjukurrpa	Pitjantjatjara term for Dreaming, Creation era (qq.v.).
tunga	Basket or container made from a single folded sheet of eucalyptus bark, sewn at the sides. Made and used by Tiwi people of Bathurst and Melville Islands.
womerah	Wooden spear-thrower; has a barb that rests in a notch on the spear-end so that it acts as an extension of the hunter's arm and increases the distance the spear travels.
Wongar	The term used to describe the Creation era (q.v.) in parts of Arnhem Land, wangar.
yarla	"Bush potato," a rounded tuber that branches underground. A staple food of Warlpiri people, it is dug by women and roasted in the ashes.
Yirritja	One of the two moieties of the Yolngu people.
Yolngu	"We people": term used by Arnhem Land communities to denote themselves.

Acknowledgments

The Book

Numerous individuals have generously provided assistance and information in the course of preparing this book. Particular thanks are due to Meredith Aveling, Kellie Robertson, and Joe Isaacs for their help in the preparation of the manuscript. Hardie Grant managing editor Tracy O'Shaughnessy and editor Jenny Lee deserve special praise for co-ordinating input from opposite sides of the globe. Kathleen Berrin and Karen Kevorkian of the Fine Arts Museums of San Francisco deserve thanks for their "need to know," which spurred me to extra efforts to explain aspects of Australian and Aboriginal culture, geography, and history. I am also indebted to my agent, Margaret Connolly, and to the designer, Michael Callaghan, for his creative and sensitive response to the images in the book.

Thanks too to Mark Ashkanasy, photographer for the Gantner Myer Collection, Joseph McDonald, Fine Arts Museums' photographer, and Richard Woldendorp, whose photographs appear on the landscape features pages. Additional photographs were provided by Kathleen Berrin, Carrillo B. Gantner, and Reg Morrison.

The Collection

Baillieu Myer conceived the idea of forming this collection when he became an active member of the National Council of the Fine Arts Museums of San Francisco. His inspiration was shared by Carrillo Gantner and Neilma Gantner, and led to the making of a truly contemporary collection that reflects their combined imagination, enthusiasm, and generosity. As collection adviser, I curated and managed the collection in Australia with help from Margaret Rennie, personal assistant to Baillieu Myer; Chris Fraser, assistant to Carrillo Gantner; and my assistant, Cressida Hall. In selecting works for the collection and subsequent exhibitions, expertise and assistance were sought from many galleries and agents, especially Ace Bourke, Karen Brown, Rodney Gooch, Helen Hansen, Peter Harrison, Donald Holt, Janet Holt, Beverly Knight, William Mora, Bill Nuttall, Gabrielle Pizzi, Roslyn Premont, and Gabriella Roy. Thanks, too, to Barbara James, Richard Kelton, Kerry Smallwood, and Peter Yates for friendship and accommodation during the project. I would also like to thank Gerald McCourt, Chris Fraser, and Christopher Fraser, Geoff Hardinge, John Guest, Simon Hartas, and Peter Velzen, who all assisted with the management of the collection.

The artists' communities on the Aboriginal lands of the Desert, Kimberley, Arnhem Land, and Tiwi Islands were most generous in their assistance. Very grateful thanks are extended to Andrew Blake of Buku-Larrnggay Mulka Arts at Yirrkala; Susan Congreve and Tara Leckey of Warlukurlangu Artists at Yuendumu; Gillian Dallwitz of Tiwi Designs, Bathurst Island; Karen Dayman of Mangkaja Arts at Fitzroy Crossing; Marina Strocchi and Wayne Eager, formerly of the Ikuntji Women's Centre in Haasts Bluff and now of Papunya Tula in Alice Springs; Felicity Green of Jilamara Arts and Crafts at Milikapiti on Melville Island; Lyn Helms of Munupi Arts at Pulurumpi, Melville Island; Samantha James of Waringarri Arts in Kununurra; Jenny Kelly and Kevin Kelly, formerly of Waringarri Arts and now of Red Rock Art, Kununurra; Tony Oliver of Jirrawun Aboriginal Art at Crocodile Hole; John Oster of Warlayirti Artists in Balgo; Libby Raynor of Bula'bula Arts at Ramingining; Una Rey of the Ikuntji Women's Centre in Haasts Bluff; Fiona Salmon of Maningrida Arts, Maningrida; Janice Stanton and Daphne Williams of Papunya Tula Artists, Alice Springs; Maxine Taylor, formerly of Warmun Arts in the Kimberley; Anthony Wallis of the Aboriginal Artists Agency; and Anna Moulton and Jonathan Kimberley of Warmun Arts, Warmun. I would especially like to acknowledge the hard work of the artists and advisers in all these communities, particularly those artists who have undertaken specific commissions for the collection. Thanks also to all those who have facilitated copyright permissions, making it possible for these works to be reproduced here. I hope that their generosity will help to foster greater public awareness and appreciation of contemporary Aboriginal art on both sides of the Pacific.

Jennifer Isaacs

Further Reading

Bardon, Geoffrey. *Aboriginal Art of the Western Desert*. Adelaide: Rigby, 1979.

———— "The Gift Time Gave. Papunya 1971–1972." In Judith Ryan. *Mythscapes: Aboriginal Art of the Desert*. Melbourne: National Gallery of Victoria, 1989.

———— *Papunya Tula: Art of the Western Desert*. Melbourne: McPhee Gribble, 1991.

Battarbee, Rex, and Bernice Battarbee. *Modern Aboriginal Paintings*. Adelaide: Rigby, 1971.

Berndt, Ronald, ed. *Australian Aboriginal Art*. Sydney: Ure Smith, 1964.

Berndt, Ronald and Catherine. *Arnhem Land: Its History and Its People*. Melbourne: Cheshire, 1954.

Berndt, Ronald and Catherine. *The World of the First Australians*. Canberra: Aboriginal Studies Press, 1996.

Berndt, Ronald, Catherine Berndt, and John Stanton. *Aboriginal Australian Art: A Visual Perspective*. Port Melbourne: Mandarin, 1992.

Broome, Richard. *Aboriginal Australians: Black Responses to White Dominance, 1788–1994*. St. Leonards: Allen & Unwin, 1994.

Caruana, Wally. *Aboriginal Art*. London: Thames and Hudson, 1993.

———— *Roads Cross. The Paintings of Rover Thomas*, exh. cat. Canberra: National Gallery of Australia, 1994.

Crawford, Ian M. *The Art of the Wandjina*. Melbourne: Oxford University Press, 1968.

Fraser, Douglas. *Primitive Art*. London: Thames and Hudson, 1962.

Flood, Josephine. *Archaeology of the Dreamtime*. Sydney: Collins/Angus & Robertson, 1992.

———— *Rock Art of the Dreamtime*. Sydney: Angus & Robertson, 1997.

Glowczewski, Barbara. *YAPA: Peintres Aborigènes de Balgo et Lajamanu*. Paris: Baudoin Lebon Éditeur, 1991.

Isaacs, Jennifer. *Aboriginality: Contemporary Aboriginal Paintings and Prints*. St Lucia: University of Queensland Press, 1989.

———— *Australian Aboriginal Paintings*. Sydney: Weldons, 1989.

———— *Australia Dreaming: 40,000 Years of Aboriginal History*. Sydney: Lansdowne Press, 1992.

———— *Bush Food: Aboriginal Food and Herbal Medicine*. Sydney: Weldons, 1992.

———— *Arts of the Dreaming: Australia's Living Heritage*. Sydney: Lansdowne Press, 1994.

———— "Bush Gardens." *Art in Australia* 35, no. 4 (1998): 157.

———— *Wandjuk Marika: Life Story as told to Jennifer Isaacs*. St Lucia: University of Queensland Press, 1995.

Johnson, Vivien. *Aboriginal Artists of the Western Desert: A Biographical Dictionary*. Roseville East: Craftsman House, 1994.

Mauss, Marcel. *The Gift: Forms and Functions of Exchange in Archaic Societies*. New York: Norton, 1967.

Morphy, Howard. *Aboriginal Art*. London: Phaidon Press, 1998.

Mountford, Charles. *The Tiwi: Their Art, Myth and Ceremony*. London and Melbourne: Phoenix House, 1958.

Mowaljarlai, David, and J. Malnic. *Yorro Yorro Everything Standing Up Alive: Spirit of the Kimberley*. Broome, Western Australia: Magabala Books Aboriginal Corporation, 1993.

Munn, Nancy. *Walbiri Iconography*. Ithaca, New York: Cornell University Press, 1973.

Myers, Fred. "Truth, Beauty, and the Pintupi Painting." *Visual Anthropology*, no. 2 (1989): 163–95.

———— "Beyond the Intentional Fallacy: Art Criticism and the Ethnography of Aboriginal Acrylic Painting." *Cultural Anthropology*, 6, no.1 (1994): 26–62.

Reynolds, Henry. *The Whispering in Our Hearts*. St Leonards: Allen & Unwin, 1998.

Ryan, Judith. *Mythscapes: Aboriginal Art of the Desert from the National Gallery of Victoria*. exh. cat. Melbourne: National Gallery of Victoria, 1989.

———— *Spirit in Land: Bark Paintings from Arnhem Land*, exh. cat. Melbourne: National Gallery of Victoria, 1990.

———— and Kim Akerman. *Images of Power: Aboriginal art of the Kimberley*, exh. cat. Melbourne: National Gallery of Victoria, 1993.

———— *Ginger Riley*, exh. cat. Melbourne: National Gallery of Victoria, 1997.

Spencer, W. Baldwin and F. J. Gillen. *The Native Tribes of Central Australia*. London: Macmillan, 1899.

Spencer, W. Baldwin. *The Native Tribes of the Northern Territory*. London: Macmillan, 1914.

———— *Wanderings in Wild Australia*, 2 vols. London: Macmillan, 1928.

Stanner, W. E. H. *On Aboriginal Religion*. Sydney: Sydney University Press, 1966.

———— *White Man Got No Dreaming*. Canberra: Australian National University Press, 1979.

Strocchi, Marina. *Ikuntji. Paintings from Haasts Bluff 1992–1994*. Alice Springs: IAD Press, 1995.

Sutton, Peter, ed. *Dreamings. The Art of Aboriginal Australia*. New York and Ringwood: Viking, 1988.

Taylor, Luke. *Seeing the Inside: Bark Painting in Western Arnhem Land*. Oxford: Clarendon Press, 1996.

Ungunmerr, Miriam-Rose. "Dadirri." *Compass Theology Review*, 22, nos. 1–2 (1988): 9–10.

Williams, Nancy M. *The Yolngu and Their Land: A System of Land Tenure and the Fight for Its Recognition*. Canberra: Australian Institute of Aboriginal and Torres Strait Islander Studies Press, 1986.

———— "Intellectual Property and Aboriginal Environmental Knowledge." *CINCRM discussion paper no. 1*. Darwin: Centre for Indigenous Natural and Cultural Resource Management, 1998.

List of Plates

List of Artists and Their Works

Index